The Inherited Lie

The Inherited Lie

Why Everything You Think About Money Is Wrong—and How to Finally Get It Right

Eleanor Whitmore

Mindful Pages

Published in 2025

ISBN: 9789371778442 (PB)
ISBN: 9789371777544 (eBook)

Published by

Mindful Pages
Imprint of Alpha Editions LLC
312 W. 2nd St #1834
Casper, WY 82601, USA

This book was developed using advanced writing tools to support the drafting and ideation process. All content has been thoughtfully curated, refined, and reviewed to ensure quality and relevance.

Content

Introduction
The Lie We Inherited

We tend to believe that our struggles with money arise from ignorance—that if only we attended the right seminar, watched the perfect financial guru on YouTube, or read one more bestselling guide on budgeting or investing, we would finally feel in control. The assumption is seductive: that the problem is informational, that a spreadsheet, app, or well-crafted plan can resolve it.

Yet this very belief is part of the difficulty.

The reality is that most financial challenges have little to do with what we know. They are rooted in what we believe—and more crucially, in what we are unaware that we believe. Beneath the transactions, the habits, and even our carefully considered goals, there exist deeply embedded narratives—cultural, familial, emotional—that shape our relationship with money. These stories are so pervasive, so internalised, that they often escape notice entirely. We mistake them for truth. Yet they are not truths; they are inherited myths.

We do not arrive in the world neutral about money. Long before earning a salary, we absorb attitudes, anxieties, and moral associations about wealth. We learn, often unconsciously, that rich people are selfish, that debt is shameful, that security resides in a "good job," or that ambition is greed. We internalise rules about frugality, worth, and aspiration through casual dinner table remarks, fleeting glimpses of neighbours' possessions, religious teachings, and societal cues. These lessons take root before we ever handle money ourselves—and they remain with us.

Most financial advice never penetrates these subterranean beliefs. It stays on the surface, focusing on how to manage money, not why we relate to it the way we do. It presumes behaviour change follows information—that those who struggle simply lack facts or discipline. If knowledge alone sufficed, the most financially literate among us would be free from anxiety, shame, and self-sabotage. They are not. Money is never just mathematics. It carries meaning, identity, emotion, power, safety, and belonging—all entangled.

This book begins where most end: with an examination of the truths we inherit without question. It invites a deep look into the psychological, cultural, and even spiritual architecture of your financial life. It asks not merely how you handle money, but what you believe it says about you. It uncovers the unconscious programming that shapes your decisions, anxieties, limits, and aspirations.

The difficult part is that many of these beliefs operate invisibly. Like background noise, they influence your entire financial reality without entering conscious awareness. You may believe you are making choices about career, spending, or saving—but often, you are reacting to inherited scripts, either conforming to them or rebelling against them. You are performing a story you did not author.

Some of these scripts are rooted in fear; others in morality, shame, loyalty, or social signalling. None of this is inherently your fault. You inherited them. But until you recognise them, you cannot change them—and without change, you remain constrained, regardless of budgeting tools or financial advice.

Consider someone raised in a household where money was scarce and the future uncertain. Phrases like "We can't afford that" or "Money doesn't grow on trees" punctuated childhood. Parents argued about bills, panicked at rent day. The lesson absorbed was that money is a source of stress, that scarcity is ever-present, that abundance invites risk. Decades later, this person may earn a secure income, yet emotionally, the same scarcity mindset persists: fear of investing, anxiety about spending, chronic concern that financial stability is fragile. No level of income rewrites a belief embedded so deeply.

Multiply this dynamic across millions, and the shortcomings of the personal finance industry become clear. It offers tools for managing money but rarely for managing meaning. It instructs on saving, investing, and planning, yet seldom addresses fear, guilt, or identity. When advice is not followed, blame quietly shifts to the individual: you didn't stick to the budget, you spent unnecessarily, you didn't try hard enough. The result is moralised failure rather than insight into the deeper architecture.

This book takes a different approach.

The Inherited Lie does not teach you to spend less or save more. It illuminates the myths you inhabit. It renders the invisible visible and the unconscious conscious. It questions moral assumptions entwined with economic thinking—the false equivalences between wealth and virtue, debt and failure, ambition and greed. It examines how the nervous system reacts to money: why some freeze at opportunity while others chase status they don't desire. Money is not rational because humans are not purely rational; we are wired for safety, belonging, identity, and meaning. Until these forces are acknowledged, no financial strategy will fully endure.

You will find no formulaic prescriptions here. Instead, you are offered a framework for reclaiming your financial identity—challenging inherited scripts, outdated myths, and entrenched emotional habits. Clarity emerges, not merely about what is broken, but about what is possible when you stop living someone else's money story and begin writing your own.

The chapters that follow dissect different aspects of the inherited lie. We explore evolutionary and psychological roots of behaviour—why brains prioritise short-term comfort over long-term gain and how this sabotages even careful planning. We examine the moral entanglements of wealth, family legacies, cultural messages, and the emotional costs of equating self-worth with net worth.

Later, we confront structural illusions: the myth of financial literacy as a cure-all, the destructive status games we play, and the flawed notion of control in an unpredictable world. We question the fantasy of the self-made millionaire, the obsession with linear success, and the promise of a fixed destination called "retirement." And ultimately, we arrive where old money stories end—at the opportunity to create something new.

The urgency of this inquiry is clear. We live amidst mounting financial anxiety: stagnant wages, soaring costs of living, relentless pressures to "succeed." Social media amplifies illusions of effortless wealth, fuelling comparison, inadequacy, and confusion about what financial success truly entails. The old paths—stable jobs, homeownership, pension security—no longer guarantee prosperity. In this context, understanding the truth about money is not a luxury. It is essential.

Yet understanding is not about memorising more financial data. It is about digging beneath the surface: examining beliefs, family legacies, and emotional triggers. It is asking courageous questions: whose voice shapes your guilt about wanting more? What lessons did you absorb by observing your parents? Which emotions attached to wealth are yours, and which are inherited? This is not therapy, strictly speaking—but it is therapeutic. Realising that your financial patterns reflect inherited stories rather than intelligence, discipline, or worth is empowering.

Ironically, the myths you inherited may once have served a purpose. Perhaps caution protected a grandmother. Perhaps relentless labour demonstrated value to a father. These beliefs arose from real histories, real fears, and real conditions. But your life is not theirs; your context is different. What once protected can now imprison.

It is time to break the cycle.

This book is neither manual nor prescription. It is a mirror—and a compass. It reflects where you have been and points to where you could go, if you stop allowing the past to dictate your financial future. You are not broken. You are not irresponsible. You are not fated to repeat the same patterns. But to change your reality, you must first see it clearly.

The lie we inherited is formidable—but so is the truth.

CHAPTER 1
Money Was Never Meant to Make Sense

It's easy to assume that money operates as a purely rational instrument—something governed by arithmetic, logic, and predictable outcomes. We approach it like a spreadsheet: input, output, balance. It ought to make sense. And yet, when we overspend despite our best intentions, avoid reviewing our statements, postpone financial decisions, or sabotage unexpected windfalls with uncanny precision, we often blame ourselves. We tell ourselves we need more discipline, sharper habits, a clearer plan. Perhaps a tighter budget, or a more sophisticated investment strategy.

This assumption, however, is misleading.

Money has never functioned solely in the realm of reason. To attempt to understand it purely intellectually is to overlook the forces that actually drive financial behaviour. Beneath each decision lies a far older engine: the human brain. Not the deliberate, calculating part we like to imagine, but the reactive, emotionally attuned system honed for survival in a world utterly unlike our own.

At the heart of this chapter is a simple yet radical idea: your brain was not designed for the modern financial landscape. It was not built to calculate compound interest, manage decades-long risk, or postpone gratification for decades. It evolved to respond to immediate threats, scarce resources, and the demands of social belonging within tight-knit tribes. In other words, your instincts are prehistoric; your bank account is not.

This explains why even intelligent, educated individuals often struggle with money in ways that defy logic. Why someone with a substantial income might feel anxiety each time they open a bill. Why another, despite ample savings, hesitates to spend on necessities. Why self-sabotage or procrastination creeps in—not from ignorance, but from deep-seated instinctual responses.

Understanding that our default wiring was forged in scarcity rather than stability sheds light on financial irrationalities. The thrill of a sale, reluctance to invest despite historical market gains, the pang of losing £50 even after earning thousands—these are not errors of judgement, but echoes of ancient programming.

A key insight emerges from neuroscience: money often activates the same circuits as survival itself. Studies reveal that financial loss triggers responses in the brain akin to physical pain, while anticipated gains stimulate reward pathways in ways comparable to food, sex, or addictive substances. This is literal biochemistry. Money is, in essence, charged with emotion.

That charge is magnified by uncertainty. Evolution favoured those who reacted cautiously to ambiguity; unpredictability was dangerous. Today, we cling to small certainties—hoarding modest savings, underpricing our work, staying in familiar but underpaid roles—not necessarily from prudence, but to avoid the discomfort of unknown outcomes.

This tendency to prioritise safety over possibility is not a moral failing. It is an inherited neurological strategy. Mechanisms once vital for survival now govern complex financial choices in abstract economic environments. It is as if we were trying to run a contemporary operating system on a Pleistocene-era processor—errors and crashes are inevitable.

Consider loss aversion, a well-documented cognitive bias: the pain of losing a sum outweighs the pleasure of gaining the same amount. £100 lost feels far worse than £100 gained feels good. This asymmetry shapes behaviour: investors retreat during downturns, savers hoard, entrepreneurs hesitate to scale. Our brains are wired to protect rather than expand, yet modern wealth creation depends on tolerating discomfort, enduring uncertainty, and resisting immediate gratification. Emotional wiring, thus, often undermines even the most carefully designed strategies.

Moreover, money touches identity. It becomes a tool for managing psychological pain—not merely the fear of insufficiency, but deeper emotions: inadequacy, shame, loneliness. Purchases often soothe, not satisfy. Generosity can affirm worth rather than abundance. Avoidance of financial conversations frequently shields us from feelings entwined with self-perception. Financial behaviour, seen through this lens, resembles emotional regulation as much as resource management.

Herein lies the limitation of conventional financial guidance. Advice may be technically sound, yet fail to produce lasting transformation because identity consistently overrides information. You can be instructed repeatedly to save, invest, or automate, but if your self-concept dictates "I am not the type to be wealthy," you will subvert progress unconsciously. Identity is tenacious. It is constructed from long-held narratives—about who we are, what we deserve, and the life we're meant to lead. Budgets are simple; rewriting those narratives demands courage, insight, and discomfort.

So when people assert they merely need to "learn more about money," we must ask: is it knowledge that's lacking, or emotional safety—the kind that allows risk, self-redefinition, and behavioural change? Rational arguments cannot override a nervous system conditioned by fear, scarcity, or shame. Yet conventional financial systems insist precisely on this: act rationally despite irrational wiring, follow the plan, ignore the emotion, trust the numbers. When such approaches fail, blame is internalised as moral weakness. The reality is far subtler: the challenge is managing a deeply human, emotionally charged system with tools ill-suited for the task.

The alternative begins with acknowledgment: financial decisions are fundamentally emotional. Beneath percentages and spreadsheets lie feelings, narratives, memories, and instincts. Without engaging these, no plan or budget will endure. Knowledge alone is insufficient; insight is required.

Next, we replace shame with understanding. Behaviours that frustrate—avoiding statements, undercharging, panicking in downturns—are not failures. They are signals of unmet needs and unresolved fears. Compassionate exploration, rather than judgment, is the path to meaningful change.

Finally, we must reframe what it means to be "good with money." It is not perfection, nor the suppression of feeling, nor robotic efficiency. It is integration: designing a financial life aligned with psychological reality, values, and lived experience—not an abstract ideal that ignores history and humanity.

The following chapters delve into culture, morality, family influence, and identity, exploring how these shape financial behaviour in ways seldom articulated. It begins with recognising a simple truth: money was never meant to make pure sense. The solution is not more information, but deeper insight—into our conditioning, our needs, and the foundations of safety, empowerment, and financial freedom.

We are not irrational. We are human. And when that is understood, it becomes the most potent foundation for wealth imaginable.

Your Brain Was Built for Survival, Not Savings

Why our ancient instincts still push us to overspend, hoard, or panic—no matter how smart we are

Money is a modern invention, but the mind that handles it is anything but. We like to imagine that financial behaviour is a matter of logic: if you earn more than you spend, save consistently, and invest wisely, you should build wealth. The formula is not complicated. And yet, the disconnect between knowing what to do and actually doing it persists across income levels, professions, and levels of education. Economists call it "irrational behaviour." Psychologists offer labels—impulse spending, risk aversion, loss aversion, financial avoidance. But these are just descriptions. To understand *why* smart people make self-defeating financial choices, we must look deeper—beyond habits and heuristics, into biology.

Human cognition did not evolve to navigate interest rates, long-term financial planning, or abstract risk modelling. It evolved to solve one problem: *stay alive today.* Our brains are wired for survival in conditions that no longer exist. The hunter-gatherer environments of the Palaeolithic era shaped not only our physical instincts but the architecture of our emotions, reward systems, and decision-making processes. The result? A mental operating system optimised for immediate threats, fleeting opportunities, and short-term gains—now attempting to navigate a world of pensions, portfolios, and economic volatility. This mismatch is not incidental. It is central.

The prefrontal cortex—the part of the brain responsible for rational planning, delayed gratification, and complex calculation—is a relatively recent development. Much of our behaviour is still governed by older systems: the limbic brain, which controls emotion and memory, and the brainstem, which manages primal responses like fight, flight, and freeze. When we experience financial stress, it is not merely a mental concern—it is a perceived threat to our safety. The same circuitry that once sounded the alarm at the sight of a predator now fires at the sight of an overdraft notice. The body does not distinguish between physical and psychological threat. The response is the same: tunnel vision, elevated heart rate, reduced executive function. In short, we become worse at making decisions *precisely* when those decisions matter most.

This explains why panic selling during market downturns is so common, even among experienced investors. It is not a failure of knowledge. It is a reversion to older, faster systems. The amygdala, the brain's fear centre, reacts much more quickly than the analytical brain. It is wired to err on the side of caution. Better to flee a rustling bush than risk a hidden snake. Applied to financial contexts, this means we will often react disproportionately to uncertainty or loss—selling when we should hold, hoarding when we should invest, or freezing when decisive action is needed.

Scarcity is particularly potent in hijacking cognition. Research in behavioural economics, notably by Sendhil Mullainathan and Eldar Shafir, has shown that the experience of financial scarcity narrows focus, reduces cognitive bandwidth, and impairs decision-making—even among those with no prior deficits in intelligence or ability. This "scarcity mindset" does not only affect the poor. Anyone under significant financial pressure is vulnerable. The brain, faced with perceived threat, reverts to immediate problem-solving. Long-term goals recede. Strategic thinking shuts down. Urgency takes over.

This is not a character flaw. It is a neurobiological response. And it is incredibly costly.

Another powerful ancient instinct at play is reward sensitivity. The dopamine system, which regulates our sense of anticipation and pleasure, evolved to motivate behaviours that supported survival—finding food, securing shelter, forming alliances. But modern consumer economies are built to exploit this system. Every sale, every notification of a deposit, every shiny new product is designed to trigger the promise of reward. Importantly, dopamine does not respond to reward itself—it responds to the *anticipation* of it. This is why online shopping can feel more pleasurable before the item even arrives. The system is primed for chasing, not possessing.

It's also why delayed gratification, so essential to saving and investing, often feels unrewarding in the moment. Telling someone to contribute to a retirement fund instead of booking a holiday is, neurologically speaking, asking them to bypass an immediate dopamine hit for a vague, abstract future gain. It's not that the decision is wrong. It's that it conflicts with the default wiring of the brain. When financial educators frame success purely in terms of willpower or self-control, they miss the underlying dynamic: people are not failing to be rational. They are responding, quite predictably, to emotional and neurological incentives.

Compounding this issue is the social context in which our brains evolved. For the vast majority of human history, status was signalled through proximity, not purchase. Belonging to a tribe, being visible, and adhering to group norms were key to survival. To be excluded was to die. While today's financial choices no longer threaten life in literal terms, they do threaten identity, belonging, and social value—concerns the brain treats with similar urgency. This is why we often spend beyond our means to signal success, conform to peer expectations, or avoid the discomfort of feeling "less than." Status anxiety is not vanity—it's a neuro-social reflex.

And then there is hoarding. In times of uncertainty, it seems rational to conserve resources. But hoarding is often not about logic. It is about control. When external circumstances feel volatile, stockpiling—money, food, even information—provides a semblance of agency. It creates a buffer against vulnerability. But it can also become maladaptive: an excessive fear of letting go, an unwillingness to invest, a reluctance to trust systems or people. The individual becomes financially "safe," but psychologically trapped—incapable of moving beyond survival mode.

Financial trauma, too, leaves neurological imprints. Repeated exposure to instability—whether through poverty, job loss, volatile markets, or parental anxiety—can create heightened sensitivity to financial triggers. The brain learns patterns and stores them. A child who grows up hearing "we can't afford that" may unconsciously associate spending with guilt, or success with disloyalty. These associations often persist long after the original context has changed. They become emotional reflexes, not rational choices.

What's striking is how little traditional financial education addresses any of this. Instead, it tends to operate on the assumption that humans are essentially rational agents who occasionally behave irrationally. In fact, the reverse may be closer to the truth: we are emotional agents, capable of rationality under the right conditions. Until those emotional conditions—safety, clarity, self-worth—are in place, no amount of financial knowledge will translate into sustainable change.

This has significant implications for how we approach financial growth. If your instinct under stress is to shut down or panic, then designing financial systems that minimise decision fatigue becomes essential. Automating savings, setting up default investment contributions, creating "if-then" rules—these are not just tools of convenience, they are tools of emotional safety. They reduce the load on the brain's executive function and lower the likelihood of reactive decisions.

Likewise, if you know that spending gives you emotional relief, the goal is not simply to stop spending—it is to understand what the spending is trying to soothe. Is it anxiety? Loneliness? Shame? Until those emotions are acknowledged and processed, they will find expression through money. Financial behaviour, after all, is rarely about finance alone. It is about emotion in motion.

The good news is that the brain, while slow to adapt, is not fixed. Neuroplasticity—the brain's capacity to rewire itself—means that with repeated patterns of reflection, behavioural adjustment, and emotional regulation, financial instincts can evolve. But the path to change does not begin with shame or sheer willpower. It begins with understanding. With recognising that the very behaviours we criticise in ourselves—impulsivity, avoidance, risk aversion—are not signs of weakness. They are signs of a brain doing its best to protect us with tools it inherited long before credit cards, markets, or retirement planning existed.

If we wish to become more effective with money, we must stop framing our irrational behaviours as failures of intelligence or character. Instead, we must learn to decode the emotional and neurological roots beneath them. Intelligence is not enough. Insight, awareness, and compassion—these are the true catalysts of transformation.

To be financially wise in the modern world is not to transcend emotion, but to integrate it. To respect the ancient instincts that helped us survive, while learning to lead them—not be led by them. The brain was built for survival. But it can be trained for something more.

The Comfort of Playing It Safe

Why we cling to small, predictable outcomes instead of risking for bigger rewards

People don't play it safe because they're weak. They do it because it works—until it doesn't. Safety is not just a preference; it's a primary operating principle embedded in the architecture of the human psyche. Predictability feels like power. Certainty feels like control. And in financial contexts, where outcomes often involve risk, delay, and ambiguity, clinging to the familiar is not just common—it's almost inevitable. The real question is not why people settle for less, but why the alternative—stretching toward something more—is so psychologically expensive, even when the potential reward far outweighs the risk.

What's striking is how many people, even those with abundant competence and opportunity, voluntarily restrict their financial lives. They underprice their work, delay investing, stay in jobs that underutilise them, or reject ideas that could scale their income. They stick with what's small, known, and proven—because it gives them a sense of order. Safety becomes the strategy, even when the underlying motive is avoidance. But playing it safe is rarely neutral. Over time, it can become a kind of slow erosion: of ambition, of growth, of self-trust. Beneath the surface lies a quiet trade-off—certainty over possibility, control over creativity, survival over expansion.

The human brain is not wired to maximise wealth. It is wired to avoid loss. This is the legacy of our evolutionary history, where the cost of a mistake could be death, and the value of reward was secondary to the importance of staying alive. The psychology of risk aversion runs deep. We overvalue immediate certainty and undervalue long-term upside. We react more strongly to potential loss than to equivalent gain. Behavioural economics terms this *loss aversion*, but it's more than a cognitive bias. It's an adaptive trait misapplied in a modern context.

In today's economic environment, this bias becomes maladaptive. Many of the most valuable opportunities—entrepreneurship, investing, negotiation, creative innovation—require tolerating uncertainty. They require an emotional posture that embraces volatility without flinching. But that posture is rarely taught, and even more rarely modelled. Most of us were raised in environments—familial, educational, cultural—that emphasised stability over expansion. We were taught to seek the predictable path, the secure job, the guaranteed income. We were not taught to discern *healthy risk* from recklessness. As a result, risk itself becomes a category mistake—anything uncertain becomes unsafe.

Consider how this plays out in everyday financial behaviour. A freelancer who underbills because they're afraid a higher rate will scare clients away. A salaried employee who stays in a role years past its expiration date, reluctant to start over or renegotiate. An investor who avoids the stock market altogether because of one painful experience or family cautionary tale. In each case, the person is not making the *wrong* decision in a vacuum. They are optimising for emotional security in a world that has trained them to fear instability.

What looks like irrational caution is often a very rational attempt to preserve identity, safety, and control.

This logic extends to income ceilings. Many people subconsciously set a financial thermostat—an internalised cap on what they're allowed to earn or accumulate. When an opportunity arises that exceeds this thermostat, they resist. Not because they doubt the opportunity, but because it threatens their constructed sense of what is "normal" for them. To want more than your familiar baseline can feel dangerous. It risks rejection, ridicule, or perceived arrogance. It disrupts loyalty to one's roots. So, we default to what is acceptable, even if it means underperforming our true capacity. Safety masquerades as humility, when in fact it is often fear.

The real threat, then, is not external loss but *internal dissonance.* Taking a bigger financial risk—starting a business, investing in oneself, scaling operations—forces a confrontation with identity. *Am I the kind of person who does this? What happens if I fail? Will I still belong?* These are not abstract questions. They shape behaviour with surgical precision. The fear of identity dislocation keeps countless people from saying yes to opportunities they intellectually understand, emotionally desire, and financially could afford to pursue.

The other hidden cost of playing it safe is opportunity blindness. When the brain is primed for threat, it cannot easily perceive potential. It narrows focus. It seeks confirmation of what could go wrong. This is not just psychological; it's neurological. The prefrontal cortex, responsible for strategic thinking and executive decision-making, becomes less active under stress. The amygdala, the threat-response centre, takes over. The result is a form of tunnel vision: we see only the immediate, the certain, the avoidable downside. The upside becomes conceptually distant, emotionally inaccessible.

This explains why financial coaching, career advice, or business mentorship often falls flat when it skips the emotional underlayer. Telling someone to "think bigger" or "just raise your prices" ignores the internal safety system they are navigating. Change is not a matter of motivation alone. It is a negotiation with the nervous system. Until a person feels internally safe enough to risk unpredictability, they will continue to cling to small certainties—even when those certainties limit their freedom.

There is also a social component. Much of what we call "risk aversion" is actually a fear of social consequence. The fear of seeming foolish, overreaching, or greedy. The fear of violating group norms. This is especially acute in environments where financial success is not culturally neutral, but morally coded. For many, making more money is not just a numbers game—it's an identity gamble. *Will people still relate to me if I change tax brackets? Will they think I've sold out?*

These are not superficial concerns. Humans are tribal creatures. Belonging matters. And when the desire for safety is rooted in the need to stay connected to a group, financial choices become acts of allegiance. The safe choice is not always the economically efficient one—it is the socially protective one. To step beyond that boundary, to opt for a path that might be lonely, misunderstood, or envied, requires more than courage. It requires a new internal framework of what safety actually means.

This is where the work begins—not in eliminating fear, but in redefining safety. Real financial safety is not the absence of uncertainty. It is the presence of internal capacity. It is the ability to withstand discomfort, navigate ambiguity, and recover from setbacks without collapsing. Paradoxically, the more one expands their *tolerance* for risk, the safer they become. Because they are no longer dependent on external predictability for internal peace.

Practical tools can support this psychological shift, but they cannot replace it. For instance, risk mitigation strategies—emergency funds, diversified investments, business reserves—are essential. But they only function well when the individual is not sabotaging them with subconscious avoidance or overcorrection. True resilience is a function of emotional preparedness as much as financial planning. It involves cultivating the self-trust required to act in the face of uncertainty, not the illusion that uncertainty can be eliminated.

The irony is that playing it safe is itself risky. The opportunity cost of over-caution is often invisible, but no less real. Income potential stalls. Creativity atrophies. Market advantages expire. Perhaps most damaging of all, a person's sense of agency slowly erodes. They begin to see themselves as someone who "just doesn't take risks," not because it's true, but because it's rehearsed. Over time, that identity calcifies. Not because it was consciously chosen, but because it was never consciously challenged.

The way out is not reckless leap-taking, but strategic discomfort. It is the repeated practice of stretching the boundary of what feels safe—financially, professionally, emotionally—without overwhelming the system. It's accepting that growth *is* uncomfortable, that the absence of anxiety is not the goal, and that the person you are becoming cannot be built inside the comfort zone of who you've been.

Financial freedom is not only about access to resources. It is about access to *range*—the psychological space to choose a bigger game without being governed by fear. That range must be developed. It cannot be downloaded. It is earned through reflection, practice, and the willingness to disappoint old narratives in service of new possibilities.

Most people are not choosing between success and failure. They are choosing between the known and the possible. And often, the known wins—not because it is better, but because it is familiar. The real work of wealth-building begins with questioning that familiarity, and with building an internal environment where bigger outcomes are not just imaginable, but emotionally accessible. Playing it safe may feel responsible. But if it costs you the fuller expression of your capacity, the greater danger may be staying small.

When Money Becomes Medicine

How we use money to soothe fear, shame, loneliness, and unspoken insecurities—and how to break that emotional cycle

Few people are truly spending money. Most are treating something. It's a diagnosis rarely offered in financial discourse, which tends to cast money as either a resource to be optimised or a problem to be solved. But for many, money serves a third, less visible function—it becomes a surrogate for emotional regulation. We spend, hoard, or give not just in response to needs or values, but in response to pain: the quiet kind that sits beneath the surface of everyday life—fear, inadequacy, loneliness, boredom, guilt. In this light, financial behaviour is often less a reflection of economic logic and more a form of psychological coping. Money becomes medicine.

Understanding this begins with recognising that financial decisions are rarely made in a vacuum. They occur within a web of emotion, memory, and identity. While economists model humans as rational actors, decades of interdisciplinary research suggest otherwise. Neurologically, financial decisions activate regions of the brain associated with emotion and threat detection. In high-stakes or uncertain scenarios, our prefrontal cortex—the rational decision-making centre—is often overridden by the amygdala, which governs fear and stress responses. This means we do not always choose what is best—we choose what *feels safest* in the moment. And safety, for many, is not about having a plan. It's about having a way to quiet what hurts.

Retail therapy is the most recognisable example. The term is casually dismissed, but its mechanisms are well documented. Shopping triggers the brain's dopamine system, offering a short-term elevation in mood. This is especially potent when life feels out of control. The act of purchasing creates a sense of agency. We choose. We acquire. We temporarily shift from reactive to proactive. But it is not the item that heals—it is the momentary reprieve from discomfort. The trouble is, the underlying pain remains unaddressed. And so, the cycle continues: trigger, purchase, relief, regret, repeat.

The same principle applies to those who hoard wealth or delay spending despite financial stability. On the surface, these individuals may appear disciplined or frugal. In reality, many are driven by chronic anxiety. Money, in this case, is not medicine but armour—a defence against the chaos of life. The logic is simple but emotionally loaded: *If I have enough, I'll be safe. If I spend, I'll be exposed.* This pattern is often rooted in childhood experiences of unpredictability—parents fighting over bills, sudden job loss, periods of deprivation. Even decades later, and even in objectively secure conditions, the body remembers what it once lacked. Fear, once imprinted, does not vanish with logic.

Others use money to buy connection. Generosity, while admirable, can mask a deeper hunger for validation or belonging. We offer gifts, cover bills, or pick up the tab—not just from goodwill, but from a desire to be liked, needed, or approved of. This becomes especially pronounced in relationships where financial giving is tied to identity: the provider, the caretaker, the one who always says yes. The cost is rarely just monetary. Over time, resentment, burnout, or imbalance can emerge, yet feel impossible to correct—because the giving was never about fairness. It was about self-worth.

On the other side of the spectrum, some use money as a substitute for personal boundaries. They say yes to every request, undercharge for their services, or avoid asking for payment. The discomfort here is not financial—it's interpersonal. Many fear that asserting financial needs will lead to conflict, rejection, or shame. So they absorb the loss. But beneath the surface, the pattern is one of appeasement. Money becomes the tool through which harmony is purchased and discomfort is avoided. It's not generosity. It's emotional outsourcing.

One of the most insidious forms of this dynamic appears in compulsive financial behaviour—not just spending, but gambling, investing with excessive risk, or chasing "get-rich-quick" schemes. These behaviours are often fuelled not by greed, but by despair. When life feels stagnant or one's self-worth is depleted, the promise of a financial breakthrough offers emotional escape. The fantasy of sudden wealth is not just about freedom—it's about transformation. But the emotional void such fantasies aim to fill is rarely financial. It's existential. And it cannot be fixed with numbers alone.

The common thread in all these cases is emotional displacement. Money becomes a proxy—a means of managing feelings we do not know how to confront directly. The problem is not the behaviour itself, but the disconnection from its root. When money is used to medicate pain, the pain inevitably returns. And because the pattern is unconscious, most people do not realise they are treating emotion with currency. They think they are being practical, generous, cautious, ambitious. But under scrutiny, the decisions reveal themselves as symptoms.

To break this cycle, awareness is the first step. Not generic awareness, but granular. Specificity is key. One must learn to ask: *What feeling am I avoiding right now? What am I trying to soothe, solve, or prove through this financial choice?* These questions are not rhetorical—they are diagnostic. They begin to map the emotional architecture beneath financial habits. Over time, patterns emerge. Spending correlates with loneliness. Saving correlates with fear. Undercharging correlates with guilt. Each behaviour becomes a clue, not a flaw.

But awareness alone is insufficient. The deeper work is to develop emotional alternatives—to build internal capacity for discomfort so that money is no longer required to regulate it. This may involve learning to sit with anxiety without fixing it, to feel shame without appeasing it, or to express a boundary without buying your way out of confrontation. This is not about becoming stoic or emotionless. It is about *decoupling money from emotion*, so that each can be addressed on its own terms.

Therapeutic support can be crucial here, especially when patterns are rooted in trauma. Financial therapy, a growing interdisciplinary field, combines psychological insight with financial education. It helps individuals understand not just how they behave with money, but *why*. This is particularly important in cases where financial self-sabotage, chronic deprivation, or compulsive giving are tied to early relational wounds. Healing in this context is not just financial recovery. It is the restoration of agency, self-trust, and internal coherence.

Cultural narratives must also be challenged. Many of us were raised with messages that linked money to morality—saving is good, spending is bad; generosity is noble, self-interest is selfish. These scripts, while well-intentioned, often confuse emotional health with behavioural compliance. They discourage inquiry. But financial behaviour is not a moral issue. It is a reflection of inner states. There is no virtue in hoarding if it comes from fear. There is no sin in spending if it reflects joy. The point is not to moralise money, but to humanise it.

In practical terms, this means building new rituals around financial decision-making. Before a purchase, a negotiation, or a giving decision, pause and check for emotion. *Am I calm or triggered? Am I grounded or grasping?* Introduce a delay between impulse and action—not as a rule, but as an inquiry. Even a few minutes of reflection can create space for clarity. Over time, this builds emotional fluency—the ability to discern when money is a tool, and when it is a treatment.

It also means building non-financial strategies for emotional regulation. Movement, connection, creativity, therapy, rest—each offers a way to process discomfort without outsourcing it to money. These are not luxuries. They are prerequisites for a healthy financial life. Without them, money remains the default mechanism for control and comfort. With them, money is freed to serve its actual purpose: to enable, not to soothe.

Perhaps most importantly, breaking the emotional cycle with money requires self-compassion. These patterns are not signs of failure. They are evidence of a system doing its best with the tools it had. Money became medicine because other options were unavailable, unsafe, or unknown. Recognising this allows for change without shame. It reframes the past not as a series of mistakes, but as a map of unmet needs.

To shift from medicating to mastering one's financial life is not a matter of perfecting spreadsheets. It is the work of integration—bringing the emotional, the relational, and the behavioural into coherence. It demands that we stop asking only, *What am I doing with my money?* and begin asking, *What is my money doing with me?*

Until we make that shift, even the most disciplined financial strategy risks being a bandage over an emotional wound. But once we do, money ceases to be a means of managing pain—and becomes a vehicle for expressing possibility.

Why Knowing More Changes Nothing

Why financial advice often fails—because information doesn't change identity

At no point in human history has financial information been more abundant or more accessible. There are bookshelves lined with personal finance bestsellers, podcasts dissecting every budgeting method, influencers publishing daily videos on how to build wealth in your sleep, and countless apps promising to automate your way to financial freedom. And yet, despite this unprecedented exposure to advice, strategies, and frameworks, the gap between what people *know* and what they *do* remains stubbornly wide. Knowledge is not the problem. Behaviour is. And behaviour, contrary to popular assumption, is not governed by information alone. It is governed by *identity.*

This is the central reason why so much well-intentioned financial advice fails. It attempts to inform, when it needs to *transform.* It targets action, while bypassing the underlying sense of self that determines what actions a person feels safe taking. A spreadsheet doesn't challenge someone's self-concept. An investment webinar doesn't recalibrate inherited beliefs about deservingness. Budgeting software doesn't address shame, scarcity conditioning, or the unconscious fear of being seen as "too much" if one earns more. Advice speaks to behaviour. But behaviour is downstream of belief. And belief is married to identity.

To put this differently: people don't simply act on what they *know*; they act on who they *believe they are.* A person who sees themselves as disorganised will unconsciously resist any system that requires order. Someone who was raised to associate wealth with corruption may self-sabotage each time their income grows beyond a familiar threshold. A woman who internalised that she must never outshine her partner may keep her pricing low, not because she lacks skills, but because her sense of identity is wired to preserve harmony through financial diminishment. These are not rational decisions. They are identity-maintenance mechanisms. And until they are examined, no amount of financial advice will produce sustainable change.

The problem, of course, is that identity is rarely addressed in financial education. In most cases, financial behaviour is treated as a matter of discipline, planning, or self-control. You didn't save? You lack willpower. You overspent? You need more accountability. You're stuck in debt? Try harder. This frame is seductive because it implies that success is within reach—just follow the formula. But when people inevitably fail to follow it, they're left not just with practical setbacks but with a deeper sense of inadequacy. The formula didn't fit. *Therefore, I must be the problem.*

What gets missed here is that people resist action not because they are lazy, but because the action conflicts with an internal identity structure. Telling someone who grew up in financial chaos to "just automate their savings" ignores the reality that for them, *certainty feels suspicious.* Asking a person who has survived on £30,000 a year for their entire adult life to suddenly embrace a six-figure opportunity triggers a sense of betrayal—not just of their past, but of the relationships and values that helped them survive it. Financial growth is not merely a behavioural shift. It's a narrative rupture.

The field of psychology supports this. Behavioural identity theory posits that individuals are motivated to act in ways that reinforce their self-concept. When an action—no matter how beneficial—contradicts that concept, it creates cognitive dissonance. The discomfort is rarely attributed to the identity itself (which feels like "who I am") but to the behaviour. So the behaviour is abandoned, and the identity is preserved. This is not failure. This is coherence. The mind's first priority is not progress—it is consistency.

This also explains why financial interventions based on information alone tend to have short-lived effects. Studies in behavioural finance show that even when people receive personalised advice, they often revert to previous patterns within months. The advice wasn't wrong. It simply wasn't *integrated.* It hadn't been reconciled with the client's emotional wiring, social context, or internalised worldview. Without that reconciliation, new strategies trigger resistance. The nervous system flags change as threat, and the person quietly—or dramatically—pulls back to the familiar.

It's worth pausing here to note that *the familiar is not the same as the functional.* People can remain loyal to deeply limiting financial patterns because those patterns confirm their place in the world. The person who always struggles gets to remain relatable. The person who never charges their worth avoids feeling selfish. The person who saves obsessively avoids the vulnerability of depending on others. These roles are often inherited, rehearsed, and reinforced for years before they are ever challenged. So when financial advice invites someone to act differently, it is also, implicitly, inviting them to *be someone different.* That's a much higher-stakes proposition.

The relationship between money and identity also plays out across cultural and intergenerational lines. For example, someone raised in a working-class family may carry implicit messages like *we're not the kind of people who get rich*, or *rich people forget where they come from*. These ideas are rarely stated outright, but they infuse behaviour. They set invisible ceilings. When a financial opportunity threatens to move someone out of their inherited class identity, it may be interpreted—consciously or not—as abandonment, betrayal, or pretentiousness. And so, the opportunity is declined. Not because it's unwise. But because it's incompatible with the story they're still living in.

Similarly, many people—particularly women, people of colour, or those from historically marginalised communities—have absorbed implicit narratives about what financial power looks like, and whether it is safe to claim it. The advice to "negotiate your salary" or "raise your rates" may sound neutral, but the underlying identity conflicts can be profound. Will I be seen as difficult? Will I be punished for asserting myself? Will I lose social capital or be judged as greedy? These are not hypothetical concerns. They are lived experiences, and they shape not just behaviour, but the willingness to *even consider* certain actions.

To shift financial behaviour in a meaningful and lasting way, we must stop treating advice as the main lever of change. Advice has its place—but only after identity has been addressed. This requires a different kind of conversation—one that acknowledges that people are not just failing to act, they are *protecting* something. A sense of belonging. A familiar emotional rhythm. A coherent narrative about what is safe, good, or acceptable. Change becomes possible not when new information is introduced, but when people begin to question whether the story they've inherited still serves them.

This is why the most powerful financial transformations rarely begin with budgeting tools. They begin with questions: *What have you learned about what's possible for someone like you? What did your parents model about money, success, or ambition? Who might you disappoint if you became wealthy?* These are not rhetorical provocations. They are the starting points for identity revision. And only through such revision does new behaviour become sustainable.

So what does this look like in practice? It means that before giving someone a strategy, you invite them to name the internal resistance. It means helping someone see how their financial choices have been shaped by emotion, not just logic. It means exploring how their current identity might be keeping them safe—but also keeping them small. And it means recognising that financial goals cannot be pursued in isolation from psychological reality.

Change requires safety. And one of the most overlooked truths in financial development is that *people do not change until it feels safe to do so.* That safety is emotional, social, and narrative. It involves building a new identity that can hold greater visibility, power, or independence without triggering dissonance. Only then does advice land as empowering rather than confronting.

The work, then, is not to find more tips. It is to ask better questions. To dig beneath behaviour and locate the belief. To understand that when someone says they "just need more discipline," what they often mean is *they need permission*—to let go of who they think they need to be, and step into who they're allowed to become. No spreadsheet will do that for them. But self-awareness might. Community might. Therapy might. Narrative repair certainly will.

If knowing were enough, we'd all be financially thriving. We are not. Because knowledge alone doesn't rewire the identity that is steering the ship. Behaviour follows belief, and belief is anchored in story. The work of financial freedom is not merely about doing more. It's about *becoming someone* who believes that more is possible—and allowed. Until that shift occurs, all the advice in the world will remain precisely what it is: optional. And mostly ignored.

CHAPTER 2
The Morality Trap

For many, money functions as more than a medium of exchange or a simple facilitator of choice—it becomes, almost imperceptibly, a gauge of moral worth. Unconsciously, we imbue financial outcomes with character assessments: the modest are "humble," those in debt "irresponsible," and the wealthy are either admired or mistrusted, depending on context. In this way, financial decisions are never merely practical; they are moralised. We judge not only the consequences of choices but the perceived integrity behind them. This moral undercurrent, largely invisible to those navigating it, exerts a powerful influence over our financial lives.

When money shapes identity, its effect is profound. Life's ledger ceases to be a record of transactions and becomes, instead, a mirror of self. The repercussions are tangible: skilled professionals underpaid, adults paralysed by the shame of debt, honest discussions about earnings stifled, and ambition rendered something to apologise for. The trap is both external and internal. Virtue is misread as limitation; caution mistaken for smallness. Many believe they must choose between moral rectitude and material prosperity, as if the two cannot coexist.

This confusion is not arbitrary. It is inherited. Religious teachings often equated poverty with piety, political narratives cast wealth as exploitation, and family traditions sometimes framed material aspiration as betrayal. These stories infiltrate how we earn, spend, save, and aspire, shaping not just our actions but our emotions. Morality is not a neutral framework applied retrospectively; it colours choices in real time, whispering into every decision, dictating what we feel entitled to seek, claim, or pursue.

The archetype of the "good poor person" runs deep in culture. Virtue validated through struggle. Living frugally is lauded as a marker of authenticity or moral fibre. From literature and film to religious and corporate narratives, the self-sacrificing teacher, the struggling artist, or the saintly figure rejecting material comfort are celebrated, often in contrast to the ostentatious or greedy. These stories do more than entertain; they embed a false binary: caring for others and caring for money are mutually exclusive.

This dichotomy is both seductive and constraining. It offers a clear moral identity, yet it traps. Wealth becomes tinged with guilt, ambition a source of inner conflict. When earnings rise, prices increase, or investments grow bolder, a quiet internal debate often emerges: Am I being greedy? Has something changed in how others see me? These are moral concerns, not rational ones. And because morality intertwines with self-worth, they are notoriously difficult to untangle.

Debt, too, carries moral weight. Though central to contemporary economies and routinely used by corporations, governments, and universities, debt remains emotionally fraught. Few regard it neutrally; shame is the common response. The messages are unyielding: debt signals failure, carelessness, indulgence. Yet this lens obscures structural realities—soaring living costs, wage stagnation, systemic inequities. Borrowing is often rational, yet guilt persists. Context is ignored; intention overlooked. A successful entrepreneur leveraging £200,000 appears strategic, whereas a graduate with £40,000 in loans is naïve. Families taking loans for emergencies may be prudent, yet social and internalised narratives rarely allow nuance. The result is hesitation, avoidance, and self-defeating choices. Debt becomes a psychological cage, not merely a financial fact.

Beneath both the poverty-virtue ideal and the debt-shame cycle lies the more insidious guilt of desire. If poverty signifies purity and debt signals disgrace, the wish for more seems dangerous. Many quietly downplay ambitions, hedging desires with disclaimers: "It's not about the money, but..." Fear of being perceived as selfish or ungrateful limits dreams. The discomfort is rarely about aspiration itself; it arises from the inherited story about ambition—that personal gain must exact social cost, that growth entails moral compromise. Often unconscious, these beliefs govern career choices, pricing, investment, and even the wealth one allows oneself to accumulate.

These moral scripts are not evenly distributed. Women frequently internalise self-sacrifice as virtue. In professional contexts, they are lauded for achieving more with less, "making it work," prioritising others. When asserting financial worth, they risk being branded aggressive or ungrateful. Biases extend beyond workplaces into self-perception: a woman may undercharge to avoid appearing greedy, a working-class man may shy from negotiation to prevent seeming superior. These are moral decisions masquerading as technical ones.

Generosity, too, is warped by moral framing. Many cultures valorise giving that involves personal sacrifice, linking virtue to discomfort. This can encourage overextension, burnout, or dependency, reinforcing the notion that wealth is justifiable only when redistributed—often to the giver's detriment. Yet guilt-driven generosity is unsustainable. True giving requires capacity; it cannot flourish where individuals punish themselves for having more than others.

Escaping the morality trap begins with recognising that money and virtue inhabit separate domains. Wealth is not a marker of goodness, nor is poverty proof of integrity. There are compassionate and selfish wealthy people alike; wise and reckless debtors. Conflating financial circumstances with moral worth oversimplifies human behaviour and sustains damaging stereotypes.

From there, introspection is key. What messages about "good" people and money did your upbringing or culture impart? Which served you, which restricted you? Awareness of these inherited scripts is foundational. Without it, new strategies remain filtered through old beliefs.

Finally, financial ambition should be embraced without apology. Desire is not the problem—ethics, execution, and intent are. Expanding income, increasing prices, building generational wealth are not inherently selfish acts. When guided by values and clarity, money becomes a tool for alignment rather than a test of character.

This chapter challenges the invisible scripts that govern our financial lives: the shame, the guilt, the false binaries. It urges nuanced understanding over rigid moralism, and the courage to grow economically without compromising character. True integrity is measured not by self-imposed limitation, but by the capacity to wield power with responsibility, clarity, and grace. Morality need not be the enemy—but entwined uncritically with money, it can become a formidable trap. It is time to step free.

The Good Person, Poor Person Myth

How our culture links wealth to virtue—and why this deeply confuses your financial decisions

There is a quiet script many people live by, rarely spoken aloud but always present: *It's better to be good than to be rich.* In this framing, wealth is not a neutral condition but a character test. If you have too much, you must have taken more than your share. If you have too little, perhaps you are virtuous for enduring it. This script shapes how people view themselves, how they judge others, and—most powerfully—how they make financial decisions. It's not simply a matter of economics. It's moral conditioning. And most of it happens unconsciously.

At the heart of this conditioning is a cultural conflation between goodness and struggle. In stories, films, politics, and religious teachings, we're taught to admire the underdog, the self-sacrificing provider, the humble worker who does the right thing despite hardship. These figures are noble *because* they endure. Their poverty—or at least their restraint—is framed as evidence of integrity. The wealthy character, by contrast, is often cast as cold, greedy, or disconnected. Whether it's Scrooge, the corporate villain, or the out-of-touch elite, the message is consistent: money corrupts. Or, if it doesn't corrupt, it certainly complicates. Better, then, to steer clear.

This dichotomy is not without historical roots. In many religious and philosophical traditions, wealth has long been treated with suspicion. In Christianity, the phrase "It is easier for a camel to go through the eye of a needle than for a rich man to enter the kingdom of God" continues to echo centuries after it was first written. In various monastic traditions, the renunciation of material wealth is seen as a pathway to spiritual clarity. Even in secular society, self-denial is often equated with virtue, while wealth—especially visibly displayed wealth—is frequently regarded with scepticism or disdain. The "good person, poor person" myth emerges from this lineage. And while the contexts may have shifted, the implications remain surprisingly durable.

This myth becomes particularly problematic when it operates below the level of awareness. People do not usually say, "I don't want to be wealthy because I'm afraid it will make me a worse person." Instead, the resistance shows up in behaviour: underpricing, over-giving, chronic hesitation around growth, refusal to invest in oneself. These are not just practical choices. They are moral negotiations. The individual may feel that to make more is to risk becoming someone else—someone less grounded, less generous, less "real." Wealth, in this framework, threatens to sever one's connection to community, identity, or authenticity. So staying small becomes a kind of loyalty. Not to a financial model, but to a moral one.

This is where the confusion becomes acute. Because financial decisions are rarely made in purely rational terms. They are made within the emotional and moral frameworks we inherit. If you believe—consciously or not—that growing your income compromises your integrity, you will find ways to delay, decline, or dilute opportunities. You'll tell yourself the timing isn't right, or that you're "not ready," or that you're prioritising balance. But often, what you're really doing is avoiding the identity shift that wealth might require. It's not the money that's threatening. It's the fear of becoming misaligned with who you think you are supposed to be.

This phenomenon is especially visible in professions that are culturally coded as altruistic: education, social work, the arts, activism. In these fields, low pay is often seen as proof of commitment. To seek more is to risk being accused—explicitly or implicitly—of "selling out." The artist who begins to earn well may be seen as compromising their integrity. The teacher who leaves the classroom to consult privately may be seen as abandoning their post. The social worker who launches a paid coaching practice may be viewed with suspicion by peers. These dynamics don't just reflect social judgments. They become internalised. The professional begins to self-regulate, ensuring they never reach an income level that might make them morally ambiguous.

It is important to be precise here. This is not an argument in favour of financial entitlement, greed, or unexamined accumulation. Nor is it a denial that systemic inequality and privilege shape financial outcomes in very real ways. Rather, it is an attempt to illuminate a subtle but powerful barrier that exists within people who already have the skill, competence, and opportunity to grow—but don't. Because they're afraid that to become rich is to become *someone else* entirely. Someone they—or the people they love—might not recognise, accept, or respect.

This internalised mythology is not unique to any one class or community. But its manifestation often tracks along cultural, gendered, and socioeconomic lines. For instance, individuals from working-class backgrounds may be taught that "people like us" don't seek excess. Wealth, in that context, is not just improbable—it's undesirable. It marks distance. It risks disloyalty. Better to be "real" and under-resourced than to be well-off and estranged. The unwritten contract is clear: financial growth is betrayal. Unless one continues to visibly struggle, one's belonging might be revoked.

Similarly, many women are socialised to perform moral virtue through self-sacrifice. To ask for more is to be "demanding." To raise prices is to be "greedy." To prioritise financial security over relational harmony is to be "selfish." These labels, even when unspoken, weigh heavily. So women shrink. Not because they lack ambition, but because ambition violates the moral script they were given. And the cost of that violation often feels greater than the cost of financial limitation.

Modern media adds another layer of complexity. On the one hand, wealth is hyper-visible—showcased through luxury lifestyles, curated images, and success narratives. On the other hand, moral suspicion lingers. Comment sections erupt when influencers monetise their platforms. Entrepreneurs are scrutinised for profiting from social causes. The tension is unresolved: we celebrate success, but we distrust the successful. The result is a paradox in which people are encouraged to pursue wealth, but not *too much*—and certainly not in ways that appear too confident, assertive, or self-assured.

To navigate this paradox, many people adopt defensive postures. They justify their financial goals by attaching them to external virtues: "I want to earn more so I can give back." "I need a bigger income to support my family." These are valid motivations. But when they are the *only* motivations permitted, something gets lost. The idea that it is acceptable to want financial growth *for yourself*—not just as a means of service, but as a form of agency, expression, or dignity—becomes taboo. And when that desire cannot be named, it cannot be claimed.

The antidote to this moral confusion is not to discard virtue, but to decouple it from deprivation. It is entirely possible to be generous and wealthy, humble and ambitious, ethical and financially resourced. But to inhabit that possibility, we must examine the scripts we've inherited. We must ask: *Who taught me what a "good" person looks like financially? What stories did I absorb about rich people? What assumptions do I carry about poverty? Whose approval am I trying to preserve by staying financially small?* These are not rhetorical questions. They are tools of liberation.

Real integrity does not require financial limitation. In fact, when wealth is pursued with clarity and consciousness, it can expand one's capacity for impact, security, and creative freedom. But that pursuit must begin with moral disentanglement. With the recognition that suffering is not a prerequisite for virtue, and that struggling financially does not automatically confer depth, insight, or goodness. It might reflect unjust systems. It might reflect bad luck. But it is not, in and of itself, proof of moral worth.

There is nothing noble about avoiding your potential. There is nothing honourable about under-earning when you have the ability to thrive. And there is nothing selfish about wanting more—if that "more" is grounded in your values, aligned with your character, and free from the shame that says you must always prove your goodness through lack.

The myth of the good person, poor person isn't just false. It's costly. It keeps capable people from stepping into their full power. It distorts financial decisions. It erodes self-trust. And it conditions us to judge one another not by integrity or impact, but by income brackets and sacrifice levels. The real question isn't whether you can be good *and* wealthy. The question is whether you've been conditioned to believe you can't—and whether you're willing to unlearn that belief before it shapes your life too narrowly to recover.

The False Religion of Debt

Why debt isn't automatically bad—and how guilt around borrowing can limit your opportunities

Debt has become one of the most emotionally charged words in the modern financial vocabulary. It does not simply describe a monetary obligation—it often invokes a moral failure. For many, to be in debt is to be irresponsible, unwise, indulgent, or undisciplined. This is not simply a practical concern about interest rates or repayment terms; it is a deeply internalised emotional judgment, shaped by cultural messaging, familial expectations, and the persistent, unspoken belief that good people live within their means and bad people borrow. Debt, in this framework, is no longer a financial tool. It becomes a test of character.

But this framing is not just inaccurate. It's dangerous. Because while it may feel noble to avoid debt at all costs, this belief system often drives people into decisions that limit their growth, erode their agency, and distort their financial potential. They delay opportunities, underinvest in themselves, reject useful leverage, and confuse deprivation with prudence. And all the while, they carry an invisible burden—not just of repayments, but of guilt.

The moralisation of debt is not accidental. It has been cultivated over centuries, particularly through religious and cultural institutions that equated debt with sin. In Christian theology, for example, debt and moral transgression are often linguistically and metaphorically intertwined. Phrases like "forgive us our debts" or the notion of being "indebted" to God reflect a tradition in which financial obligation is linked to spiritual shortcoming. Similarly, in some strands of Islamic jurisprudence, debt is viewed as spiritually undesirable, even though Islamic finance offers structured alternatives. Across many cultures, to be in debt is to be beholden—to owe not just money, but dignity.

These messages filtered into economic and social norms. By the mid-20th century, particularly in Western societies, being debt-free was promoted as a badge of honour. The disciplined family that saved up for every purchase stood in contrast to the reckless spender who borrowed to get ahead. This dichotomy was aggressively reinforced by media, public policy, and financial advice industries that framed credit use as dangerous and debt as inherently shameful. Even today, personal finance content often recycles these tropes, casting all debt as suspect and debt-free living as inherently virtuous.

The result is an environment where many people view debt not as a neutral financial instrument but as a personal stain. Even when the debt was accrued strategically—say, to fund higher education, launch a business, or access housing—borrowers internalise shame. They avoid talking about it, delay seeking advice, and carry a sense of failure even when their actions were justified and economically sound. They do not simply want to repay what they owe—they want to redeem their moral standing.

This moral overlay creates significant distortions in behaviour. People routinely turn down low-interest loans that could meaningfully expand their capacity, simply because they fear "being in debt." They avoid using credit to invest in their careers or acquire appreciating assets, opting instead to pay out of pocket or delay action until they can afford it "outright"—even when the cost of waiting is higher than the cost of borrowing. Others overpay their debts at the expense of building emergency savings, contributing to pensions, or funding important life goals. The logic here is not financial. It is emotional. *It just feels better to owe nothing—even if it makes no sense on paper.*

But debt, in its most useful form, is not a problem to be eliminated. It is a tool to be understood. When used intentionally, debt allows access to resources that would otherwise be out of reach—capital to grow a business, tuition to access education, financing to secure property, or bridging loans to navigate transitions. In a well-structured financial life, strategic debt can act as a catalyst, not a curse. What matters is not whether you borrow, but *why*, *how*, and under what terms.

This does not mean all debt is good, or that one should borrow indiscriminately. High-interest consumer debt, such as credit cards used to fund lifestyle inflation or compulsive spending, often reflects deeper emotional patterns that need addressing. But to treat *all* debt with the same suspicion is intellectually lazy. It collapses nuance. It equates financial activity with moral identity and leaves people either frozen in fear or chasing absolution through accelerated repayment, often at the expense of other priorities.

The pressure to eliminate debt as quickly as possible is often presented as a marker of discipline. But in practice, it can become an act of financial self-harm. People drain savings to pay off debt faster. They decline investment opportunities that could outpace their loan interest. They ignore inflation, opportunity cost, and portfolio diversification in the name of becoming "debt-free." And perhaps most damaging of all, they reinforce the false belief that debt is incompatible with stability, freedom, or maturity.

This belief is particularly harmful for entrepreneurs and self-employed professionals. In the business world, debt—more neutrally referred to as *capital*—is often essential. Few businesses scale without outside funding. Whether through loans, lines of credit, or structured finance, access to borrowed resources is what allows a business to hire, market, develop infrastructure, or pivot strategically. Yet when individuals bring their personal shame-based relationship with debt into their business, they sabotage growth. They self-fund too slowly, underprice their services, or limit operations unnecessarily. They avoid the very leverage that could increase their earnings, all in the name of playing it safe.

Higher education presents another example. In many countries, particularly the United States, student debt has become a lightning rod for broader systemic critiques of education, inequality, and predatory lending. These critiques are valid. But in the discourse, it is easy to forget that *not all educational debt is misguided.* For many, it is the only path into professions that would otherwise remain inaccessible. The real issue is not the existence of debt, but its structure—its terms, cost, and the level of informed consent at the point of entry. To conflate all educational borrowing with regret is to miss the nuance—and to discourage those for whom education is still a powerful lever for upward mobility.

The shame around debt also has a chilling effect on dialogue. Because debt is treated as failure, people avoid talking about it openly. They suffer in silence, compare themselves to a distorted version of others' finances, and internalise a sense of personal inadequacy. This secrecy reinforces isolation. It prevents collective learning. And it fuels the false impression that everyone else is managing perfectly, while they alone are mismanaging their lives. But in reality, debt is ubiquitous. What differs is not the presence of debt, but the level of honesty around it.

To move beyond the false religion of debt, we need a more emotionally intelligent, contextually aware framework. We must separate financial choices from moral panic. We must ask not "Do I have debt?" but "Does this debt serve a clear purpose, under terms I understand, with a repayment plan I can sustain?" That's not a moral question. It's a strategic one. And it opens the door to agency, rather than shame.

Critically, we also need to develop the emotional resilience to hold complexity. You can carry debt and be financially responsible. You can borrow strategically and act with integrity. You can leverage other people's capital without selling your soul. And you can choose *not* to borrow—not because you fear moral contamination, but because you have made a clear-eyed assessment that it's not the right tool for your goal. The difference is not in the action, but in the clarity and confidence behind it.

There is nothing inherently virtuous about deprivation. And there is nothing inherently shameful about needing or using debt. Financial integrity is not about moral purity. It is about informed consent, aligned values, and conscious choice. When we untangle our self-worth from our balance sheet, we free ourselves to think strategically, act courageously, and build resources in service of our goals—not our guilt.

To do that, we must stop treating debt as a confessional booth and start treating it as a lever. Not a moral failing, but a decision to be made wisely. Not a symbol of deficiency, but a potential source of mobility. Not a scarlet letter, but a neutral instrument that, like any tool, can be used well or poorly—but should never define the person who holds it.

The Guilt That Keeps You Small

How invisible feelings of undeservingness sabotage your income, pricing, and negotiations

There is a category of financial limitation that cannot be explained by lack of knowledge, strategy, or opportunity. It's the quiet, persistent feeling that you're not supposed to have more. Not because it's impossible, but because something in you whispers it would be *wrong*—to charge that much, to ask for more, to take up that much space in a room, to profit from your work without apology. This feeling isn't always loud. In fact, its power lies in its subtlety. It operates in the background of your pricing, your earnings, your negotiations. It masks itself as modesty, responsibility, ethics, or pragmatism. But at its root is a simple, often unspoken belief: *I don't deserve more than this.* And that belief quietly governs the shape of your financial life.

The experience of undeservingness is often so internalised that it's invisible to the person experiencing it. They may have every external marker of competence—qualifications, track record, accolades—but still hesitate to invoice what their work is worth. They downplay their needs in salary conversations. They defer to the budgets of others. They use phrases like "I just want to be fair," or "I don't want to be greedy," or "It's not really about the money." These may sound like ethical principles, but more often, they are emotional escape routes—ways to avoid the discomfort of fully owning one's value.

This guilt doesn't emerge from nowhere. It is cultivated over time, often from childhood, where money is rarely discussed explicitly but always taught implicitly. Children absorb not only what is said, but what is felt. They notice whether their parents were stressed or ashamed when asking for a raise, whether generosity was prized over stability, whether ambition was celebrated or criticised. A parent who constantly said, "We can't afford that," may have passed on more than financial caution—they may have taught the child to limit their wants, to equate aspiration with risk or selfishness. The message is rarely stated outright, but it lands all the same: *you are better—safer, nicer, more lovable—if you don't ask for too much.*

This emotional pattern is especially common among people from marginalised or historically disadvantaged backgrounds. When your identity, culture, or family history includes experiences of exclusion, discrimination, or economic precarity, the very act of asking for more can feel like overstepping. Success may carry the weight of representation. You are not just negotiating for yourself—you are negotiating against the implicit question of whether people like you are "allowed" to succeed. In this context, guilt is not irrational. It is protective. It shields you from the perceived risk of standing out, being resented, or judged as arrogant.

Guilt can also be relational. In families or communities where financial struggle has been normalised, the prospect of earning significantly more than your peers or relatives can feel like betrayal. It may not be safe to out-earn your siblings. It may feel disloyal to price yourself above what your parents ever made. And so, without ever discussing it, you cap your income to preserve connection. You subconsciously stay within the bounds of what is culturally or emotionally acceptable. The goal is no longer to thrive, but to belong.

Even within professional settings, guilt plays a powerful role. Employees routinely fail to negotiate salaries that reflect their value, not because they lack leverage, but because they feel uncomfortable "making it about money." Entrepreneurs and freelancers set their prices by asking, "What would I pay for this?" instead of "What is the market willing to pay, and what do I need to be sustainable?" They build pricing models around their emotional comfort, rather than the structural needs of their business. And then they wonder why they are overworked, underpaid, and silently resentful.

One of the most telling signs of guilt-driven earning is the compulsion to over-deliver. The person who stays late, adds extras, or refuses to enforce boundaries is often not simply generous—they are trying to *earn* what they've already charged. They worry the client or employer will think they're not worth it. So they compensate by giving more than they were paid for, hoping to quiet the inner dissonance between what they received and what they feel they deserve. This is not just inefficient. It is unsustainable. It leads to burnout, bitterness, and a distorted sense of worth.

What complicates this further is the cultural double bind around money and morality. In many societies, we are taught to associate financial modesty with integrity. The "good" person is expected to be humble, undemanding, and generous. Assertiveness is often recast as aggression. Financial ambition becomes synonymous with greed. The result is a confused value system in which people genuinely fear becoming *less good* by becoming *more wealthy*. So they stay in roles that are too small, accept compensation that is too low, and negotiate terms that are unfair—all in the name of remaining ethically intact.

But guilt is not an accurate moral compass. It is a learned emotional reflex. It tells you what feels familiar, not what is fair. And it is particularly unreliable when it comes to financial decisions, because it confuses your past experiences with your present reality. It convinces you that to want more is to take more, that to assert your value is to devalue someone else, and that to step into abundance is to lose some essential part of your identity. None of this is true. But all of it feels true if you've never interrogated where the guilt came from, or whose rules you are still playing by.

To begin dismantling this pattern, the first step is not strategy. It is self-inquiry. Ask yourself: *When did I learn that asking for more was dangerous? Whose comfort am I protecting by staying small? What would I do differently if I didn't feel I had to justify my worth?* These are not abstract questions. They are diagnostic tools. They help reveal the emotional contracts you are still honouring—contracts that may have kept you safe in one phase of life, but are now keeping you stuck.

It's also important to separate humility from self-erasure. Humility is the recognition that your value does not make you better than others. Self-erasure is the belief that acknowledging your value makes you worse. Many people conflate the two, believing that to be good is to be invisible, or that to have integrity is to expect less. But there is nothing virtuous about pretending to be less competent, less skilled, or less deserving than you are. Undercharging does not make you honourable. Over-accommodating does not make you noble. It makes you exhausted, under-resourced, and—ironically—less able to serve at your highest level.

Releasing guilt is not about swinging to entitlement. It is about arriving at clarity. About recognising that your work, your time, and your contribution have value—not because you are flawless, but because you are offering something real. When you price accordingly, negotiate assertively, and allow yourself to receive without apology, you are not taking from others. You are allowing a fair exchange to occur. You are respecting the ecosystem of value, which only works when people are honest about what they need and what they bring.

This shift does not happen overnight. It requires practice. It means noticing the moment you shrink in meetings. Catching the reflex to add discounts before the client has even objected. Pausing before you say yes to "just one more thing." It means learning to hold the discomfort of asking without cushioning it. Learning to trust that what feels risky may actually be necessary. And learning to replace guilt with responsibility—not to stay small, but to step fully into your role, your voice, and your rightful financial seat at the table.

You are not better for earning less. You are not selfish for asking more. And you are not greedy for wanting enough—not just to survive, but to breathe, build, and expand. The guilt that keeps you small is not a reflection of your ethics. It is a story that's ready to be rewritten. And the first line of that new story begins the moment you stop confusing deservingness with discomfort. You are allowed to earn what sustains you. You are allowed to grow. And you are allowed to do so without guilt.

Afraid to Want More

The hidden shame many people carry around the desire for wealth—and why ambition isn't greed

There's a conversation that rarely happens in public but often plays out in private, whispered not aloud but within the architecture of one's own mind. It sounds like this: *Is it okay for me to want more?* Not more convenience, not more security, not more breathing room—but *more.* More wealth. More financial power. More material freedom. For many intelligent, capable people, the desire for more does not inspire motivation—it activates shame. The longing itself feels suspect, even before a single step is taken. And in that shame, a dangerous equation takes root: *If I want more, I must be greedy. If I want more than others, I must be selfish. If I go after more, I may not be the person I believe myself to be.*

This emotional equation is one of the most under-acknowledged barriers to financial growth. It doesn't show up as a lack of ambition. In fact, many who carry this internal conflict are highly driven. But the drive is often re-routed—towards causes, towards others, away from the self. Outwardly, they may be accomplished, but inwardly, they are negotiating with guilt. They feel that their ambition must be justified, restrained, or camouflaged. Otherwise, they fear it will be misinterpreted—not just by others, but by themselves.

The roots of this shame are social, cultural, and often deeply personal. In many cultures, especially those shaped by collectivist values or spiritual traditions, desire for wealth is framed as morally precarious. To want is to deviate from the ideal of contentment. To accumulate is to risk becoming detached, arrogant, or ethically compromised. From religious teachings that extol the virtues of the meek, to political narratives that frame wealth as exploitation, the message is consistent: *the desire for more must be watched closely.* It is not neutral. It is dangerous.

These messages are then reinforced by early family dynamics. If someone grew up in a household where money was a source of conflict, fear, or lack, they may have learned that wanting more causes stress. If wealth was framed as unattainable, unjust, or the result of moral compromise, they may have internalised that it is safer—not just practically, but ethically—to expect less. Even families that were financially comfortable may have passed down the belief that modesty is a virtue, and aspiration beyond one's station is tacky, shallow, or disloyal.

These inherited narratives do not remain intellectual. They become embodied. When someone who carries this conditioning begins to make more money, they may experience discomfort that feels disproportionate to the change. They may sabotage success through underpricing, avoidance, or impulsive spending. They may rationalise their decisions in moral language: "I don't need that much," or "Money isn't everything." These statements are often sincere, but what they mask is a deeper discomfort with the *permission* to have more. It is not the money that causes distress—it is what the money symbolises: autonomy, separation, visibility, and change.

What makes this dynamic especially complex is the social tension between aspiration and acceptance. People are often encouraged to pursue success, but only in ways that do not challenge collective expectations. A woman who wants to out-earn her partner may feel that her ambition threatens the emotional balance of the relationship. An entrepreneur who grows up in a working-class family may fear being resented for "forgetting where they came from." A person of colour in a predominantly white professional environment may feel that seeking wealth reinforces stereotypes. These are not abstract fears. They are real emotional calculations made daily by people who must constantly choose between fitting in and rising up.

As a result, many people create emotional loopholes. They allow themselves to pursue wealth only if it is immediately linked to sacrifice or service. "I want to earn more so I can give back." "I need financial freedom to help my family." These motives are valid. But they are often the *only* motives permitted, as though wanting more *for oneself* is inherently suspect. The implication is that self-interest must always be translated into altruism before it becomes acceptable. And in that translation, many people lose clarity about what they actually want.

This guilt around wanting more also distorts decision-making. It creates a ceiling—not just on income, but on imagination. People stop themselves from applying for certain roles, launching certain businesses, or exploring new markets, not because they lack competence, but because they feel the desire itself makes them a different kind of person—less virtuous, less principled, less true to their roots. This is not simply limiting. It is a form of internal exile, where one banishes their own aspirations in order to maintain a moral self-image.

The irony is that the desire for wealth is often misread as greed when, in fact, it can stem from a deep wish for agency, dignity, and freedom. Wanting more does not necessarily mean wanting to take from others. It can mean wanting more choice, more stability, more ability to respond to life without fear. It can mean wanting to experience life more fully, to stop calculating the cost of every decision, to move through the world with confidence rather than contraction. None of these are inherently unethical. What makes them feel that way is the surrounding narrative that any material desire must be immediately suspect.

Reframing ambition begins with decoupling it from moral panic. Ambition is a psychological drive, not a declaration of greed. It reflects the human capacity for vision, for growth, for agency. Like any drive, it can be distorted—but it is not inherently corrosive. It becomes toxic only when fused with unconscious scarcity, unresolved trauma, or unchecked narcissism. In its healthy form, ambition is expansive. It enables people to lead, create, solve, and contribute at a scale that limited thinking does not allow. And that includes financial ambition.

To move past shame, people must examine their stories about wealth at the level of identity. What does being wealthy mean to you? Who told you that wanting more was dangerous? What image comes to mind when you think of a rich person—and do you see yourself in that image? These are not superficial questions. They reveal the subconscious scripts that govern what you believe is safe, possible, and appropriate. Until those scripts are made visible, no financial strategy will feel comfortable for long.

Crucially, this work must include emotional permission—not just logical justification. You cannot rationalise your way into feeling worthy of more. You must *allow* it. That means making peace with the discomfort of visibility, the friction of standing apart, the reality that some people *will* judge you, misread you, or fall away. It means holding the tension of wanting more while still honouring your values, your relationships, and your integrity. It means becoming someone who can hold both ambition and ethics without apology.

This kind of growth is not loud. It does not require performative wealth, hollow bravado, or status signalling. It requires self-trust. The quiet confidence to say: *Yes, I want more. And that doesn't make me greedy. It makes me honest.* And when that honesty is integrated—when people can finally want more without moral collapse—they begin to move differently. They ask for the raise without shrinking. They raise their rates without over-explaining. They take up space, not to dominate, but to breathe. They stop outsourcing their self-worth to social approval. And in doing so, they unlock not just more money—but more power, more peace, and more permission to live on their own terms.

There is no virtue in self-denial for its own sake. And no shame in desiring more than subsistence. What matters is *how* you pursue what you want, *why* it matters to you, and whether you can do so without compromising the values that ground you. Ambition is not the enemy of ethics. It is their amplifier—if you are willing to release the shame that taught you otherwise. You are not wrong to want more. But you may need to unlearn the idea that you are. And when you do, you will find that wanting more is not a threat to who you are—it is a return to what you were always allowed to become.

CHAPTER 3
Scarcity Thinking: The Old Family Curse

Most people do not encounter money in classrooms or textbooks. Instead, they learn it by observation, by absorbing the atmosphere around it. They pick it up in fragments: an overheard conversation at the dinner table, the tension behind a slammed door when the bills arrive, the subtle change in a parent's tone when something irreplaceable breaks. Long before they earn, spend, or save their first pound, they are internalising a script. And for many, that script is soaked in scarcity—not merely as a material reality, but as an emotional climate. A world where there never seems to be quite enough—of money, of time, of the security to feel at ease.

This chapter delves into that climate with care, examining it not as metaphor or mindset, but as an inherited psychological pattern with tangible consequences. Scarcity thinking is not simply having less; it is the belief that less is the natural order. That stability is fleeting, risk is dangerous, success is suspicious, and generosity must always be tempered by the shadow of disaster. It is a worldview passed quietly across generations, often without a single explicit lesson—and precisely because it is largely invisible, it is rarely questioned.

The central idea is straightforward yet unsettling: your present relationship with money still echoes the earliest impressions of emotional and financial safety. Not merely what you were told, but what you felt. For some, scarcity was obvious—poverty, evictions, hunger, the grind of debt collectors. For others, it was subtler: a parent's persistent anxiety about employment, the unspoken shame of depending on extended family, strict rules on what counted as waste. These impressions do not vanish; they become encoded, shaping not only how you handle money but what you believe is possible for you.

Consider how often people restrain their ambitions not due to evidence, but inherited doubt: "People like us don't get ahead." "Better to be safe than sorry." "Comfort invites disaster." These are not financial lessons—they are survival codes, passed down by those navigating conditions you may no longer face. Yet these codes continue to govern, long after their original context has vanished. You might earn more than your parents ever did, yet still fear falling behind on rent. You might hold savings, yet feel guilty with every spend. Opportunities may abound, but hesitation, downscaling, and hoarding persist. Scarcity, in many cases, is vigilance passed down, not actual lack.

The modern world does little to counteract this pattern; indeed, it often magnifies it. Consumer culture promises abundance while engineering dissatisfaction. Every advert, algorithm, and trend cycle whispers that you are one purchase away from completeness—and that what you have is already obsolete. This is structural, not accidental. The economy thrives on engineered inadequacy. Many now inhabit a state of chronic scarcity, chasing, acquiring, and yet perpetually feeling behind. Even those with plenty live in fear of loss; enough is always shifting.

This sensation is not greed, but psychological hijacking. When self-worth is intertwined with performance, appearance, or status—as culture encourages—contentment becomes elusive. Scarcity transforms from an external reality to an internal default: anticipatory grief, a quiet dread that you are always a few steps behind.

One of scarcity's most paradoxical expressions is fear of letting go even when resources exist. As earnings or savings rise, many freeze. They resist spending, delay investment, hoard cash—not out of avarice, but out of anxiety. The stability they have achieved feels precarious, unfamiliar. Security does not soothe; it magnifies unease. So they protect rather than expand, stockpile for catastrophe, and overlook opportunities that might enlarge freedom in the present.

Traditional advice rarely addresses this. The assumption that more money equals more confidence is misleading. In reality, income often intensifies pre-existing fears. Someone raised amidst financial chaos may excel at survival but struggle to relax, living perpetually as though disaster is imminent.

Breaking free demands more than positive thinking; it requires a psychological reorientation. And it must be precise: abundance thinking is not magical thinking. It is not pretending risk does not exist or reciting platitudes. True abundance is trust in one's capacity to meet life's demands—to earn, adapt, and recover if necessary. It is built from internal capability, not external assurance.

This chapter guides that work. It traces the lineage of financial mindset—not only what was taught, but what was absorbed. It examines scarcity-driven habits, unpacks their emotional logic, and offers pathways to replace inherited vigilance with grounded confidence. The aim is not to swing from deprivation to fantasy, but to cultivate resilient abundance: a form of psychological wealth capable of holding both opportunity and uncertainty.

You will be challenged to reconsider assumptions about safety, risk, and sufficiency. Many remain underpaid, decline investments, or resist scaling their work not because the numbers do not add up, but because their internal thermostat signals "this far and no further." That thermostat was set by history, not reason—and it will not recalibrate until you consciously intervene.

There is no single formula here; scarcity manifests differently. Compulsive spending, obsessive saving, underpricing, avoiding investment—these behaviours are linked not to money itself, but to fear. Fear, left unexamined, contracts vision, constrains choice, and encourages smallness "just in case."

Scarcity thinking is not blameworthy. It is an inherited survival strategy, reinforced by culture and nervous systems, originally designed to provide control. But like many inherited beliefs, it may no longer serve the life you wish to build. Recognising this is not betrayal—it is liberation. It is the first step toward choosing your own financial identity rather than repeating someone else's.

The family legacy of scarcity is not broken by income alone. It is broken by altering one's understanding of having more: separating peace from punishment, stability from threat, worth from struggle. This chapter does not teach budgeting or minimalism; it invites a fundamental rewiring of assumptions about enough, risk, and the morality of financial ease.

It begins with seeing old stories clearly: "Suffering proves success," "People like us don't advance," "Spend too much, lose everything." These narratives once safeguarded someone—perhaps your parents, grandparents, or younger self. If they now keep you small, anxious, or disconnected from potential, it may be time to acknowledge them—and leave them behind.

Scarcity is not a money problem. It is an identity problem. It defines what life you permit yourself, which risks you allow, how much peace you accept. Until that belief shifts, financial education alone cannot free you.

This chapter does not promise quick solutions. It offers frameworks, insights, and reflections aimed at cultivating clarity—clarity that manifests not merely in your bank account, but in your body, decisions, and sense of security. True wealth begins there—not in digits, but in nervous systems; not in income, but in identity. From that grounded space—not fear, not fantasy, but clarity—real abundance becomes possible.

The Stories You Absorbed as a Child

How our parents' financial fears—spoken or unspoken—shape our beliefs today

Before we understand money as numbers, we feel it as energy. Children do not need financial literacy to sense economic tension. They absorb the emotional weight of money long before they can calculate compound interest or interpret a payslip. A slammed door after a bill arrives. A strained smile at the supermarket checkout. A parent's sudden change of tone when asked for something "extra." These moments teach more than any financial workshop ever could. They form the scaffolding of belief—about what is safe, what is allowed, what is likely, and what must be feared.

This is how financial psychology is passed down: not through direct instruction, but through atmosphere. Parents rarely sit their children down to formally explain interest rates or retirement planning. But they teach constantly—through reaction, omission, and tone. Some families weaponise money. Others wrap it in silence. Some model extravagance to mask lack. Others over-function to project control. Few explain. Fewer still reflect. But children, as attuned social learners, adapt anyway. They develop rules. Often unspoken. Often rigid. And these rules linger long after they leave home.

For many adults, those early scripts become unconscious operating systems. You may find yourself struggling with money not because of your current circumstances, but because you are running a set of beliefs you never consciously chose. Beliefs that once protected your emotional environment, but now limit your financial autonomy. These inherited narratives are not inherently "wrong." Many were built under real constraints. But the tragedy lies in how often they remain unexamined—quietly controlling decisions, expectations, and identity.

One of the most common inherited stories is this: *money is hard to come by*. For some, this was explicitly stated: "We can't afford that," "Money doesn't grow on trees," "Rich people are different from us." For others, it was encoded in the rhythms of daily life—the constant budgeting, the worry over petrol prices, the panic when something broke. Children exposed to this climate often internalise the idea that money is unstable, elusive, and always on the edge of disappearing. As adults, they may become hyper-vigilant, emotionally frugal, or paradoxically, compulsive spenders—attempting to soothe financial anxiety through consumption.

Equally damaging is the story that *money is morally suspect*. This is especially common in families that value modesty, self-sacrifice, or spiritual virtue. Wealth is portrayed as inherently corrupting. Financial success is viewed with suspicion. Generosity is praised only when it involves personal deprivation. In this narrative, financial ambition becomes a character flaw. And so children raised within it often grow up conflicted. They want to succeed, but fear becoming "one of them." They feel pulled between aspiration and belonging—unsure whether wealth will affirm their identity or betray it.

There is also the story that *money equals safety*. This one is often born out of trauma—historical poverty, forced migration, economic displacement. In these families, money becomes the central metric of control. Every pound is accounted for. Every decision is filtered through future risk. Children in this environment often grow up with an overdeveloped sense of financial responsibility. They become the careful ones. The planners. The savers. But they may also become paralysed—afraid to invest, spend, or pursue uncertain opportunities. For them, risk is not a strategic calculation. It's a threat to survival.

These stories often intersect with class, race, gender, and immigration history. A Black British child watching their parents navigate workplace discrimination while trying to keep food on the table learns that success comes with emotional cost. A first-generation immigrant observing their family hustle for every marginal gain learns that money must always be earned the hard way. A girl growing up in a household that subtly privileges male leadership absorbs the idea that her financial independence is optional, or worse, threatening. These nuances matter. They shape what people believe they are allowed to earn, spend, and build without apology.

Importantly, the stories we inherit aren't only learned through hardship. Even in affluent households, distorted money narratives thrive. A child who grows up with wealth but without emotional attunement may learn that money is a substitute for love. That approval must be bought. That personal worth is tethered to financial status. These children may become high achievers—accumulating credentials, promotions, and assets—but still feel hollow. Because they never learned how to separate *being resourced* from *being valuable.*

What's most pernicious about these inherited narratives is how easily they masquerade as personality traits. Someone raised in a family that feared loss may describe themselves as "just cautious." Someone raised with moral suspicion of wealth may insist, "I'm not motivated by money," even as they undercharge and overwork. Someone raised in economic chaos may believe they "thrive under pressure," when in fact they have never felt safe enough to relax. These are not traits. They are adaptations.

Unpacking these adaptations requires more than financial education. It demands *emotional inquiry.* Asking questions like: *Whose voice is this in my head? Who taught me that security must come with sacrifice? Why do I feel guilty when I spend on myself, even if I can afford it?* These are not abstract reflections. They are investigative tools. They expose the hidden contracts we've signed with our past—agreements we can no longer afford to honour.

This does not mean blaming parents. Most did the best they could with the knowledge, resources, and emotional tools available to them. Many passed down these narratives as a form of love—attempting to protect their children from the unpredictability they themselves endured. But good intentions do not make those narratives right for your current life. Respecting the past does not require re-enacting it.

Nor does rewriting your financial story mean swinging to the opposite extreme. Rejecting your family's frugality by embracing reckless spending is not healing. It's rebellion disguised as freedom. Real transformation lies in integration. Taking what was useful—discipline, awareness, resilience—and discarding what is no longer necessary—fear, guilt, limitation. It's not about rejecting your inheritance. It's about *choosing which parts to keep.*

This work is especially urgent now, as many people confront global instability while carrying personal histories of financial stress. Economic uncertainty tends to reactivate old narratives. When the markets crash, when layoffs loom, when inflation rises, people revert to what's familiar. They shrink. They postpone. They brace. But without awareness, they can't tell whether they are responding to present reality or ancestral programming. They confuse the two. And in doing so, they give their inherited fears full authority over their current choices.

This chapter will help you interrupt that confusion. It will show you how to recognise the fingerprints of the past on your financial identity. It will offer frameworks for understanding how familial beliefs shape emotional responses. And it will guide you in beginning the difficult, necessary work of rewriting those scripts—without shame, without fantasy, and without abandoning the wisdom embedded in your history.

You are not responsible for the stories you inherited. But you are responsible for the ones you live by. And if those stories are keeping you in patterns of avoidance, scarcity, guilt, or paralysis, then you are not honouring your past—you are being ruled by it. True financial maturity means stepping out of the role of inherited child and into the role of intentional adult. It means moving from unconscious repetition to conscious authorship.

Every financial decision you make is part of that authorship. Every time you negotiate a rate, choose to invest, or spend without shame, you are either reinforcing the old story or writing a new one. The goal is not perfection. It's *awareness.* Because awareness, when sustained and integrated, becomes power. And that power is how you break the cycle—not just for yourself, but for those who follow. The story you absorbed as a child does not have to be the story you pass on.

The "Never Enough" Illusion

How consumer culture feeds a constant hunger for more—and leaves us perpetually dissatisfied

The modern economy is not driven by need—it is driven by dissatisfaction. Our financial system thrives not on what people genuinely lack, but on what they *feel* they lack. This distinction is subtle but transformative. For most people in developed societies, the essentials of survival are no longer the defining economic challenge. Yet the experience of "not having enough" remains pervasive. It's a paradox of abundance: the more we accumulate, the more we seem to crave. Not because we are greedy or undisciplined, but because we have been conditioned—systematically, psychologically, and relentlessly—to believe that contentment is always just one more purchase away.

This illusion is not accidental. It is the outcome of a sophisticated ecosystem built to manufacture desire. From the moment we wake to the moment we sleep, we are bombarded with narratives that suggest something is missing from our lives—something we can acquire. Advertisements do not merely sell products; they sell identity, aspiration, and belonging. A phone is not just a tool—it is sleekness, status, competence. A car is not just transport—it is power, prestige, arrival. Clothing is not about fabric—it is about visibility, admiration, aesthetic fluency. Each purchase is framed not as a transaction, but as a step closer to the version of yourself you ought to be.

What makes this system so powerful is that it exploits a deeply human tendency: the psychological bias toward *hedonic adaptation.* This is the phenomenon by which the emotional impact of any gain—material, professional, romantic—diminishes over time. The new house becomes normal. The new salary is quickly allocated. The novelty of the latest gadget fades within days. What once thrilled us becomes baseline. So we seek the next upgrade. Not because we are broken, but because our brains evolved for survival, not satisfaction. In a world of scarcity, dissatisfaction was adaptive—it kept early humans scanning for more. But in a world engineered to overstimulate those instincts, it becomes a trap.

This is the essence of the "never enough" illusion: a manufactured hunger that cannot be satisfied, because it is not rooted in lack—it is rooted in identity dislocation. We don't buy things merely to possess them; we buy them to become someone. And because that "someone" is always just out of reach—cooler, wealthier, thinner, more admired—the pursuit is endless. Every acquisition solves a problem that marketing first invented. Every solution plants the seed of a new inadequacy. It is not just an economic cycle. It is an emotional treadmill.

Nowhere is this more evident than in the modern relationship between social media and consumption. Platforms that once promised connection have become arenas of curated envy. The algorithms reward visual excess—holidays, luxury goods, lifestyle markers. Even authenticity is now a branded aesthetic. The result is a hyper-personalised feed of comparative inadequacy. We are not just trying to keep up with the Joneses—we are trying to keep up with thousands of invisible avatars of "better." The damage is subtle but profound. What once felt sufficient—a decent job, a modest home, a well-worn jacket—now feels inadequate under the glare of algorithmic perfection.

Crucially, the illusion of "never enough" doesn't only impact what we buy. It shapes how we *feel* about what we already have. It corrodes gratitude. It destabilises self-worth. It creates a default state of quiet panic—an internal dialogue that whispers, *You should be doing more, having more, being more.* And when that voice becomes chronic, it doesn't just lead to poor financial decisions—it leads to emotional exhaustion. People work longer hours not always to survive, but to sustain a lifestyle that numbs their discontent. They take on debt to fund status symbols that temporarily mute their shame. They defer rest, play, and presence, convinced that fulfilment lies just beyond the next purchase, promotion, or pay rise.

This is not a moral failing. It is the predictable result of an economy that requires dissatisfaction to remain profitable. The average consumer is exposed to thousands of marketing messages per day. Each one finely tuned to elicit a sense of lack. Over time, that lack calcifies into identity. You are not merely *without* a product—you are *less than* until you own it. The consequence is chronic undercurrents of shame, comparison, and anxiety that masquerade as financial goals. What's marketed as "aspiration" is often just socially sanctioned insecurity.

Counterintuitively, even the self-help and productivity industries—ostensibly designed to empower—can become entangled in this cycle. The pursuit of better habits, better tools, better routines can morph into a perfectionistic loop. You are not just buying software; you are buying the promise of becoming someone who has it all together. But when progress becomes another vehicle for comparison, self-development collapses into self-criticism. Ambition, untethered from clarity, becomes a form of financial and emotional escapism.

Escaping the "never enough" illusion does not mean rejecting all aspiration. It means becoming conscious of the scripts you're living by. It means interrogating whether your desires are truly yours—or if they've been shaped by algorithms, adverts, and ambient pressure. It means distinguishing between *fulfilment* and *accumulation*, between *self-expression* and *status signalling*. This requires deliberate pause. A slowing down. A reorientation around values that cannot be bought—peace, presence, autonomy, creative flow, relational depth.

One useful distinction is between *growth* and *grasping*. Growth is rooted in purpose. It is expansive, generative, and often slow. Grasping is compulsive. It is reactive, brittle, and urgent. Much of consumer culture encourages grasping—act now, don't miss out, upgrade or be left behind. But true financial peace comes from aligning your choices with your internal compass, not external noise. It is the capacity to say, *This is enough. Not because I've settled, but because I've chosen.*

That choice, however, must be supported by structures. Psychological insight alone is not enough. You cannot out-think a billion-dollar advertising industry with willpower. You must design your life to make enough *feel* like enough. This might involve curating your digital environment, limiting exposure to aspirational content, or setting concrete thresholds for spending that reflect your actual values, not your performative self. It might involve redefining what success means to you—not in abstract terms, but in measurable, emotionally grounded ways.

It also requires examining the *fear* behind the hunger. Many people pursue more not because they are greedy, but because they are scared. Scared of irrelevance. Of being left behind. Of discovering that even with more, they still feel empty. These fears are legitimate. But they are not solved by consumption. They are solved by coherence—by living in integrity with what matters to you. And that often begins not with addition, but with subtraction. Subtracting noise. Subtracting comparison. Subtracting the assumption that your value is contingent on visual success.

What emerges in the absence of the illusion is not complacency, but clarity. You realise that you can want more without needing more. That ambition does not require chronic dissatisfaction. That wealth, in its richest sense, includes your time, attention, energy, and ability to be fully alive in the moment—not just your net worth. This shift does not diminish your goals. It dignifies them. Because they are no longer built on shame. They are built on agency.

The "never enough" illusion will not disappear overnight. It is reinforced daily, subtly and powerfully. But it can be interrupted. With awareness. With honesty. With a refusal to outsource your sense of worth to systems that profit from your insecurity. That is the work this chapter invites. Not a retreat from growth, but a reclamation of authorship. Because when you finally stop chasing what you were never missing, you make space to build what you truly need. And that is where wealth begins—not with what you acquire, but with what you no longer believe you lack.

The Fear of Letting Go

Why some people hoard money, avoid investing, or freeze financially even when they have plenty

For many, the great obstacle to building wealth isn't scarcity—it's paralysis. Not because they don't earn enough, but because they can't bring themselves to *use* what they have. They save compulsively, resist spending on things that would improve their quality of life, and avoid investments that could grow their money—despite having ample resources. Outwardly, they appear responsible, even prudent. But beneath the surface lies an emotional tension that reveals a deeper truth: fear, not logic, is in control. Their financial decisions are not shaped by opportunity, but by the psychological grip of security-seeking. And that grip can be just as limiting as poverty.

This fear is not easily dismissed. In many cases, it is generationally reinforced, culturally praised, and internally rationalised as wisdom. We are taught to admire the saver and pity the spender. To delay gratification, accumulate "just in case," and measure maturity in restraint. But when saving turns to hoarding, when planning becomes avoidance, and when prudence crosses into self-denial, the strategy begins to undermine the very wellbeing it's meant to protect. The financial fortress becomes a cage.

The roots of this fear are often found in lived experience. People who have known real hardship—whether in their own lives or in those of their parents—carry an internalised narrative: money disappears. It cannot be trusted. Its presence is temporary, fragile, and conditional. Even when circumstances change, the emotional script does not. A six-figure bank balance cannot override a childhood spent watching parents argue over unpaid bills. A successful career does not erase the imprint of financial instability.

This is not irrational. It's survival memory. And until it is examined, it continues to govern choices unconsciously.

The paradox is that many people who fear losing money are not actually *risk-averse*—they are *uncertainty-averse.* They don't necessarily shy away from change. They shy away from the feeling of vulnerability that accompanies it. Investing, for example, is not scary because it's complex. It's scary because it forces you to let go of control. You must part with something tangible (cash) in exchange for something intangible (potential). That space between action and outcome triggers every dormant fear: *What if I lose it? What if I was wrong? What if I never recover?* These questions are emotional, not technical. And they cannot be answered by data alone.

Even more subtly, the fear of letting go is often moralised. People associate financial restraint with virtue. Frugality is seen as discipline; spending is seen as indulgence. But this binary thinking ignores a crucial dimension of financial maturity: intentionality. Spending, when aligned with values and well-being, is not failure—it is freedom. Refusing to spend out of guilt, fear, or shame is not prudence—it is paralysis. When people defer every joy "until it feels safe," they often discover that safety is a mirage. No number ever feels high enough. No scenario ever feels certain enough. As a result, life is postponed indefinitely.

One of the most telling examples of this dynamic can be observed in people approaching retirement. After decades of saving and sacrificing, many find themselves unable to shift gears. They have "enough," but feel emotionally bankrupt when it comes to enjoyment. They don't trust the numbers. They don't trust themselves. And they certainly don't trust the world to remain stable. So they downsize their aspirations, not because they must, but because they don't know how to feel safe letting go. Their identity has become entangled with financial restraint. To spend is to lose who they are.

This same pattern is common among high-income professionals. They defer investing in their business, in experiences, in health or rest—not because they can't afford it, but because *spending still feels like a threat.* The guilt that accompanies financial release is not about the amount; it's about what it symbolises. For some, spending feels selfish. For others, it feels reckless. For many, it simply feels unfamiliar. And because our brains interpret unfamiliarity as danger, they freeze—defaulting to hoarding, hesitation, or hyper-control.

Breaking this cycle requires more than practical advice. It requires a shift in orientation—from scarcity to stewardship. The goal is not to spend for its own sake, but to spend in alignment with purpose. To understand that money is not security—it is *potential*. Left inert, it does not protect you. It stagnates. Financial security is not found in the pile—it's found in the confidence to use that pile wisely, flexibly, and meaningfully. The true mark of financial maturity is not how much you accumulate, but how fluently you can deploy what you've earned without betraying your peace of mind.

One of the most effective ways to retrain this fear is to engage in structured, intentional acts of release. This could mean investing a small portion of your savings—even if the return is uncertain. It could mean spending on something that enhances your life—even if you've been conditioned to "tough it out." It could mean giving generously—not because you're overflowing, but because you understand that generosity expands capacity, not depletes it. These practices are not financial in the narrow sense—they are psychological training grounds for trust. Trust in yourself. Trust in your future. Trust in your ability to regenerate wealth, rather than merely preserve it.

Critically, this process must be accompanied by a re-evaluation of your internal thresholds. Many people operate with outdated scripts about what constitutes "enough." They set arbitrary numbers—"I'll feel safe once I have X"—but those numbers often move. Not because reality changes, but because the fear hasn't been addressed at its root. It's not that they don't have enough—it's that they don't *feel* like enough. And that dissonance will not be resolved by more accumulation. It must be resolved by integration: learning to hold your financial resources and your emotional reality in the same hand, without letting one distort the other.

This is particularly relevant in relationships. Couples often clash not over the *amount* of money, but over the *feeling* of money. One partner may want to invest in a home renovation, while the other hesitates—not because they disagree on the value, but because the act of spending feels threatening. When this fear goes unnamed, it can breed resentment, misinterpretation, or power struggles. But when it's recognised as fear—not stinginess, not control, not irresponsibility—it opens space for compassionate negotiation. The question shifts from "Can we afford this?" to "What does this choice mean to each of us emotionally?"

The broader societal narrative does little to help. Financial media tends to amplify either panic or greed. We're told to save obsessively *or* to chase the next big win. There is little support for the nuanced middle ground: thoughtful, values-based financial release. The kind of choices that allow you to grow without gambling, to give without guilt, and to live without fear that one misstep will collapse your future. In the absence of this narrative, many default to what feels safest—inaction.

But financial inaction is not neutral. It has consequences. The cost of not investing is lost opportunity. The cost of hoarding is psychological rigidity. The cost of avoidance is stagnation—not just of wealth, but of life. Money is a tool, and tools are meant to be used. When we allow fear to keep that tool locked in the drawer, we limit not just our financial outcomes, but our personal evolution.

Ultimately, the fear of letting go is not about money—it is about trust. And trust is built not in theory, but in practice. It is built by making one conscious, values-aligned financial decision at a time, even when your nervous system wants to hold on tighter. It is built by recognising that your past does not have to dictate your future, and that your identity is not defined by your capacity to delay pleasure, but by your capacity to use money as a force for expansion—not just protection.

If wealth is to serve your life, rather than dominate it, then at some point, you must learn to release. Not recklessly. Not blindly. But wisely, with awareness, and with the full understanding that *having enough* is not just a mathematical condition—it is a psychological skill. A skill that must be learned, practised, and embodied if you are ever to move from survival into sovereignty.

Building Real Abundance

(Without Magical Thinking) – How to rewire your mind for healthy growth, grounded confidence, and long-term peace:

Real abundance is not a mood. It's not a meme. It's not about pretending to be wealthy until the universe catches on. And it certainly isn't created by reciting prosperity affirmations while ignoring the balance in your bank account. What most people call "abundance thinking" has been so thoroughly diluted by pop-spirituality and influencer culture that the term now rings hollow. The problem isn't that the idea is invalid—it's that it's been stripped of rigour. True abundance isn't about magical thinking; it's about mental conditioning rooted in clarity, responsibility, and resilience. It is not about wishing, but about wiring. To experience sustainable abundance, you must rewire how your mind relates to growth, risk, worth, and control—especially when your past has taught you to fear all four.

To start, we must abandon the myth that abundance is a mood state you can manifest through sheer positivity. That framing is not only misleading—it's psychologically reckless. It implies that negative thoughts repel wealth, that fear blocks success, and that doubt itself is a form of sabotage. This line of thinking doesn't foster abundance; it manufactures shame. If you've grown up around instability, trauma, or scarcity, doubt and fear are not character flaws—they are *adaptive.* They evolved for a reason. Abundance does not come from suppressing those instincts. It comes from understanding them, integrating them, and retraining the nervous system to tolerate more than it has historically been able to hold.

The nervous system, in fact, is central to any serious discussion of abundance. Most people assume that the capacity to receive more—more money, freedom, impact—hinges on external readiness. But the real threshold is *internal.* If your body associates expansion with danger—because past experiences of growth led to conflict, burnout, loss, or isolation—it will resist prosperity even when your conscious mind desires it. You'll delay opportunities, downplay your capabilities, undercharge your work, or overwork until you're depleted. Not because you don't want more—but because your system isn't wired to *feel safe having more.* This is not a problem solved by spreadsheets or hustle. It's solved by slowly expanding your tolerance for safety inside growth. And that takes deliberate emotional work.

This leads us to a hard truth that most financial advice avoids: psychological set points are often more powerful than knowledge or willpower. A person who feels safe with £50,000 in the bank may feel immediate anxiety at the thought of £500,000—because more money introduces new identity questions, new social expectations, and new decision-making demands. The result is often self-sabotage, disguised as pragmatism: "Now isn't the right time." "I don't really need it." "It's not about the money." But this isn't modesty—it's a subconscious strategy for self-protection. Abundance begins when we recognise these internal negotiations and refuse to let them dictate our ceiling.

Healthy abundance also requires a complete reframe of what growth actually means. In the hustle-driven model of capitalism, growth is synonymous with acceleration: more clients, more hours, more output, more visibility. But in an emotionally integrated model, growth means *deepening*. It's about increasing the quality of decisions, the alignment of your work, the spaciousness in your calendar, and the richness of your impact. It often involves *earning more by doing less but better*. That transition, however, requires an ego shift—from being the hero who saves the day by doing everything, to being the strategist who designs systems, builds boundaries, and stops equating effort with worth. The refusal to make that shift is what keeps many talented professionals stuck in chronic under-earning, despite their intelligence and experience.

At the cultural level, abundance is further complicated by narratives that glorify scarcity as virtue. We admire the person who sacrifices. We respect those who live "humbly." But we rarely interrogate what that humility costs. When financial contraction is seen as moral high ground, the pursuit of prosperity is pathologised as greed. This internalised moral friction creates a psychological bind: wanting more feels selfish, but staying small feels suffocating. The only way out is to disentangle money from morality. Abundance is not a character flaw. It is a resource amplifier. When you have more, you can give more, build more, rest more, and influence more. But that begins with permission—not from society, but from yourself.

And permission cannot thrive in an environment of chronic comparison. One of the most corrosive features of modern financial culture is the endless benchmarking of personal progress against curated online metrics. People don't just compare net worths—they compare lifestyles, holidays, partners, kitchen renovations. The result is a distorted sense of what is "normal," and a deeply fractured sense of personal sufficiency. Abundance, by contrast, is inherently *non-comparative*. It emerges when your values, strategies, and goals are internally coherent—regardless of external performance. You're not trying to *win*. You're trying to *align*. And that alignment is what produces long-term peace.

Importantly, real abundance does not ignore risk—it incorporates it. Magical thinking often assumes that once you're "aligned," things will simply flow. But alignment does not protect you from volatility. What it does is make you more *resilient* to it. The abundant mind does not seek to eliminate uncertainty—it seeks to increase optionality. That might mean diversifying income streams, cultivating skills that travel across industries, or building cash reserves that offer breathing room. These are not glamorous moves, but they are foundational. They turn abundance from a hope into a strategy. Because ultimately, abundance is not about the absence of risk—it's about your capacity to remain grounded inside it.

This brings us to perhaps the most misunderstood element of abundance: sustainability. It's easy to feel abundant for a moment—after a big launch, a bonus, or a windfall. But the real work is *staying* there. And staying requires systems. It requires you to stop relying on adrenaline and start relying on rhythm. Abundant people don't wait to feel motivated—they build routines that reinforce emotional clarity, financial intelligence, and strategic action. They make decisions not just for today's goals, but for tomorrow's energy. They don't just protect their money—they protect the mindset that earned it.

One powerful tool in this process is reflective review. Instead of only measuring external gains (revenue, assets, reach), train yourself to also measure *internal gains*: Do I feel more at ease when I spend? Do I recover faster from setbacks? Do I notice opportunities sooner? Do I ask for what I'm worth without panic? These are the real signs of abundance. And they are not always visible from the outside. But they are felt—deeply, quietly, and sustainably. They indicate that your mind is no longer fixated on survival, but is oriented toward creative expansion.

And that's the ultimate goal. Abundance is not about arriving at a number—it's about inhabiting a mode of being. A mode where your financial life reflects your values, not your fears. Where your strategy is grounded in reality, not fantasy. Where your goals are rooted in sovereignty, not shame. And where your relationship with money feels like partnership—not punishment, not performance, and not projection.

Rewiring for real abundance is not glamorous. It's not overnight. It doesn't look good on social media. But it is *liberating*. It is the disciplined art of retraining your psychology to hold more peace, more trust, and more capacity than your past would have predicted. It's slow, strategic, and deeply personal. But once done, it produces the kind of quiet confidence that no market crash, policy change, or algorithm shift can take from you. And that is what makes it real.

CHAPTER 4
Self-Worth Is Not Net Worth

Beneath the surface of modern financial life—beyond spreadsheets and statements—lies a quietly pervasive assumption: "My income reflects my value." Rarely articulated, even more rarely questioned, it nonetheless shapes careers, fuels anxiety, distorts relationships, and bends life trajectories in subtle but relentless ways. The notion that self-worth and net worth are inseparably linked is not merely cultural; it is institutional. From grades to salaries, from social media profiles to investor presentations, our modern selves are constantly appraised in economic terms. And yet, when identity fuses with financial output, the effect is distortion rather than empowerment.

This chapter investigates one of the most corrosive myths in contemporary financial psychology: that personal value can be measured by earning capacity, financial stability, or productivity. This belief does more than dictate work habits; it shapes self-perception. It underpins overwork, burnout, impostor syndrome, underpricing, and financial shame. It turns a failed project into a personal indictment, leaves the objectively successful feeling hollow, and prompts self-sabotage when fortunes begin to rise. The conflation of identity and income may appear rational—it is ubiquitous, after all—but it is among the costliest psychological errors one can make.

We begin with the identity crisis money quietly triggers. For many, the conviction "I am what I earn" is not conscious; it is inherited. Childhood rewards—good grades, compliant behaviour, helpfulness—often came tethered to love and approval. Over time, these early associations migrate onto productivity and earnings: produce, and you belong; succeed, and you matter. Ambition itself is not the danger; the peril lies in its fragility. When worth is contingent on results, failure feels existential. Risk becomes a threat to being. And the pressure to validate oneself through earnings becomes relentless.

Central to this trap is impostor syndrome—not a passing insecurity, but a structural feature of an economy where worth is measured in financial terms. The more accomplished someone becomes, the more they fear being "found out," not due to incompetence, but because internalised worth lags behind external achievement. They overwork to compensate, undervalue their time, and constantly reassert their right to earn through over-delivery. This is not a personality flaw; it is systemic. When self-respect depends on proof, overextension and under-advocacy become inevitable—and quietly tragic.

The "deservingness deficit" exacerbates the problem. While many presume financial blocks stem from opportunity or knowledge gaps, the deeper obstacle is often psychological: "I'm not ready for more," "Others deserve it more," "I haven't done enough yet." These are rarely objective truths; they are internalised scarcity, shame, or inherited guilt. Money becomes emotionally charged terrain, a symbol of permission. Denied that permission—through culture, class, family, or trauma—one cannot safely receive more, regardless of ability or diligence. The consequences manifest subtly: deflecting praise, discounting prices, avoiding negotiation, or sabotaging success to align with a self-identity anchored in struggle or self-sacrifice.

This leads to a widely misunderstood principle: compensation is rarely for effort; it is for value. Time spent, seniority, or hard work are not the currencies of remuneration—perceived impact is. A consultant who saves a firm £100,000 in a single call has created enormous value, irrespective of hours invested. Designers, therapists, coaches, entrepreneurs—the same principle applies. The distinction matters. Recognising that worth is tied to impact rather than output reshapes self-perception, pricing, and advocacy.

Separating self-worth from net worth does not diminish ambition; it clarifies it. Healthy ambition is not about proving oneself—it is about expressing oneself. It distinguishes working to be someone from working to do something meaningful. The ramifications are profound. Those who decouple worth from financial validation take smarter risks, negotiate assertively, set boundaries without guilt, and rebound more quickly from setbacks. Their confidence is sturdy, not brittle.

Achieving this shift requires deep introspection. It means confronting inherited scripts about money and value, often unexamined for decades. Perhaps money was a source of conflict in your upbringing, leaving you anxious around wealth. Perhaps you observed a parent fuse identity with job performance, and now mirror that pattern unconsciously. Perhaps applause for effort shaped a fear that slowing down equates to invisibility. These beliefs are not irrational—they are unexamined. The chapter aims to illuminate them.

Context matters. We live in a culture that equates success with visibility, productivity, and affluence. Social media rewards display, not depth. Economic systems reward scale, not soul. In such a milieu, rejecting the self-worth/net worth linkage may feel countercultural—or even precarious. Yet it is also the doorway to freedom. Untethered from performance, agency grows. You stop needing to prove, and begin choosing. You stop chasing external validation, and start defining value on your own terms.

This chapter offers no instant fixes. It does not suggest abandoning ambition or detaching from financial goals. Rather, it invites grounding selfhood in something steadier than market forces. It encourages reflection: Who am I when I am not earning? What is the value of my work beyond money? How would my financial life change if I recognised that I am already enough?

These are practical, not abstract, questions. Until they are answered, income alone cannot provide security, raises will feel unearned, and success will ring hollow. Decoupling self-worth from net worth is both emotional and strategic: it enables wiser decisions, healthier boundaries, and sustainable stability. Most importantly, it cultivates a relationship with money that is grounded, generous, and sovereign.

As the following chapters unfold, the goal is not to shrink ambition but to expand psychological capacity. Not to ignore money, but to prevent it from defining identity. Freed from that entanglement, energy is liberated. In that space, money ceases to be a mirror of self-worth; it becomes a tool of expression. A means, not a measure. A resource, not a referendum on value. And it is there—in that delicate separation—that real power begins.

The Identity Crisis of Money – Why so many people secretly believe: "I am only as valuable as what I earn."

Walk into a room full of high achievers, and ask them to introduce themselves without mentioning their job title, income, or professional accolades. You will witness visible discomfort. For many, such a request is disorienting—because without the metrics of productivity or financial success, they're unsure who they are. This discomfort reveals something deeper than professional pride: a cultural equation that binds personal worth to economic performance. We are taught to measure ourselves not by character, integrity, or contribution, but by output. And money, being the most legible signal of output, becomes the shorthand for identity.

This belief—that our value is proportional to our earnings—is rarely stated so plainly. But it lurks in language, incentives, and social norms. Children are praised for being "hardworking." Teenagers are encouraged to pursue "high-paying" degrees. Adults are assessed by job title, car model, postcode. Even spiritual or creative communities that claim to reject materialism often reproduce the same dynamic in subtler forms—using impact, reach, or influence as alternative currencies of self-worth. In this context, financial success isn't just a goal—it's a proxy for meaning. And financial struggle becomes not just a hardship, but a personal failing.

This distortion begins early. Many people grow up in homes where money wasn't just a practical concern—it was a moral one. When a parent lost a job or faced debt, the household atmosphere shifted. Anxiety filled the gaps that words couldn't. Even in affluent families, children often learn that being "good" means being productive, useful, or high-achieving. Over time, this morphs into a belief that being loved, safe, or respected is something that must be earned—usually through performance. The adult version of that performance is financial. We hustle not just to pay bills, but to prove we are enough.

The implications are far-reaching. People with this belief system tend to over-identify with their work. They stay in toxic jobs because quitting would feel like erasing a part of their identity. They tie their emotional state to financial metrics: a good month brings pride; a dip in income brings shame. Entrepreneurs set aggressive goals not from strategy, but from insecurity. Employees accept low pay because they think they must "deserve more" before asking. Creatives hesitate to charge market rates because they fear their worth hasn't yet been "proven." These are not business decisions—they're emotional distortions disguised as logic.

This identity crisis also explains why financial growth often doesn't yield emotional satisfaction. If self-worth is hitched to achievement, then no amount of money ever feels secure. Each milestone simply raises the bar for the next one. You earn six figures, then feel behind because others are earning seven. You buy the house, then compare yourself to someone with three. The comparison trap is endless—because the underlying hunger isn't for more money, but for internal validation. And that can't be solved by external metrics.

At the same time, this belief system makes financial setbacks feel catastrophic. When income drops or a project fails, the emotional fallout is disproportionate—not just stress about bills, but shame, panic, and identity collapse. It's not just "I lost money." It's "I am a failure." This over-identification creates rigidity. People avoid risk not because they're risk-averse, but because failure would threaten their sense of self. Ironically, this fear of losing status often leads to self-sabotage—holding back from negotiating, undercharging, or overworking to the point of burnout, just to sustain an identity that was never stable to begin with.

There's also a social layer to this. In many cultures, particularly capitalist ones, the myth of the "self-made success" is deeply revered. We idolise stories of financial ascent not just for their strategy, but because they validate the belief that effort equals worth. As a result, those who struggle financially are often treated with contempt or condescension—not because of what they lack, but because of what we project onto them. Poverty becomes pathologised, and wealth becomes idealised. This creates a double bind: those who succeed feel pressured to sustain a façade of perfection, and those who don't feel ashamed to ask for help. Both suffer from the same illusion: that money is the measure of a person.

But if money is not our measure, what is? This question can't be answered with slogans or affirmations. It requires a rewiring of our internal value system. That process begins by recognising that economic value and personal worth are not the same. They are correlated in a market, but not in meaning. A teacher shaping the lives of hundreds may earn less than a hedge fund analyst, but their contribution is not lesser. A parent raising children may earn no income, but their labour sustains generations. A writer working for a decade on an unpublished manuscript may earn nothing from it, yet still be engaged in meaningful creation. Value, in the human sense, is not always visible on a payslip.

To disentangle money from identity, we must shift the lens. Rather than asking, *What am I worth?*, a more useful question is, *What am I offering?* What impact does my work create? Who benefits from my presence, expertise, or perspective? These questions orient us towards contribution, not comparison. They help us ground value in substance, not performance. And they open the door to more sustainable financial decisions—ones that are aligned with integrity, not insecurity.

Of course, this reframing must be supported by systems. A person cannot detach self-worth from net worth in isolation if they are embedded in communities, industries, or families that constantly conflate the two. It helps to create environments—personal or professional—that celebrate effort, growth, and honesty over appearance. It helps to consume media that models a diversity of success stories, not just the financially glamorous ones. It helps to have conversations—real ones—about failure, fear, and the emotional cost of living in a performance-driven world. Cultural myths only lose power when they are named aloud.

Some might argue that tying identity to money motivates excellence. But that argument collapses under scrutiny. There's a difference between being motivated by purpose and being fuelled by fear. The former energises; the latter depletes. People who ground their worth internally are often more innovative, generous, and resilient—not less. They're more willing to say no to exploitative deals, more likely to ask for help, and more capable of recovering from setbacks. They're not trying to prove they're valuable—they already believe it.

Ultimately, the goal is not to reject money or ambition. It's to free both from the burden of identity. Money, at its best, is a tool: for creation, for security, for possibility. It becomes dangerous only when it's asked to do emotional labour it was never designed for—like proving your worth or earning your place in the world. That labour must be done elsewhere: in therapy, in community, in honest self-examination.

Because the real identity crisis isn't about how much you earn—it's about what you've come to believe it means. Undoing that belief is not weakness. It's maturity. It's the foundation for a financial life that's not just strategic, but sane. One where you can pursue growth without sacrificing self-respect. One where your wins are satisfying, not hollow. And one where your value, finally, is yours to define.

The Silent Killer: Imposter Syndrome – How self-doubt keeps you undercharging, overworking, and holding yourself back.

There is a peculiar irony that afflicts some of the most capable, accomplished people in the world: the more they achieve, the less they believe they deserve it. This is not modesty. It's a quiet terror that whispers, *Any moment now, they'll find out you're a fraud.* This is imposter syndrome—one of the most insidious forms of psychological self-sabotage in modern professional life. And while it's often treated as a harmless confidence issue or a quirky rite of passage, its consequences are far more damaging than they appear. It's not just that imposter syndrome makes people feel small—it shrinks their income, their influence, and their long-term capacity to lead.

In a culture obsessed with credentials, performance, and visibility, many professionals live with the gnawing suspicion that they don't truly belong at the tables they've earned their way into. They second-guess their expertise, attribute success to luck, or dismiss their achievements as flukes. This internal dissonance doesn't stay confined to self-esteem. It quietly leaks into money decisions. People with imposter syndrome routinely underprice their services, hesitate to negotiate, over-deliver to prove worth, and avoid visibility to minimise risk. These behaviours are not irrational—they are survival strategies designed to avoid exposure. The fear is not just failure; it's discovery.

What's striking is that imposter syndrome rarely correlates with actual competence. Research shows that it disproportionately affects high-performing individuals, particularly those in underrepresented groups—women, people of colour, immigrants, and first-generation professionals. When the cultural template of what success "should" look like excludes you, even earned achievements can feel counterfeit. The further your identity deviates from the default norm—whether in gender, background, accent, or experience—the harder it is to believe that your presence is fully legitimate. The system may say yes; your nervous system says, *Not yet. Not really.*

This internalised doubt becomes particularly potent in financial settings. Take pricing, for instance. People struggling with imposter syndrome often avoid charging market rates because they feel their work isn't "worth" it—regardless of its objective value. They may pre-emptively discount, apologise for their fees, or pad their work with unnecessary extras to justify the price. Behind each of these behaviours is the false belief that they must overcompensate for their perceived illegitimacy. The result? A chronic mismatch between value delivered and value received. And over time, this financial incongruence compounds—not just in income lost, but in self-trust eroded.

It's not just entrepreneurs and freelancers who suffer from this. Inside organisations, imposter syndrome drives professionals to overwork in silence. Employees take on extra hours, avoid asking for raises, or decline promotions out of fear they won't be able to "prove" themselves. They say yes to every task, hoping that effort will mask insecurity. Ironically, many of these individuals are seen by others as high-performers. But inside, they are haunted by the sense that they're winging it—and that one mistake could unravel everything. The cost here is both personal and organisational: burnout, stalled careers, and the invisible loss of potential leadership.

Compounding the issue is the fact that imposter syndrome often masquerades as humility. People mistake it for being grounded, self-aware, or not wanting to appear arrogant. But there's a crucial difference between humility and self-erasure. Humility acknowledges limits without denying ability. Imposter syndrome denies ability altogether—or insists it's not enough. And the more competent someone is, the more irrational this self-doubt becomes. A surgeon who feels inadequate after saving hundreds of lives. A CEO who attributes success to luck despite a decade of growth. An artist whose work touches thousands, yet feels undeserving of praise. These are not isolated cases. They are structural patterns.

What fuels this phenomenon is not just internal psychology, but external reward systems. Many industries, particularly those driven by knowledge, creativity, or performance, operate in environments of chronic uncertainty. There are no fixed metrics for excellence—only feedback loops shaped by subjective validation. When the rules are ambiguous, and praise is inconsistent, even high achievers can feel like they're faking it. Add to this the rise of social media, where success is curated and comparative, and the result is a perpetual crisis of authenticity. People don't just wonder if they're good enough—they wonder if anyone is.

So how does one dismantle the grip of imposter syndrome without falling into the trap of overcompensation? First, by acknowledging that it's not a personal flaw—it's an adaptive response to inconsistent validation in a high-stakes world. It's not proof that something is wrong with you. It's proof that you've internalised a system that rewards performance over presence, confidence over competence, and polish over process. The problem is cultural, not characterological. That distinction alone is liberating.

Second, by redefining what "enough" looks like. Imposter syndrome thrives in vagueness. The more abstract your standards of success, the more likely you are to feel that you haven't met them. One antidote is specificity. What are the actual indicators of your effectiveness? What evidence exists that you're creating value? What feedback, outcomes, or results have you received that contradict the voice of self-doubt? Bringing your achievements into conscious awareness—not as ego fuel, but as data—helps anchor self-perception in reality, not rumination.

Third, by separating financial value from emotional validation. People with imposter syndrome often conflate charging more with being more. This makes every fee adjustment feel existential. But money is not a verdict on your worth—it's a tool to exchange value. Your prices should reflect the transformation you offer, not the level of confidence you feel on any given day. This requires a shift from self-esteem-based pricing to results-based pricing. You're not paid because you feel qualified. You're paid because you solve problems. That distinction frees you to price strategically, rather than emotionally.

Fourth, and most challengingly, by learning to tolerate visibility. Imposter syndrome often leads to hiding—playing small, staying quiet, or avoiding opportunities that might spotlight your work. But influence requires exposure. And exposure requires risk. The goal is not to feel fearless, but to act despite fear. Courage, in this context, is not loud. It's the quiet act of showing up, again and again, even when your inner critic screams. Each time you do, you build internal proof: not that you're perfect, but that you're capable—and that's enough.

Finally, by seeking environments that affirm your reality. Imposter syndrome is often reinforced by isolation. When you're the only one in the room who looks, sounds, or thinks like you, self-doubt thrives. Community is essential—not just for encouragement, but for perspective. Talking openly about imposter syndrome with peers, mentors, or therapists breaks the illusion that it's a personal failing. It reveals it for what it is: a common distortion that loses power when named aloud.

The paradox is this: many of the world's most valuable contributors live with the sense that they have nothing to offer. They wait to feel "ready," not realising that readiness is rarely a feeling—it's a decision. And the work of transformation begins not when you silence the inner critic, but when you stop letting it make your choices. You may never fully eliminate imposter syndrome. But you can learn to stop giving it the final vote.

Because the question isn't *Do I feel like I belong?* The question is *Will I act as if I do—even when I don't?* That shift—from internal validation to behavioural alignment—is where freedom lives. It's where careers expand, incomes rise, and real authority is built—not from pretending to be someone you're not, but from owning who you already are.

The Deservingness Deficit – How feelings of unworthiness block wealth—and how to finally feel ready for more.

There's a question that rarely makes it into spreadsheets or financial planning tools, yet it quietly governs the way millions approach money: *Do I believe I deserve more?* Not *can I earn more*, *am I capable*, or even *do I want it*—but *do I feel fundamentally worthy of it?* Beneath polished resumes and ambition-fuelled goal setting, this invisible layer of self-concept silently shapes financial outcomes. It is one of the most overlooked forces in wealth psychology: the deservingness deficit.

On the surface, many people appear driven and confident. They show up, deliver, and outwardly participate in economic life like everyone else. But beneath the activity lies a persistent undertow—a low-grade sense that more is for other people. Others can raise their rates, ask for the promotion, build scalable income. Others can live with ease. *I can't ask for that much. I haven't earned it yet. I should be grateful for what I already have.* These aren't conscious strategies. They're embodied beliefs—deeply internalised and often inherited.

Deservingness is not a matter of competence or effort. It's a felt sense of value, rooted in early experiences and reinforced by culture. Many people learn from childhood—explicitly or by omission—that asking for more is selfish, indulgent, or dangerous. Some were raised in environments where scarcity was moralised: money was tight, and those who had it were suspect. Others absorbed subtler cues: the parent who never bought anything for themselves, the unspoken rule that "we don't talk about money," or the cultural message that wanting too much is greedy. These narratives do not fade with adulthood. They calcify into default programming.

And this programming doesn't just affect how people *feel* about money—it dictates what they believe they're *allowed* to have. If someone has unconsciously concluded that wealth is incompatible with goodness, or that abundance will isolate them from their family, or that they must suffer to earn, then no amount of financial advice will override that story. They might nod along in agreement during a budgeting seminar or a business workshop, but when the time comes to take bold action—raise fees, invest in growth, decline an underpaid offer—they freeze. Not because they don't know what to do. Because deep down, they don't believe they're allowed to do it.

The tragedy of the deservingness deficit is that it often afflicts the most conscientious people. Those who care deeply, serve generously, and operate with integrity are frequently the ones most plagued by doubt. This is no coincidence. Their sense of responsibility becomes a double bind: *Because I care so much, I shouldn't ask for more. Because others are struggling, I must downplay my needs.* Empathy turns into self-erasure. Altruism becomes a mask for low self-worth. And the economic consequence is not just reduced income—it's chronic under-living.

This phenomenon shows up across industries. Therapists undercharge because "my clients can't afford more." Creatives hesitate to invoice because "this was fun for me—it feels wrong to make money from it." Employees delay salary negotiations because "I don't want to seem pushy." Entrepreneurs avoid scaling because "what if I can't deliver?" In each case, the surface explanation appears rational. But beneath it is the same unspoken belief: *I am not yet enough to deserve more.*

The internal logic of deservingness is irrationally perfectionistic. It says, *Once I feel confident, once I've proven myself fully, once everyone approves—then I'll be ready.* But confidence does not arrive before action. It is the result of action. And worth is not a certificate to be earned through suffering. It is the baseline condition for healthy economic participation. You don't need to qualify for value. You are already valuable. The real task is *acceptance*—not acquisition.

But here's the dilemma: telling someone they deserve more doesn't automatically make them feel it. Worthiness is not an idea. It's a nervous system state. And that means the path to healing the deservingness deficit is not just cognitive—it's relational, behavioural, and embodied. It requires unlearning old stories, building new habits, and gradually proving to yourself—through experience—that more is safe, more is possible, and more is *not* an act of betrayal.

Start with this: notice your reflexive resistance to expansion. When you receive praise, do you downplay it? When an opportunity arises, do you defer, delay, or explain it away? When you set financial goals, do they feel exciting—or shameful? These micro-moments of contraction are diagnostic. They reveal where your self-concept lags behind your reality. The work is not to override them with toxic positivity, but to interrogate them with compassion. Ask: *Whose voice is this? What am I afraid will happen if I have more?*

Often, the fear is not failure—it's disconnection. More money might mean separating from your peer group, outgrowing familial patterns, or confronting envy and judgement. And if your belonging has always been tied to sameness or self-sacrifice, then prosperity may feel threatening. But it's worth asking: *Is the version of belonging I'm preserving actually nourishing me?* If not, then perhaps the real growth is not in getting more—but in becoming the kind of person who can hold more without guilt.

To shift deservingness at the root, one must practice receiving—not just intellectually, but practically. That means charging fair rates, accepting compliments, saying yes to help, and allowing yourself to rest without justifying it. It means building a life where your wellbeing is not a reward for exhaustion, but a non-negotiable foundation. These small acts of allowance accumulate. They send a message to your psyche: *I am safe to expand. I am worthy of support. I do not need to suffer to earn.*

This shift is not about entitlement. It's about integrity. Because refusing to receive—when you're creating real value—is not humility. It's imbalance. The economy depends on the circulation of value, and withholding yourself from that exchange doesn't serve the world. When you under-earn, undercharge, or over-give, you diminish your capacity to sustain the very contributions you care about. Worthiness is not a luxury mindset. It's a prerequisite for sustainable impact.

There's a concept in behavioural finance called "loss aversion"—the tendency to fear loss more than we value gain. But deservingness introduces another form of aversion: *value aversion.* The subconscious fear of being seen, being rewarded, or being celebrated for what we offer. And it is this aversion—not a lack of skill or effort—that keeps many people playing small. Until that pattern is addressed, no amount of strategic advice will land. Because strategies are only as effective as the person who believes they're allowed to use them.

The good news is that worthiness is not fixed. It can be reclaimed. But it won't happen through thinking alone. It will come from repeated, embodied decisions that contradict the old narrative. Say yes to the opportunity you don't feel ready for. Raise your rates before you feel confident. Delegate even if you think you should "do it all." These aren't just business moves. They are therapeutic acts of reparenting. They say to your nervous system: *It's safe to grow.*

Ultimately, the most radical act of financial healing is not building wealth. It's believing you're allowed to. Not as a reward for suffering. Not as compensation for trauma. But because you are inherently worthy of a life that supports, nourishes, and expands you. That belief, once internalised, changes everything. Not just what you earn—but how you live.

Redefining What You're Actually Paid For – Why you're not paid for your time or effort, but for the unique value you create.

Most people assume they are paid for time. That assumption is quietly baked into our daily vocabulary—hourly rates, day jobs, time sheets, billable hours. The equation is straightforward: I put in X hours, I earn Y pounds. For many, it feels fair, almost moral. Hard work equals fair pay. Time equals worth. But this tidy logic conceals a deeper, more disruptive truth: *in most real-world markets, people are not actually paid for their time or their effort—they are paid for the value they generate.* And that value has little to do with how long something takes, or how hard it feels.

This is not a semantic distinction. It's a paradigm shift—and one that radically alters how we think about pricing, performance, income potential, and self-worth. If you still believe you're earning money because you worked a long day or pushed through fatigue, you are measuring your economic contributions through a lens that no longer serves you. Not because time and effort don't matter, but because they are not the unit of value that buyers, clients, or companies ultimately care about.

Consider this: if you hired a lawyer to help you resolve a legal dispute and they solved your problem in 20 minutes—because they knew precisely what to do—you would not demand a discount. In fact, you might be relieved. You are not paying for their time. You are paying for the years of skill, judgement, and pattern-recognition they compressed into that one call. Likewise, if you needed brain surgery, you would not choose the surgeon based on how long the operation takes or how exhausted they'll be afterwards. You want the best outcome delivered as efficiently as possible. In high-trust, high-stakes domains, we intuitively understand: *value is not measured by labour—it's measured by impact.*

Yet most people—especially those in knowledge work, consulting, coaching, and the creative industries—struggle to apply this principle to themselves. They chronically undercharge, over-deliver, or feel guilty for earning well if the task "didn't take that long." This confusion stems from a cultural overattachment to visible effort. We are conditioned from school age to value outputs we can observe: hours logged, tasks ticked off, time spent in the chair. But markets do not reward effort. They reward outcomes. And those outcomes often come from expertise, not endurance.

This misunderstanding becomes especially dangerous in a post-industrial economy. In agricultural or factory work, labour hours did largely determine productivity. More hands on deck meant more units produced. But in the modern economy—dominated by tech, service, and intellectual work—*leverage* matters far more than labour. A single insight, innovation, or system design can generate disproportionate results. A software engineer can write code in an afternoon that powers a million-dollar product. A designer can create a brand identity that drives conversions for years. A strategist can restructure a business model that unlocks new revenue streams. The economic value of these acts is *not* time-dependent. It's outcome-dependent. And often, the more senior the contributor, the faster they can create it.

Yet people still discount themselves if it "didn't feel hard." If they found it easy, they assume it must not be worth much. This is a catastrophic misreading of value. Ease is often a sign of mastery. You are not paid for how much strain you feel. You are paid for the difference you make. And the better you get at something, the more natural it becomes to create results that others can't replicate—not because you try harder, but because you know more, see more, and trust yourself more.

This shift also reframes how we think about pricing. If you charge for time, you are setting a ceiling on your income that is mathematically non-negotiable: 24 hours a day. You will eventually hit a wall. But if you price based on the value you provide, you decouple income from hours—and open up a far more scalable model. This doesn't mean overcharging arbitrarily. It means aligning your pricing with the actual change, relief, insight, or transformation you deliver. And if your work generates real, lasting results, then that value is often far higher than the amount of time it took to produce.

Of course, this model requires honesty, not hype. You must *understand* what your value is before you can communicate or charge for it. That means asking: *What improves because of my presence? What problem do I solve? What decision do I accelerate? What risk do I reduce? What pain do I eliminate?* These are not esoteric questions. They are the foundation of value articulation. And they're the only reliable way to build sustainable pricing structures that reflect reality, not guilt or guesswork.

Many professionals—particularly those who identify with caring, creative, or service-based identities—resist this shift. They fear that charging for value is manipulative or mercenary. But that fear is usually misplaced. Valuing your contribution does not mean exploiting others. It means taking responsibility for the real economic impact of your work. Undercharging is not humility. It is distortion. And it can unintentionally erode the perceived quality of your offering. Price signals value. When your rates are incongruent with your results, people either become suspicious—or they unconsciously undervalue what you do.

Understanding that you are paid for value also forces you to confront a more uncomfortable question: *Am I actually creating outcomes worth paying for?* This is where the distinction between busyness and effectiveness becomes vital. You can work long hours, stay overwhelmed, and produce nothing that materially moves the needle. Or you can work intentionally, focus on what matters, and create asymmetric value in short bursts. The former earns sympathy. The latter earns income.

This model also recalibrates what growth looks like. In a time-and-effort economy, growth means doing more—more hours, more clients, more hustle. But in a value-based model, growth means doing *better*. That might involve improving your skill, deepening your niche, designing smarter systems, or cultivating stronger client relationships. In this framework, rest is not laziness—it's strategic. Reflection is not indulgence—it's capacity-building. You're not trying to squeeze more out of the same hour. You're trying to become the kind of person whose hour produces ten times the result.

The implications for negotiations and career advancement are equally profound. If you walk into a salary conversation anchored to time, you're limited to arguing for incremental raises based on how long you've stayed or how hard you've worked. But if you walk in anchored to value, you shift the conversation to *impact*. You show your manager or client how the business is different because of your contributions. And in doing so, you reclaim agency in an economy that otherwise treats you as interchangeable.

There's a psychological cost to ignoring this truth. When you base your worth on effort alone, you tether your self-esteem to exhaustion. You feel validated only when depleted. You subconsciously seek struggle as proof that you're earning your keep.

This is not only unsustainable—it's corrosive. Over time, it diminishes your joy, your health, and your strategic clarity. But when you root your worth in value created, you liberate yourself from the tyranny of busyness. You can work with focus, rest without guilt, and scale without breaking.

This is not theory. It is the real engine behind the world's most resilient earners. Top consultants don't bill by the hour—they bill by the outcome. Elite freelancers don't quote based on time—they quote based on the business result. Visionary creators aren't paid for effort—they are paid for insight. The common denominator is simple: they understand what they're actually being paid for. And they structure their offers, schedules, and identities accordingly.

To embrace this shift, start by tracking outcomes, not hours. Document what improves when you're involved. Study what people thank you for. Ask where your clients or colleagues were before, and where they are after. And above all, stop apologising for the ease with which you create value. That ease is not an accident—it's the result of everything you've learned, lived, and earned. You're not paid for your fatigue. You're paid for your effect.

If the old model said, *I must work harder to earn more,* the new model says, *I must understand, articulate, and expand the value I create.* It is a quieter, more empowered path—one that does not glorify hustle, but honours clarity. And in that clarity lies the freedom to earn without exhaustion, grow without guilt, and step fully into the economic expression of your worth.

CHAPTER 5
The Myth of Financial Literacy

Ask someone struggling financially what they think they need, and the answer often comes without hesitation: "I just need to get better with money." On the surface, it sounds perfectly reasonable. Sensible, even. Yet under closer inspection, it is a half-truth at best. Our culture's obsession with financial literacy—countless books, charts of compound interest, personal finance seminars—creates an illusion: that knowledge alone guarantees better outcomes. That if people simply understood what to do, they would act accordingly. That bad financial decisions spring from ignorance, and good ones from education. But experience, both collective and individual, tells a different story. People who can recite the Rule of 72 still max out credit cards. MBA graduates may live paycheck to paycheck. Financial literacy alone does not reliably predict financial wellbeing. Something subtler governs behaviour.

What is missing is integration, not information. Not a clever spreadsheet, but a deeper engagement with emotion, identity, and habit. Most financial tools are designed to help us think, yet the majority of financial behaviour is driven by feeling. Until this mismatch is confronted, even the most informed individuals repeat patterns that defy rationality—because these patterns were never rational in the first place. They were familiar, emotionally coded, inherited from family narratives, or tied to identity in ways rarely examined.

This explains why budgets so often fail. Not due to laziness or lack of discipline, but because traditional budgeting assumes people are calculators. Categorise expenses, allocate funds, and behaviour will follow—so the logic goes. But spending is rarely purely cognitive. People shop when lonely, avoid bills when ashamed, splurge when powerless, and hoard when unsafe. Behaviour does not bend to spreadsheets; it bends to internal states. When budgets ignore this, they become either performative rituals or guilt-inducing exercises, fleeting in effect at best.

Worse, the modern financial self-help landscape is clogged with superficial fixes. Advice like "stop buying lattes" or "set SMART goals" may seem practical, but they fall flat for anyone confronting deep emotional resistance. Financial literacy as popularly delivered is tactical—it lives in the head. What is needed is financial embodiment: knowledge that permeates the nervous system, the stories we tell ourselves, and the environmental cues that reinforce or undermine habits.

If knowledge were sufficient, the most educated would be the most financially secure. Time and again, this is not the case. Long-term financial wellbeing correlates more strongly with behavioural fluency—the capacity to act consistently in alignment with goals, even under pressure. This fluency is learned, not from textbooks, but through the interplay of emotion, habit, and self-concept. It requires not just knowing what to do, but believing oneself to be the kind of person who does it. Identity-level change is therefore not optional—it is essential.

Consider the under-earner who intellectually understands their worth but hesitates to quote a rate without guilt, or the professional adept at analysing balance sheets who overspends under stress. These are not failures of logic. They are misalignments between internal state and external information. Until the nervous system feels safe to act differently, new knowledge rarely yields new outcomes.

The financial industry seldom addresses this, favouring tactics over transformation. Quick-fix tools are easier to sell than identity-level work. Yet for genuine, long-term progress, one must confront the emotional scaffolding beneath financial choices, recognising when behaviour reflects patterned emotional responses rather than rational calculation. Only then does leverage become possible.

This chapter invites a reframing: to examine not just money, but the assumptions driving behaviour. It begins by challenging the mythology of budgeting as a cure-all, then explores why knowledge alone often produces identical results, and why enduring change must begin with self-concept. Identity governs action; early emotional conditioning echoes through adult financial life; true transformation requires integration, not insight alone.

At the heart of this reframing is the idea of a Personalised Financial Identity. This is not branding; it is practical alignment between financial systems and psychological wiring. A traditional spreadsheet may fail a visual learner, whereas a colour-coded dashboard could thrive. Social reinforcement may be essential for some, while solitary tracking suffices for others. Customising systems to temperament is not indulgent—it is necessary. Reliance on willpower alone is a long-term losing strategy.

Behavioural finance supports this. Studies on loss aversion, sunk costs, and temporal discounting demonstrate that humans routinely act against their financial interests—not from ignorance, but from wiring designed to avoid pain, seek comfort, and preserve identity. Industry advice often ignores this, offering correctional mantras like "be more disciplined" or "delay gratification," which fail and deepen shame.

By contrast, this chapter offers a compassionate, rigorous approach. It does not pathologise struggle, nor reduce financial behaviour to willpower. It situates behaviour within memory, nervous system responses, environment, and belief. Any attempt to transform financial life without addressing identity is doomed. No budget, however meticulous, will overcome an internal self-image that resists change.

This reframing shifts the question from "What should I do?" to "Who am I becoming through these decisions?" Money ceases to be merely transactional; it becomes a mirror of self-trust, agency, responsibility, and desire. Avoidance reveals lingering shame; compulsions indicate unprocessed emotion; spending maps unmet needs; aspirations show self-concept expanding beyond current identity.

The aim is not to make you a budgeting evangelist. It is to explain why traditional methods often fail and what works better. It encourages noticing invisible emotional patterns behind behaviours, stopping self-blame, and approaching financial transformation as a deeply human process—logic, memory, emotion, and desire in conversation, not conflict.

The promise is this: when you stop striving for literacy in someone else's terms and begin building systems coherent with your psychological landscape, transformation occurs. Not because you have gained more knowledge, but because you are living from a financial identity that is coherent, aligned, and self-authored. That is not literacy. That is liberation.

Why Budgets Don't Work for Most People – The truth: budgets don't fail because people are weak—they fail because they ignore emotion.

If budgets worked the way financial experts claimed, we'd see far fewer people in financial distress. The premise is elegant in its simplicity: spend less than you earn, allocate funds to clear categories, monitor your progress, and success will follow. But for millions of people, budgets are not a lifeline—they are a recurring source of failure, guilt, and shame. Not because these individuals are irresponsible or mathematically illiterate, but because traditional budgeting systems are emotionally tone-deaf. They operate on the assumption that people make financial decisions like machines—detached, rational, and fully self-controlled. That assumption is not only incorrect; it is profoundly damaging.

Budgets fail not because people are weak-willed, but because budgets—as they are typically designed—ignore the emotional complexity of human behaviour.

Conventional budgeting operates like a software patch for a hardware issue. It attempts to fix behaviour by imposing structure, rather than understanding the deeper operating system that governs financial choices. In reality, people don't spend according to neat allocations—they spend to relieve stress, to signal identity, to cope with shame, to feel momentarily in control. A budget that fails to address these internal dynamics becomes just another tool of self-punishment: a device to track how often you disappoint yourself.

Consider this: nearly every budget is designed around categories—housing, groceries, transport, entertainment. But these categories rarely capture *why* someone spends. They ignore the context in which spending decisions are made. They don't track the late-night impulse buy that follows a stressful work week, the overspending on gifts driven by guilt, or the monthly self-reward ritual born of emotional depletion. Instead, they treat these decisions as "failures" to stay within limits, rather than as expressions of unexamined emotional needs.

A telling example can be found in the experience of high-functioning professionals. Many such individuals, despite earning healthy incomes and understanding the mechanics of budgeting, find themselves perpetually veering off course. It's not for lack of knowledge or planning. It's because budgeting systems rarely account for identity conflict. The professional who was raised with scarcity narratives may hoard money, feeling terrified to spend even on legitimate needs. Another might overcompensate for childhood lack by overspending the moment they feel flush. The budget becomes a surface-level intervention on a deep emotional imprint. Until those imprints are addressed, the behaviour will not shift sustainably.

This failure of budgeting logic extends into how we conceptualise financial self-control. Most people internalise the idea that going over budget is a personal defect. They imagine that if they just had more willpower or discipline, they would finally "get it right." But willpower is not a sustainable strategy. It is a short-term override mechanism, not a structural solution. Relying on it daily is like navigating a city without a map—exhausting, inefficient, and prone to breakdown under pressure. When emotional regulation is weak, willpower collapses. And when willpower collapses, people fall back on old behaviours that provide immediate psychological relief, even if they sabotage long-term goals.

Financial coaches and institutions often misread this pattern. They respond with tougher measures: stricter budgets, more granular tracking, shame-based motivators. But this only amplifies the problem. The real barrier isn't a lack of strategy—it's the absence of *emotional congruence.* If a budgeting system contradicts someone's emotional needs or identity, it will be resisted, either overtly or covertly. Progress is then misinterpreted as "discipline," and setbacks as "failure," when both are merely signals of whether the system resonates at a deeper level.

The more productive question isn't "Why can't I stick to a budget?" but "What part of me is this budget ignoring?" Is it the anxious inner child who fears scarcity? The burned-out adult who seeks reward? The socially conditioned self who needs to appear successful? Until these parts are acknowledged and integrated, no financial tool—no matter how sophisticated—will produce consistent results.

Another layer of complexity is the misalignment between budgeting and how people experience time. Budgets are typically structured around monthly periods, but financial behaviour does not unfold in tidy cycles. It is irregular, stress-sensitive, and often reactive. People may behave one way at the start of the month—optimistic, focused—and another by week three, when fatigue, unexpected expenses, or emotional depletion shift their internal state. A static budget doesn't adapt to these fluctuations, which means it quickly becomes irrelevant or oppressive. As soon as it no longer matches lived experience, it becomes easier to abandon altogether than to renegotiate its terms.

Moreover, budgets often set fixed limits on flexible behaviours. Take food spending. A budget might allocate £300 for groceries, but what happens when your mental bandwidth is low and you resort to takeaways? Or when you're emotionally drained and grocery shopping becomes an act of self-care? These deviations are not irrational. They are responses to unmet psychological needs. The budget, however, registers them as failure. And so, over time, the person comes to associate budgeting with a cascade of guilt and self-judgement, making it even harder to re-engage.

There's also a cultural dynamic at play. In many societies, budgeting is framed as a moral act—a marker of responsibility, adulthood, and virtue. Deviating from the budget, then, doesn't just feel like a misstep; it feels like a character flaw. This moral lens obscures the truth: that financial behaviour is not a referendum on your worth, but a mirror of your emotional regulation and belief systems. Until we decouple budgeting from morality, we will continue to weaponise it against ourselves.

What, then, is the alternative?

It starts with recognising that *money management is not a data problem—it is a behaviour problem.* And behaviour is always downstream of emotion. Instead of trying to control spending through restrictions, we must first understand *what function* that spending serves. Emotional tracking—recording what you feel when you spend—is often more insightful than tracking pounds and pence. Noticing that you tend to spend when anxious, or withhold money when ashamed, gives you actionable insight. You're no longer fighting yourself. You're working *with* yourself.

Secondly, any financial system must be customised to the individual's emotional architecture. Some people are wired for structure; others need flexibility. Some thrive on visuals and dashboards; others need tactile tools like cash envelopes. Some need accountability from a coach or peer; others prefer quiet reflection. The one-size-fits-all budgeting paradigm collapses under the weight of human variance. True financial agency comes from designing systems that honour your psychological wiring—not suppress it.

Another shift involves moving from goal-based budgeting to *values-based* allocation. Traditional budgets ask, "What do you need to spend?" A values-based framework asks, "What matters most to you right now?" It invites conscious trade-offs rather than rigid constraints. Instead of feeling imprisoned by categories, you are guided by priorities. This creates a sense of autonomy, which is one of the most powerful drivers of consistent behaviour.

Importantly, emotional literacy must become a central pillar of financial literacy. Understanding your triggers, shame patterns, and coping mechanisms is not ancillary to budgeting—it's foundational. Without this awareness, financial strategies become futile exercises in self-control. With it, they become tools of self-clarity and empowerment.

Ultimately, the goal is not to abandon all structure, but to build one that breathes. A budget that acknowledges that some months are emotionally heavier. That recognises that people don't make decisions in spreadsheets—they make them in grocery aisles, during stressful meetings, after difficult conversations. A budget that evolves with your life stage, energy levels, and psychological needs. A budget that is not a cage, but a compass.

So the question is not whether you can stick to a budget. The question is whether your financial system reflects the *truth* of who you are—not just your income and expenses, but your history, your temperament, your inner landscape. Because if it doesn't, it will always feel like an imposition. But when it does, something remarkable happens: your financial behaviour begins to feel less like effort and more like alignment. Not because you've become more disciplined—but because you've become more honest.

That is the missing link. Not knowledge. Not tools. Not willpower. But emotional congruence. When your financial system honours your internal world, consistency becomes possible. And when consistency becomes possible, transformation is not far behind.

More Knowledge, Same Results - Why even financially educated people still struggle—and what they're missing.

It's a quiet embarrassment among the financially literate: knowing all the right things to do, and still not doing them. The shame is often acute, because unlike those who plead ignorance, these individuals don't have the excuse of not knowing better. They've read the books, taken the courses, memorised the principles. They understand compound interest, diversification, inflation, behavioural biases, tax brackets, and emergency funds. They could give a flawless PowerPoint presentation on financial best practices—and yet their bank accounts, stress levels, or daily behaviours suggest something is still off. And this is not an anomaly. It's a pattern.

The uncomfortable truth is that *financial knowledge alone rarely changes financial outcomes*. The assumption that more information leads to better results is a seductive fallacy—comforting, linear, and widely perpetuated by financial institutions and educational systems. But in reality, money is not merely a knowledge problem. It is an emotional, behavioural, and identity-driven one. And until those deeper forces are confronted, no amount of technical education will bridge the gap between understanding and execution.

This is not to undermine the value of financial literacy. It's necessary—but it's not sufficient. The most common misinterpretation of financial struggle is that it stems from ignorance. It often doesn't. It stems from misalignment—between what a person knows and what their internal wiring permits them to act on. A person might fully grasp that spending £200 on a spontaneous weekend away will delay their debt payoff plan. But in the moment, the need for escapism, connection, or self-worth outweighs the abstract value of prudence. Knowledge bows to emotion. Logic is eclipsed by lived experience. And later, they'll criticise themselves as though it was merely a lapse in judgement, rather than a conflict of unmet needs.

To understand why knowledge doesn't always translate into transformation, we need to look at the mechanics of human behaviour. Decisions are rarely driven by conscious intent alone. They are shaped by subconscious scripts formed in childhood, by unresolved emotional patterns, by the stories we tell ourselves about what money means. These scripts operate below the surface of awareness, quietly vetoing our best intentions. No spreadsheet, however well-formatted, can override a person's internalised belief that they are not the kind of person who builds wealth, deserves ease, or can be trusted with prosperity.

Take, for instance, the case of a financial planner who knows precisely how to manage risk, diversify assets, and construct a long-term wealth strategy. Professionally, they are trusted to guide others. But privately, they may be over-leveraged, under-saving, or compulsively overspending. Why? Because their identity—perhaps shaped by scarcity-driven parenting, or an internalised need to appear successful—drives them to self-sabotage in subtle ways. Their behaviour is not incongruent with their knowledge. It's entirely congruent with their unspoken emotional needs.

This gap between knowledge and behaviour isn't unique to finance. Doctors who smoke, psychologists in dysfunctional relationships, nutritionists with disordered eating—all are examples of how professional expertise does not immunise against personal complexity. But in money, the fallout is particularly severe, because the discrepancy often carries moral judgement. A person who knows better and still "fails" feels not just ineffective, but inauthentic. The guilt is layered: guilt over the financial choices themselves, and guilt over the perceived hypocrisy of making them despite knowing better.

It's also critical to acknowledge the role of environment. Many financial education programmes operate on the assumption that people exist in stable, rational ecosystems. They don't. They exist in high-pressure jobs, unstable economies, exploitative labour markets, and social media landscapes designed to weaponise comparison. They live with partners who may not share financial goals, in cultures that glorify status over sustainability, and in bodies and minds shaped by anxiety, trauma, or chronic fatigue. A budget doesn't operate in a vacuum. Neither does a plan. Knowing the "right" thing is only the first step; executing it consistently in a chaotic context is an entirely different challenge.

One particularly misunderstood element is the impact of identity. People act in accordance with who they believe they are—not just what they know. If someone sees themselves as "bad with money," "a spender, not a saver," or "just not the finance type," they will unconsciously filter all decisions through that lens. They may resist systems that contradict this identity, even if those systems are objectively beneficial. In contrast, when someone internalises a new identity—say, as a steward of wealth, a conscious investor, or someone who honours their future self—their behaviour shifts, often without coercion. The knowledge hasn't changed. The self-concept has.

This is where most financial education fails. It teaches facts, not frameworks for identity change. It tells people what to do, but not how to become the kind of person who does it naturally. It doesn't ask: *What would need to shift in how you see yourself for this strategy to feel natural?* Instead, it assumes that behavioural change is the inevitable consequence of awareness. This assumption is both lazy and incorrect.

We must also talk about emotional safety. Acting on financial knowledge often requires confronting deep fears—of not having enough, of being judged, of failing publicly, of becoming someone your friends no longer relate to. If implementing financial strategies threatens a person's emotional safety, they will unconsciously avoid doing so. For example, someone who grew up hearing that wealthy people are greedy may hesitate to grow their income, not because they lack ambition, but because doing so risks violating a tribal loyalty to their family's values. No amount of budgeting advice addresses this dissonance.

Then there is the issue of pacing. Financial education tends to be delivered in cognitive sprints: workshops, seminars, content-heavy books. But behavioural change happens in slow, iterative cycles. People need space to reflect, apply, fail, regroup, and reapply. They need to experiment with small shifts, not be overwhelmed by comprehensive plans that don't account for psychological readiness. In this sense, financial transformation is not a curriculum—it is a relationship. One that requires trust, safety, and time.

The missing ingredient, then, is not knowledge—but *integration.* Integration means that information is not just understood intellectually, but metabolised emotionally and aligned with identity. It means that strategies are filtered through personal context, emotional safety, and behavioural readiness. It means that instead of piling on more information, we pause to ask: *What is blocking me from acting on what I already know?*

This also means replacing shame with curiosity. When someone fails to act on their financial knowledge, the question is not "What's wrong with me?" but "What unmet need was I trying to meet?" Financial behaviour is often a proxy for emotional coping. Until those needs are addressed, the behaviour will not change—regardless of how much someone knows.

So what works?

First, self-awareness. Not generic insight, but precise articulation of your money beliefs, emotional triggers, and identity narratives. What do you believe wealth says about you? What financial behaviour do you use to regulate discomfort? What part of you resists financial clarity, and why? These questions are not ancillary—they are diagnostic.

Second, emotional literacy. Being able to name, sit with, and respond to emotions without outsourcing them to money. Most people are financially dysregulated not because of greed or ignorance, but because they haven't learned to be emotionally self-regulating. They use spending to soothe, saving to feel in control, or avoidance to escape shame. Teaching financial tools without teaching emotional regulation is like giving someone a map without teaching them how to walk.

Third, values-based strategy. Instead of abstract goals like "get out of debt" or "build wealth," anchor financial action to values that feel personally meaningful—freedom, contribution, security, integrity. This creates emotional coherence and makes discipline feel like alignment, not deprivation.

Fourth, community and modelling. People need to see others like them successfully embodying new financial identities. Representation matters—not just demographically, but psychologically. When you see someone who shares your fears, history, or worldview navigating money with grace, it expands what feels possible.

And finally, permission. Permission to go slow. To fail without self-punishment. To rewrite your identity in real time. To act before you feel completely ready. Because transformation does not begin with more knowing—it begins with safer being.

Financial knowledge is valuable. But it is not the whole picture. It is the scaffolding. The structure. What makes it functional is the architecture of the self that it rests upon. Until that architecture is addressed—emotionally, behaviourally, and psychologically—most people will keep learning more, and living the same.

And the problem isn't them. It's the assumption that knowing is the same as becoming. It never has been. And it never will be.

Behavior Over Information – The missing piece: changing your identity and emotional wiring around money.

Ask most people what they need to improve their financial lives, and the answer you'll often hear is: *more information.* A new budgeting app. A better investment strategy. A course in passive income. The assumption behind this reflex is almost never questioned: that more data equals better decisions. But this is a dangerous oversimplification. If information alone created transformation, every financially literate person would be wealthy, calm, and secure. They are not. Because the central driver of behaviour is not knowledge—it's identity. And the architecture of identity is built far below the cognitive surface.

The financial industry has long treated behaviour as a technical issue, solvable through education and tools. This approach fails because it does not account for how deeply emotional money is. *You do not manage money in a vacuum of logic—you manage it through the lens of self-perception, emotional patterns, and deeply embedded scripts about what is safe, what is possible, and who you are.* No budget can override a nervous system trained to panic at the idea of scarcity. No investment framework can operate on a belief system that quietly equates wealth with selfishness, or ambition with betrayal. This is the hidden infrastructure behind our actions, and until it is addressed, behaviour change will remain shallow, short-lived, or self-cancelling.

This is not a moral failing. It is a mismatch between the systems we are taught and the way human beings actually work. The financial education paradigm trains people to be good calculators. But people are not calculators—they are meaning-making creatures, driven by emotional salience and identity consistency. You will not act out of alignment with who you believe you are. And this is precisely where financial transformation must begin: *not with what you do, but with who you are allowed to be.*

Consider the person who repeatedly builds up savings, only to find themselves draining it within months for reasons that don't quite make sense even to them. They may cite emergencies, "once-in-a-lifetime" opportunities, or simply that life got expensive. But underneath, there may be something more fundamental at play: a belief that having money creates vulnerability. Perhaps they were raised by someone who hoarded wealth and used it to control others. Perhaps they internalised a story that to have money is to attract resentment, obligation, or scrutiny. So the nervous system does its job: it discharges the money before it becomes dangerous.

This is not poor reasoning. It is brilliant protective patterning. The financial leak is not a budgeting issue—it is a nervous system issue wrapped around an identity issue, masquerading as a math problem. And unless the underlying story changes, no amount of strategy will stick.

Identity-driven money work asks different questions. It doesn't begin with spreadsheets. It begins with curiosity: *Who do you believe you are when it comes to money? What roles do you perform in order to feel safe, accepted, or in control? What core emotions do you use money to regulate—guilt, shame, anxiety, pride? What part of your financial life feels dissonant with who you think you're allowed to be?*

These questions are not tangents. They are the core curriculum. Because once someone sees the pattern they've been reenacting—perhaps being the "responsible one" who carries everyone, or the "humble one" who doesn't ask for more—they can begin to decide whether that role still serves them. *Change doesn't come from forcing new behaviours onto an old identity. It comes from rewriting the identity itself.*

And that rewriting is not done through affirmations or willpower alone. It happens through repeated experiences of emotional safety—where a new behaviour does not feel like a threat to connection, stability, or self-worth. A person who believes that charging more for their work will lead to rejection will only do so when they experience a different outcome often enough that the nervous system updates its expectations. This is slow work, but it is real work. It replaces fear with familiarity. And familiarity is what the nervous system calls safety.

We also must acknowledge how emotion shapes perception. When a person feels shame, the brain narrows its options. It reduces risk tolerance, limits creativity, and makes the future feel abstract. This is why many people can plan well for others—clients, colleagues, even family—but sabotage their own plans. Their knowledge isn't faulty. Their emotional context is. They are not resisting discipline; they are reacting to emotional pain.

This has massive implications for how we teach financial decision-making. Instead of frontloading data, we must begin with emotional literacy. Instead of incentivising behaviour through shame, we must cultivate identity safety. Instead of assuming people will act rationally if only given enough tools, we must understand that rationality is often the reward of emotional regulation—not its precursor.

A growing body of psychological and neurobiological research supports this. Studies in behavioural economics, affective neuroscience, and trauma-informed psychology all point to the same insight: *behaviour follows identity, and identity is shaped by emotional safety, not logic.* When people feel unsafe, they do not optimise. They defend, hide, and default to familiar scripts. Even when those scripts are costly.

Real financial progress, then, requires a shift from information-heavy interventions to *identity-sensitive environments*. This includes how we structure conversations about money, the metaphors we use, and the assumptions we hold. For example, saying "you need to get your spending under control" implies recklessness. It activates shame. But asking "what need is this spending helping you meet?" opens the door to insight and choice. One invites resistance. The other invites responsibility.

Importantly, this also challenges our cultural narratives around money as a pure meritocracy. The idea that good choices equal good outcomes ignores the emotional and systemic barriers that shape access to those choices in the first place. It flattens complexity and punishes struggle. But when we recognise that money behaviour is a mirror of internal state—not simply external skill—we can begin to work at the level that actually matters.

Identity-shifting financial work also invites us to question what "success" looks like. For some, it may be about earning more. For others, it may be about releasing chronic hyper-vigilance and allowing rest. For some, it might mean becoming visible in their work. For others, it means letting go of over-performance. *There is no one-size-fits-all wealth plan—because there is no one-size-fits-all identity.* Behavioural change must be rooted in personal values, not social norms.

One of the most potent frameworks here is the concept of *future self-building.* Rather than simply planning for retirement or financial milestones, this asks: *What kind of person do I want to become, and how does that person think, feel, and act with money?* This reframes action as an expression of becoming. It turns each financial decision into a vote for the identity you are choosing to inhabit.

This approach is powerful because it creates coherence. When your actions align with a self-concept that feels meaningful, they don't require discipline—they feel natural. This is what makes some people naturally inclined to save, invest, or grow: they're not forcing those behaviours; they've absorbed them into their identity.

Contrast this with someone trying to follow a prescriptive plan that conflicts with their internal wiring. It feels like friction. It depletes willpower. And eventually, it collapses. Not because they are weak—but because they are misaligned. *Behaviour change that conflicts with identity is always temporary. Behaviour change that reflects identity is sustainable.*

To support this kind of transformation, we need tools that go beyond charts and calculators. We need reflective journaling, emotional coaching, community modelling, somatic awareness, and financial narratives that acknowledge nuance. We need to teach people how to recognise emotional triggers, rewrite self-limiting beliefs, and develop internal safety for new patterns to emerge.

We must also offer permission—for messiness, for slowness, for imperfection. Because money work that honours identity is not linear. It's cyclical. Some days you will feel powerful and clear. Other days, old fears will resurface. That's not failure. That's the nervous system doing its job—protecting you based on outdated data. And that's why compassion is not optional. It is the foundation on which real, durable change is built.

In the end, the financial revolution that matters most is not in the market, the policy, or the product. It is in the self. The version of you that can calmly say no without guilt. That can price your work according to value, not fear. That can invest in the future without punishing the present. That version already exists. It is not waiting for more information. It is waiting for your permission to lead.

And that shift—from knowledge to embodiment—is what changes everything.

Your Personalised Financial Identity – A new approach: designing your money life around who you truly are, not who you've been told to be.

Most financial advice begins with numbers. Rarely does it begin with *you.* The implicit assumption is that there is a correct way to manage money—a model that, once learned, will make you more responsible, disciplined, or successful. But here is the uncomfortable truth: *most financial systems are designed to standardise behaviour, not personalise it.* They prioritise compliance over self-awareness, technique over fit. And this is precisely why many intelligent, educated, even well-earning individuals still feel disempowered around money. They are following a template that does not match who they are.

Your financial identity—how you think, feel, and behave with money—is not a by-product of rational planning. It is a psychological construct built from years of internalised messaging, emotional conditioning, and social modelling. You didn't choose it so much as absorb it. You inherited beliefs from your parents, expectations from your culture, and constraints from your environment. Over time, these inputs calcify into something that feels like fact. You begin to mistake your conditioning for your character.

So when you repeatedly avoid your bank statements, undercharge your work, or impulsively spend as a form of relief, the issue is not that you are irrational or irresponsible. The issue is that your money behaviours are in conflict with the identity you were trained to inhabit. *It is very difficult to build a sustainable financial life while living inside someone else's expectations.*

A personalised financial identity begins with reclaiming authorship. Instead of fitting your life into someone else's spreadsheet, you design your financial strategy to reflect your real psychology—your values, needs, sensitivities, motivations, and strengths. This is not about indulging every preference. It is about crafting a money life that is psychologically congruent. *Congruence is what enables consistency. And consistency—not force—is what sustains wealth.*

Consider two people earning the same income. One thrives on structure and finds peace in meticulous tracking. The other feels suffocated by granular budgeting and makes better decisions when given spacious parameters. Conventional advice would reward the former and label the latter as irresponsible. But the deeper truth is that *both can thrive—if their financial systems align with their identity.* Problems arise not from a lack of knowledge, but from an incongruence between tool and temperament.

A personal financial identity also requires confronting the roles you've unconsciously learned to play. Were you the child who had to be "the saver" because the adults were financially chaotic? Have you built an identity around being low-maintenance, afraid to take up too much financial space? Are you performing the script of the high achiever, tying your worth to output and constantly reinvesting in growth, even when your nervous system is exhausted? These roles may once have protected you. But now they may be distorting your decisions.

Financial healing is not merely about setting new goals. It's about questioning old scripts. If you believe you are someone who is "just bad with money," your brain will filter experiences to validate that narrative. You will discount your wins, magnify your stumbles, and remain in a loop that feels self-fulfilling. To break it, you must ask:

Who do I believe I am when it comes to money? Where did that belief come from? And is it still useful?

This process often uncovers contradictions. You might aspire to financial independence while simultaneously feeling guilty about abundance. You might crave ease while equating wealth with pressure. These are not flaws. They are fragments of identity formed under different emotional conditions. *Reintegrating them is not a mindset hack—it is a developmental process.* One that asks you to hold complexity, not eliminate it.

Modern behavioural finance is finally beginning to catch up with what many therapists and coaches have long known: *money decisions are identity decisions in disguise.* We spend to feel a certain way. We save to feel safe. We invest—or avoid investing—based on the stories we believe about control, worth, risk, and responsibility. The most influential forces in your financial life are rarely financial. They are psychological, relational, and often invisible until questioned.

Designing a personalised financial identity means moving beyond default scripts. It means noticing what truly matters to you—without the noise of social comparison. Perhaps you value autonomy over luxury. Or flexibility over accumulation. Perhaps you want a simple, peaceful life that doesn't require constant optimisation. Or maybe you feel most alive when taking bold risks in pursuit of big ideas. *The point is not to follow a predetermined ideal, but to clarify your own.*

And here is where many people stumble: they've never been invited to do this kind of reflection. Most financial planning begins with external benchmarks—how much to save, what to earn, where to invest. Rarely does it begin with internal alignment. But *internal alignment is not a luxury—it is the foundation for lasting behavioural change.* When your money systems reflect your core identity, you no longer need to rely on motivation or willpower. You simply act from who you are.

To design your financial identity, begin not with goals, but with questions. What do I fear when it comes to money? What am I trying to prove—or avoid proving? What am I silently seeking through my financial life: approval, security, freedom, power? Which financial behaviours energise me? Which deplete me? Where do I feel most authentic in how I engage with money? Where do I feel most performative?

This is not about pathologising your current behaviour. It is about understanding its logic. Every financial pattern you've developed serves—or once served—a function. Overspending may regulate emotional distress. Under-earning may avoid perceived conflict. Chronic saving may shield against vulnerability. These are not problems to be punished. They are *adaptive strategies* that lose effectiveness as you grow. When you stop shaming them, you can start updating them.

Importantly, this approach does not ignore practical skills. Strategy still matters. But skills are only as useful as the context in which they're applied. Telling someone to build a high-yield portfolio while they fear being resented for wealth is like teaching someone to run while their shoelaces are tied together. Personalisation means sequencing the work correctly: *psychological safety first, then financial structure.*

The result is a money life that is no longer driven by avoidance, obligation, or unconscious imitation. It is animated by clarity, dignity, and ownership. You save because it feels empowering—not punitive. You earn in ways that honour your value—not inflate your ego. You spend in ways that affirm your priorities—not react to boredom or pressure. This is what it means to move from financial conformity to financial sovereignty.

To be clear: this is not a fast process. Identity work is nuanced, layered, and often slow to unfold. You may revisit the same themes multiple times. You may regress before you stabilise. That is not failure—it is integration. Growth does not always look like forward motion. Sometimes it looks like making the same decision with a little more awareness, a little less shame, and a little more agency.

The future of financial literacy will not be about distributing more data. It will be about helping people develop self-knowledge. It will recognise that people don't just want more money—they want *money that feels aligned with their lives, their values, their relationships, and their aspirations.* And to achieve that, they must be allowed to stop performing who they were told to be—and start becoming who they actually are.

Personalised financial identity is not a trend. It is a liberation. A refusal to contort oneself into frameworks built for someone else's life. A commitment to aligning the visible (your financial outcomes) with the invisible (your inner truth). Because when you bring your full self into your financial decisions, *you stop managing money—and start relating to it.*

And that changes everything.

CHAPTER 6
The Status Game

It is entirely possible to enjoy financial stability and yet harbour a gnawing sense of inadequacy. You might earn more than your parents ever did, reside in a safer neighbourhood, indulge in better food, and still find yourself quietly haunted by the suspicion that you are somehow behind. A scroll through the curated shopfronts of modern life—designer handbags, bespoke holidays, choreographed "unboxings" of luxuries you didn't even know you lacked—can quickly invite the question: what am I missing? This unease has little to do with genuine scarcity. It springs instead from a deeper fear of falling short. Welcome, then, to the status game: an economy where the true currency is not utility, but signal.

Today's money struggles are rarely just arithmetic. They are entangled with meaning, visibility, identity. What are you if you do not upgrade? What does your car, your watch, your choice of restaurant whisper about you? And perhaps more disquieting—what happens when those whispers are not your own but echoes of constant comparison? The most corrosive financial burdens are often incurred not in pursuit of need, but in the theatre of success.

At its root, this is an old story. Humans have always craved belonging and recognition. In earlier times, status was bounded and legible: lineage, craft, religious standing, civic duty. Now, it is fluid, digital, and endlessly recalibrated. Platforms such as Instagram, TikTok, even LinkedIn, have turned status into an always-on algorithmic loop. The scoreboard is public, the comparisons relentless, and the cost of keeping up increasingly unbearable—both to the psyche and the wallet.

But the matter is larger than social media. What we are confronting is a cultural merging of consumption with selfhood. Luxury goods no longer merely promise quality—they promise association. Fitness clubs market not exercise, but membership in a certain tribe. Financial products themselves—platinum cards, investment apps with sleek minimalist interfaces, cryptocurrencies shrouded in exclusivity—are framed less as tools, more as badges. We are not just buying services or goods. We are buying confirmation that we belong.

This chapter examines the scaffolding of the status game—its mechanics, its distortions, and the ways one might begin to disentangle from it without retreating from contemporary life. Its claim is simple yet provocative: people rarely overspend out of ignorance or greed. More often, they are scrambling to uphold a narrative that equates visibility with worth.

Take the cost of looking successful. For those in high-prestige industries, image and competence become indistinguishable. The watch, the car, the restaurant—all read as credentials. At first, such purchases may feel strategic, an "investment" in credibility. But soon, the performance ossifies into expectation. What was once a costume becomes a cage, draining the very security the individual labours to create.

Research on conspicuous consumption consistently shows that it is not the securely wealthy who spend most feverishly, but the aspiring affluent—the ones close enough to glimpse status, but not firmly established within it. The nearer the promise, the louder the signalling. Which is why high earners can still drown in debt, why influencers borrow outfits for photo shoots, and why even financially literate individuals overshoot their means. Status today is not about access—it is about projection.

The psychological toll of comparison compounds this. Our ancestors might have measured themselves against a village. We, by contrast, are bombarded daily with more images of others' curated lives than they would have seen in a lifetime. And these images are hardly neutral: they are aspiration, staged. You rarely see the overdraft beneath the exotic trip, the inheritance behind the "self-made" home purchase. You see the reveal, not the reality. The consequence is a warped sense of what is normal, and a persistent suspicion that you, alone, are lagging.

Social media, in particular, subtly recalibrates our baseline of "enough." It does not merely inflate desire—it deflates self-worth. And shame, once seeded, tends to germinate financial sabotage.

Convinced you are behind, you make rash gestures to prove otherwise. Feeling unseen, you overspend to be noticed. Sensing exclusion, you purchase entry into spaces that never accounted for your reality. The relief lasts only briefly; the debt lingers much longer.

Equally insidious is the dynamic of buying belonging. Few acknowledge how much of financial life is shaped by social pressures. The annual phone upgrade, done not for need but for parity with peers. The employee saying yes to every costly lunch to avoid seeming standoffish. The student buying luxury trainers, not for function, but to sidestep ridicule. These are not simply indulgences—they are social strategies. In many environments, money functions as a proxy for safety.

Escaping this cycle demands more than discipline. It requires a redefinition of wealth itself. Genuine wealth is not a performance but a steady coherence between values and resources. It asks for financial frameworks tailored to your actual life, not a dream cobbled from feeds and adverts. It means naming the status symbols you inherited, identifying those you still chase, and learning which no longer serve you. Sometimes opting out is not deprivation—it is reclamation.

This need not mean rejecting aspiration wholesale. Ambition and refinement have their place. The question is one of origins: are your goals authentic, or are they residues of comparison? Is that promotion aligned with your personal trajectory, or a lingering contest with an audience long gone? Does the new wardrobe reflect your evolving self, or a fear of fading relevance? The house—security, or social proof?

Such questions are not indictments. They are liberations. For once you become aware of the game, you need not play it blindly. You can curate your environment instead of being curated by it. You can choose when to signal, when to abstain. You can make purchases that affirm you internally, not merely validate you externally. You stop bleeding wealth into appearances.

There is profound dignity in setting your own terms of success. It doesn't mean abandoning beauty, elegance, or ambition. It means refusing to let them dictate your worth. Your identity steadies, your spending sharpens, your self-respect thickens. And perhaps most significantly, your financial life begins to reflect not what looks impressive, but what actually sustains.

In the chapters ahead, we will look at ways to disengage from the status economy without becoming a recluse from modern culture. We will trace the mechanisms that keep people snared in cycles of performative consumption, and sketch practical routes toward autonomy. The aim is not frugality for its own sake. The aim is integrity—spending in a manner that honours your values, secures your future, and speaks your truth.

The status game may dominate the stage, but it is not destiny. See it clearly, and you may finally set down the mask—and begin to live.

The Price of Looking Successful

How much of our spending is really about signalling to others that we've "made it"

Most people don't buy a luxury handbag to carry things. They buy it to carry a message. The same is true for the latest smartphone, a designer watch, an over-leased car, or the kitchen renovation that swallows half a year's salary. These are not purely functional decisions—they are statements. In societies where money and identity are deeply entangled, how we spend becomes how we are seen. And how we are seen too often dictates how we feel about ourselves.

There's a quiet but corrosive force that shapes our financial choices—status anxiety. We rarely name it, but it hums beneath much of our consumer behaviour. The impulse to spend is not always about utility, desire, or even comfort. Often, it's about performance. The performance of competence, desirability, sophistication, or upward mobility. When money becomes a proxy for validation, we start paying for illusions. And the price is far higher than the receipt suggests.

What we call "financial freedom" is often just social performance wrapped in personal finance language. The dream house isn't just a home; it's proof. The first-class ticket isn't just a seat—it's a signal. Many people chasing wealth aren't chasing security—they're chasing admiration. The irony is cruel: the more we spend to *appear* successful, the more we erode the very stability and autonomy that true financial wellbeing requires.

To be clear, there is nothing inherently wrong with luxury, indulgence, or aesthetic pleasure. The problem begins when consumption becomes theatre—when the audience, real or imagined, starts directing the script of our financial lives. That is when autonomy collapses into performance, and authenticity is displaced by comparison.

Status-driven consumption is not new. What is new is its speed, saturation, and subtlety. The 19th-century economist Thorstein Veblen coined the term "conspicuous consumption" to describe the spending habits of the wealthy elite who bought lavish goods to demonstrate their social superiority. But in Veblen's world, status signalling was largely confined to the visible rich. Today, it has become democratised—and dangerously accessible. With credit, leasing, and buy-now-pay-later schemes, we no longer need to *be* wealthy to look like we are. This illusion comes at the cost of financial fragility.

Modern status anxiety has mutated in step with the rise of digital life. On Instagram, everyone appears to be doing better than you—earning more, travelling further, looking sleeker, and living in brighter, more curated spaces. These aren't just posts; they're performances of value. As a result, we live with a constant whisper: *you are behind.* You are not enough. You are not there yet.

This "there" is a moving target, designed to perpetuate dissatisfaction. It's not an endpoint—it's a marketing strategy. The entire machinery of consumer capitalism is built on the cultivation of lack. Once you own the handbag, you'll need the watch. Once you buy the car, you'll need the new kitchen. Once you redo the kitchen, you'll need the holiday to recover from the stress of the renovation. Consumption rarely satisfies; it stimulates desire for the next round.

And because social status is always comparative, the more you have, the more you notice those who have more.

A 2022 study by researchers at the University of Pennsylvania found that people systematically overestimate how well others are doing financially. This misperception is amplified by visibility: we see others' spending far more than we see their saving. We see the car, not the monthly payment; the vacation, not the overdraft; the ring, not the resentment it may mask. This creates what scholars call "positional externalities"—your consumption doesn't just affect your life; it changes the reference point for everyone around you.

Here is where the cost of signalling becomes systemic. If one neighbour renovates their home, the others begin to feel theirs is outdated. If one parent sends their child to a prestigious (and costly) private school, others feel pressure to follow—even if it strains their resources. A single act of conspicuous consumption can ratchet up the baseline of what is considered "normal", thereby escalating collective stress, debt, and emotional strain. These are not isolated behaviours; they're contagious expectations.

The psychology of status is deeply rooted in evolutionary biology. Humans are social creatures wired to seek inclusion and respect. Historically, status conferred survival advantages—it provided access to resources, protection, and mates. But the environments we evolved in were not saturated with advertising, influencers, or digital performance metrics. Our neural circuitry hasn't caught up to our economic context. And this mismatch makes us vulnerable. We are using primitive social instincts to navigate a hyper-commercial world that's engineered to exploit them.

To step outside the status game requires more than frugality or budgeting. It requires a redefinition of what success looks and feels like on your terms. This is not about minimalist puritanism or rejecting all luxury. It is about clarity. *Am I buying this because I truly want it—or because I want to be seen wanting it?* Am I building a life—or building a brand?

Consider the research from Elizabeth Currid-Halkett, who coined the term "aspirational class" to describe affluent professionals who no longer flaunt their status through flashy goods, but rather through more subtle, socially validated markers: organic food, private education, wellness regimens, and curated experiences. These forms of consumption are less visible but equally performative. Even anti-consumption can become a form of elitist signalling. A Tesla might signal one kind of success; a second-hand vintage bicycle with ethical provenance might signal another. Either way, the motivation is status-oriented.

None of this is about moral purity. It's about recognising when our decisions are being hijacked. The question is not *should I buy luxury goods* or *should I reject consumerism altogether.* The question is whether we're being governed by internal values or external scripts. Financial health begins with sovereignty—the ability to choose from alignment, not anxiety.

We must also acknowledge the structural layer. Some people feel pressure to perform success not out of vanity but out of necessity. Marginalised groups, for example, may invest more in status markers to signal competence, legitimacy, or belonging in spaces where their worth is otherwise questioned. For them, status signalling is a form of protection. This makes the status game not just a matter of personal psychology but of social survival.

Still, the remedy begins in awareness. When we name the invisible incentives shaping our spending, we reclaim our agency. When we interrogate the emotional drivers beneath our purchases, we soften the grip of shame, envy, and insecurity. And when we detach our self-worth from other people's perceptions, we can begin to redefine wealth as something more durable than visibility.

True wealth is not about what others see when they look at your life. It's about how deeply rooted you feel inside it. A secure, aligned financial life may never look impressive on Instagram—and that's precisely the point. It's not about optics. It's about ownership. Not just of assets, but of your values, your vision, and your peace.

To escape the high cost of looking successful, we must begin with a different kind of audit—not of our bank statements, but of our motivations. What are we truly trying to buy when we buy? Respect?

Relevance? Reassurance? Until we can answer that with honesty, no amount of income will ever feel like enough.

This chapter invites you to examine not just what you spend, but what your spending says—for you and about you. It is an invitation to reclaim the mic in a world where everyone is performing. Because real freedom isn't in the applause. It's in no longer needing it.

Social Media's Money Mirage — How Instagram and TikTok Distort Our Sense of What's Normal and Fuel Toxic Comparison

There is a quiet shift taking place in how we understand wealth—not through spreadsheets or statements, but through screens. Every day, millions of people swipe through curated glimpses of other people's lives. A leased Lamborghini, an oceanfront villa, a £15,000 designer handbag in the crook of a manicured arm. It's not just content—it's currency. And it's profoundly distorting how we perceive financial reality, ambition, and our own adequacy. Platforms like Instagram and TikTok no longer merely reflect lifestyle—they manufacture aspiration. In doing so, they've created what might be the most effective illusion of wealth ever constructed: a mirage of prosperity that rewards presentation over possession, and envy over introspection.

We are not rational when we scroll. The human brain evolved to learn by observation. We mimic, compare, and emotionally benchmark ourselves against others—not against spreadsheets, economic data, or actuarial tables. In the offline world, financial comparison was naturally constrained. You might compare your car to a neighbour's, your salary to a colleague's, or your holiday to a sibling's. But these comparisons, while occasionally painful, at least occurred within a recognisable context. Social media annihilates that context. You now compare your Tuesday night dinner to a chef's plated masterpiece in Bali. Your living room to a Soho House suite. Your £30,000 salary to someone flashing stacks of cash in Dubai with no disclosed source of income. What was once rare is now routinised. The extraordinary becomes the expected. And the average—your life, your choices—begins to feel like failure.

Importantly, the damage isn't just emotional. The pressure to keep up with a fantasy has real financial consequences. Research from the National Bureau of Economic Research has shown that visibility of others' spending (even fictionalised or exaggerated versions) can increase your own spending on status goods—regardless of income or savings. Credit card debt, luxury purchases, buy-now-pay-later schemes—all rise in environments of heightened visibility. And while this might feel intuitive, what's less obvious is how deeply this need to be seen as successful overrides personal financial logic. People aren't just spending beyond their means—they're organising their entire financial architecture around appearances. Saving less, investing later, taking fewer career risks, even selecting jobs based on perceived prestige rather than long-term fulfilment or economic fit.

But this isn't just about envy or ego—it's about identity. Social media has changed the very function of money in daily life. Once a medium of exchange, money is now also a medium of self-construction. Posting your latest purchase isn't simply sharing—it's performing. The product is rarely the goal; the perception is. What matters is not whether the holiday was restful or the meal tasted good—but whether it photographed well. This performative layer distorts not just what we want, but why we want it. You may believe you want a new watch or an upgraded kitchen, but look closer: do you want it, or do you want to be the kind of person who has it—and can show it?

What makes this landscape particularly treacherous is that the images we're responding to are not financially transparent. Most people do not disclose the debt behind the sports car, the influencer deal behind the free stay, the desperation behind the third credit card. What's presented as effortless luxury is often engineered, indebted, or entirely fabricated. Yet our brains treat these images as real data points. This is what wealth looks like, they whisper. This is what success should feel like. But the models are flawed, the data is corrupted, and we're running calculations with false inputs. And so, people begin to work not toward true financial health, but toward digital plausibility—an income that looks good online, not a portfolio that protects them offline.

This dynamic is even more pronounced among younger users. Surveys conducted by financial firms in the UK and US consistently show that Millennials and Gen Z feel under more pressure to display wealth than previous generations. One 2023 study by Credit Karma found that nearly 40% of Gen Z respondents had made financial decisions—often unwise ones—specifically to appear more successful on social media. This includes everything from taking holidays they couldn't afford to delaying crucial expenses like insurance or savings to buy visible status goods. The currency of credibility has changed. Success is no longer only measured in net worth—it's measured in impressions, likes, and the envy it can reliably generate.

However, the solution is not a rejection of social media. It is naïve and ineffective to suggest people simply "log off." These platforms are now part of our informational infrastructure, our social fabric, even our professional ecosystems. But what we need is a more sophisticated understanding of how they shape perception—and how to immunise ourselves against the contagion of comparison. The antidote is not abstinence but awareness. We must learn to audit not just our bank statements but our internalised financial scripts: Where did this desire come from? What do I believe this item will *say* about me? Who am I performing for, and at what cost?

To do that, we must start differentiating between performative wealth and authentic prosperity. Performative wealth is externally constructed, dependent on validation, and often debt-fuelled. Authentic prosperity is quieter. It's defined by financial resilience, freedom of time, alignment with personal values, and the ability to make decisions uncorrupted by social coercion. The irony is that authentic prosperity often doesn't look impressive. It looks like a modest house that's paid off. A ten-year-old car without a monthly payment. A career path that earns less than it could but allows for evenings with family, mornings without panic, and holidays not posted online because they're actually restful.

The tragedy is that many people have achieved or are within reach of this authentic wealth—but abandon it in pursuit of digital approval. They refinance homes to afford new kitchens, not because the old ones don't function, but because they no longer "read" aspirational. They chase higher-paying but more soul-crushing jobs, not because they need the income, but because "founder" sounds better than "freelancer." In the process, they erode the very financial and emotional stability they once aimed to protect.

There is also a darker, more subtle outcome: over time, these false signals corrode our capacity for gratitude. If every scroll reminds you of what you lack, you will rarely feel peace with what you have. And financial contentment is not a product of income—it's a product of perspective. Gratitude is not some soft psychological virtue—it is a practical economic tool. It delays unnecessary upgrades, tempers impulsive spending, and fosters satisfaction independent of display. But in a digital economy where visibility equals value, gratitude often feels insufficient. And so, we spend—not because we need more, but because we no longer feel enough.

Ultimately, the greatest cost of the money mirage may be what it steals from us invisibly: trust in ourselves, confidence in our path, and clarity in our definition of success. Social media cannot—and will not—do that work for you. It will never ask whether this purchase fits your values. It will not nudge you toward long-term wealth over short-term status. It will not reward you for restraint. That responsibility is yours. And the first step is to understand that what you're seeing is not neutral. It's a performance. The second step is to decide whether you want to spend your real money trying to keep up with someone else's fiction.

The answer isn't to silence ambition—it's to reclaim authorship. To build a life that is not filtered through envy, but filtered through meaning. To understand that true wealth is not what's flaunted, but what's *felt*—when the doors are closed, the phone is off, and you know, privately, that you're okay.

Buying Belonging — Why We Spend to Feel Included, Validated, or Accepted—and How to Break the Cycle

Few financial behaviours are as misunderstood as the urge to spend for acceptance. Often dismissed as superficial or indulgent, this pattern is in fact deeply human—rooted not in vanity, but in vulnerability. At its core, the desire to belong is not a luxury; it is a biological imperative. For most of human history, exclusion meant danger. Acceptance wasn't just socially gratifying—it was survival. This ancient wiring still governs much of our emotional life today, including how we relate to money. And in modern consumer societies, where identity is often shaped and expressed through consumption, *we've learned to buy our place in the tribe.*

From the clothes we wear to the restaurants we visit, the gym memberships we choose to the holidays we post, financial decisions are rarely just about utility. They are about *proximity.* To status, to culture, to community. Whether it's a teenager saving up for a pair of trainers that will earn him approval at school, or a professional upgrading her wardrobe before a promotion cycle, the logic is the same: *if I spend in the right ways, I will be seen as enough.* Financial decisions become social ones. And the consequences are more profound than we often admit.

Modern consumer culture capitalises on this emotional vulnerability. Branding is no longer just about quality—it's about identity. Marketers sell more than products; they sell belonging. You don't buy a pair of Lululemon leggings—you buy the perceived discipline, health, and lifestyle of a certain aspirational archetype. You don't just buy the electric vehicle—you buy into a persona of environmental consciousness and modernity. Luxury brands, in particular, are expert at weaving cultural codes into their products: exclusivity, refinement, recognition. What you are really paying for is not function but *membership.*

The psychological costs of this dynamic are significant. When we tie self-worth to financial display, we become trapped in what sociologist Zygmunt Bauman called "liquid modernity"—a state of perpetual insecurity, where identity must be constantly reaffirmed through external signals. And because culture is always shifting, so too are the metrics of inclusion. What worked last season feels inadequate now. Belonging becomes a moving target, and we chase it with our wallets.

The emotional root of this cycle is not greed, but fear. *Fear of being left out. Fear of being underestimated. Fear of invisibility.* And in an increasingly atomised world, where traditional communities have weakened and social media intensifies comparison, these fears are constantly reinforced. You're not just trying to keep up with the neighbours—you're trying to keep up with the algorithmically amplified lives of influencers, celebrities, and even curated friends. The result is a distorted sense of what's "normal," and a growing anxiety about falling behind socially, professionally, or aesthetically.

This dynamic shows up everywhere. People stretch beyond their budgets to attend destination weddings they can't afford, fearing they'll seem ungrateful or distant. Colleagues say yes to post-work drinks, even when it strains their finances, because saying no feels like opting out of the informal network that drives promotion. Parents buy into extracurriculars, uniforms, and gifts not just for their children's development, but to avoid the shame of seeming inattentive or "less-than." These aren't frivolous decisions—they're attempts to stay close to the centre of the group. And the cost isn't just financial. It's psychological depletion, relational tension, and often, a lingering sense of being out of alignment with one's values.

There is also a class dimension at play. For those from working-class or marginalised backgrounds, there can be an added layer of pressure: the need to perform belonging in spaces that were not originally built for them. The right clothes, accents, gadgets, or social cues become tools of survival. Spending, in these contexts, is not indulgence—it is adaptation. To judge such behaviour without understanding its social function is to miss the point entirely. *Spending to belong is often a rational response to irrational expectations.*

So how do we break the cycle? Not through shame or austerity, but through awareness and redefinition. The first step is to *interrogate the emotional function of our purchases.* What am I really buying? Safety? Approval? Proximity? Am I saying yes out of genuine desire—or to avoid exclusion? These are not easy questions. But they are necessary ones. Because until we understand what money is doing emotionally, we cannot change what it's doing behaviourally.

Next, we must consciously redefine belonging on our own terms. Real belonging does not require constant financial signalling. It requires mutual respect, aligned values, and emotional presence. In authentic relationships, showing up is more valuable than showing off. Yet we often spend more time and money trying to impress those who wouldn't miss us if we disappeared, than nurturing the relationships that genuinely sustain us.

Building a more intentional relationship with money and belonging also requires boundaries. This may mean declining social events that are financially misaligned—even when uncomfortable. It may mean being transparent with trusted friends about financial priorities, rather than silently overextending. It may even mean re-evaluating certain friendships or environments that consistently require you to contort yourself financially to be accepted. *True community doesn't demand economic conformity—it respects economic diversity.*

This reorientation isn't just about spending less. It's about reclaiming authorship over what defines connection and worth. It's about understanding that *belonging is not something you can purchase—it is something you cultivate.* And when you free your financial life from the burden of constant social signalling, you open space for something richer: alignment, confidence, peace.

The paradox is that when you stop trying to belong everywhere, you begin to belong more deeply somewhere. You find people who resonate with who you are—not what you wear, earn, or post. You discover that money, when disentangled from performance, becomes a tool for support, not spectacle. And you remember that your place in the world is not rented through consumption—it is built through presence, contribution, and clarity.

This is not a rejection of aesthetics, ambition, or generosity. It's a shift in direction—from externally imposed metrics of acceptance to internally held standards of authenticity. Because the people who are worth staying close to won't require you to go broke proving you're worthy of their company. And the more your spending aligns with your truth, the more your life—quietly but powerfully—starts to reflect it.

Choosing Authentic Wealth Over Appearance — How to Build Financial Goals Rooted in Personal Meaning, Not Social Performance

We live in a world where financial optics have become a primary form of self-expression. The car in your driveway, the postcode you inhabit, the label stitched into your jacket—each has been transformed into a proxy for competence, status, and even moral virtue. And yet, beneath this glossy architecture of economic performance, many people are quietly anxious, underprepared, and emotionally unfulfilled. They may look affluent on the outside, but their goals are hollow—shaped more by external expectations than internal clarity. What we call "success" has, in many cases, become a mirage: *something to be seen in, not something to be sustained by.* Authentic wealth offers a fundamentally different path. It prioritises meaning over mimicry, alignment over applause, and long-term peace over short-term praise.

The problem begins with a simple but pervasive confusion: we often mistake *the appearance of wealth* for *the reality of it.* This confusion is not an accident—it is the product of a financial culture engineered to reward visibility over viability. From advertising and influencer culture to aspirational media and professional networking platforms, we are surrounded by signals that suggest wealth is what can be *seen.* And so we build goals that reflect this. We aim for income brackets that sound impressive, not ones that enable our values. We strive for upgrades we're told we should want, not outcomes that would actually stabilise or fulfil us. We conflate high earnings with good planning. But *wealth is not income—it is what remains when the performance ends.*

To begin building authentic wealth, we must start by decoupling financial planning from social mimicry. This means rejecting the idea that your goals should be shaped by comparison. The house your peers bought at thirty is not a relevant benchmark. The holidays your colleagues post each summer are not indicators of life satisfaction. Financial goals should be grounded in the real constraints, opportunities, and values of your life—not in someone else's highlight reel. This requires both intellectual honesty and emotional courage. It is far easier to adopt society's default goals—buy a house, get promoted, retire early—than to ask what success *genuinely* means to you.

Authentic wealth begins with an internal audit. What do you actually want your money to *do*? Provide freedom? Create impact? Buy time with family? Reduce anxiety? Fund creative risks? These questions are often absent from traditional financial advice, which tends to prioritise optimisation over introspection. But without this introspective clarity, you will inevitably build a life that looks good on paper but feels off-centre in practice. You will chase milestones that exhaust you. You will hit financial targets and feel strangely hollow when you arrive. Because the numbers were never the point—the *meaning* was.

Consider the concept of *financial success*. For some, it might mean early retirement. For others, it might mean flexible work, a modest but paid-off home, and time to pursue passions. One is not superior to the other. But only one of them will resonate with you. And until you define success on your own terms, you will remain susceptible to the pull of financial theatre—goals that exist primarily to signal status rather than serve your life.

This misalignment can have concrete consequences. People overextend on mortgages for properties they don't actually enjoy living in. They pursue high-paying careers that drain them emotionally and leave little room for health, family, or creativity. They say yes to expensive lifestyles that create private stress in exchange for public approval. These trade-offs are not failures—they are symptoms of a system that equates visibility with value. *But value is not measured in square footage, job titles, or likes. It's measured in alignment—between your resources and your real priorities.*

Recalibrating toward authentic wealth also means interrogating your relationship to time. Time is the ultimate currency, and yet most people spend it as if it were infinite—sacrificing hours, years, even decades in service of goals they don't deeply care about. What if your definition of wealth included time affluence? What if you built a financial life that allowed you to be present for your children, to read books slowly, to walk instead of commute, to create instead of consume? These are not abstract luxuries—they are legitimate, measurable outcomes that can and should be factored into your financial planning. *If your money isn't buying you the life you want, then it doesn't matter how much of it you have.*

This is not a call to reject ambition, nor to romanticise poverty. Rather, it is a call to reimagine ambition as something rooted in meaning, not performance. You can still earn well, invest wisely, and build security. But do it from a place of personal coherence, not external competition. When you set goals from within—when you choose to prioritise your actual needs, curiosities, and dreams—you become more resilient to economic turbulence and less reactive to social noise. You build systems that nourish your life instead of draining it.

A powerful exercise for reconnecting with authentic wealth is to list your five core values and ask: *Is my financial life structured to support these?* If your top value is freedom but your finances keep you tethered to rigid obligations, that's misalignment. If your top value is creativity but all your income goes toward maintaining appearances rather than fuelling expression, that's misalignment. Wealth, in this context, becomes a form of infrastructure—not a finish line, but a foundation. Not a spectacle, but a strategy.

It also helps to understand that authentic wealth is often *quiet.* It doesn't beg for validation. It doesn't need to announce itself. That's why it's so often overlooked. It looks like the family that lives beneath their means in a modest home and has no debt. The freelancer who works four days a week and spends the fifth with their children. The couple who invests aggressively in their 30s and quietly retires at 50 without ever flashing a designer label. These people aren't failing at wealth—they've simply chosen not to perform it.

This is particularly important for those navigating spaces where appearance has professional consequences. In industries where image is tied to credibility—consulting, media, real estate—there may be pressure to perform financial success as a prerequisite to opportunity. Here, authenticity must be balanced with strategy. But even in these contexts, clarity matters. You may choose to invest in optics—but do so *consciously*, not compulsively. Know the trade-off. Calculate the ROI. Protect your baseline.

Ultimately, choosing authentic wealth means asking one of the most subversive questions in modern finance: *What would enough actually look like for me?* Not hypothetically. Not aspirationally. Practically. This question dismantles the treadmill. It allows you to step off the endless climb toward "more" and begin designing a life that fits. A life where money becomes a supportive tool—not a source of chronic performance anxiety. A life where your goals are intelligible to you, even if they're invisible to others.

In a culture obsessed with visibility, choosing authentic wealth is a radical act. It is a return to sovereignty. It is a reminder that the real richness of life does not reside in aesthetics, metrics, or digital applause. It resides in clarity, integrity, and peace of mind. And that kind of wealth, once built, doesn't just look good—it *feels right.*

CHAPTER 7
The Lie of Financial Security

Ask most people what they truly want from money, and the answer is rarely flamboyance or excess. It is security. Not yachts, not multiple properties, not the social currency of wealth—but the quiet assurance that one is safe, stable, and shielded from risk. Security lurks beneath every financial aspiration, often unspoken yet profoundly motivating. And yet, paradoxically, the more we chase it, the more elusive it becomes. High earners lie awake fretting over bills. Millionaires refresh portfolios compulsively, dreading a minor dip in the market. Even those with paid-off homes and decades of savings can feel exposed, anxious, or somehow behind. The unspoken reality of modern finance is stark: security is not a balance sheet figure—it is a state of mind.

This chapter asks us to reconsider one of the most persistent illusions of our financial age: the notion that money can ever truly guarantee safety. It cannot. And while that may initially unsettle, it is in truth liberating. For when security is no longer pursued solely through accumulation, we open ourselves to cultivating it in ways that are psychologically sustainable, emotionally anchored, and practically viable.

The idea that financial security is a matter of accumulation is not new, yet today's economic landscape—volatile markets, vanishing pensions, and the instability of employment—renders it more fragile than ever. Degrees no longer guarantee careers. Jobs offer no promises of loyalty. Property is not always a safe harbour. Savings may erode against inflation. The traditional markers of stability no longer deliver peace of mind. And yet, in defiance of evidence, we cling to the fantasy that a higher balance, a fatter portfolio, or a larger insurance policy will finally bring calm.

The first myth to confront is the belief that security resides in quantity. We are conditioned to imagine thresholds—£50,000, £500,000, £5 million—as magical lines of comfort. Yet observation, and experience, tell another story. Those with substantial assets frequently report the same, if not greater, anxiety than those with modest means. Why? Because financial worry is rarely proportional to reality. It is a construct of perception, identity, and habituated emotional patterns—not an equation solvable by spreadsheets. If scarcity was the backdrop of your upbringing, or if worth was always tied to financial success, your nervous system governs your sense of safety far more than your net worth.

A second pervasive illusion is that security is certainty. Much of what we call financial security is really a flight from the unknown, a desire to construct a life so insulated that nothing might go wrong. Yet this aspiration is fundamentally unattainable. Markets are unpredictable. Employers, industries, governments—all fluctuate beyond our control. To believe otherwise fosters paralysis: delaying decisions, hoarding cash, obsessing over control. Ironically, in chasing safety, we often create fragility.

Psychologically, the fear of uncertainty eclipses even the fear of poverty. It explains why people cling to stagnant roles, avoid necessary investments, or shrink ambitions even when resources exist to expand. The brain interprets ambiguity as danger—even absent actual threat. Modern finance triggers fight-or-flight responses that evolved to manage survival, not balance sheets. Consequently, many act from over-caution or reflexive fear rather than reasoned strategy.

To reconceive financial security, the conversation must extend beyond money. The crucial question is no longer "How much do I need to feel safe?" but rather, "What engenders a genuine sense of safety within me?" For some, it may be a cash buffer. For others, diversified income streams, simplified living, or acquiring timeless skills. Across all cases, the most durable security is resilience. Not the brittle comfort of a precise figure, but the emotional and behavioural capacity to adapt, recover, and act decisively under pressure.

Resilience is seldom taught in financial education. It is invisible on your balance sheet, yet it may be your most vital asset. A resilient individual can lose a job and immediately recalibrate. A resilient entrepreneur can endure failure and rebuild. A resilient saver can stay the course amid market turbulence. Resilience cultivates creativity, mobility, and confidence rooted not in external assurances but internal capability. This is the security that endures.

Another enduring myth is the "safe job." Traditional financial planning has long presumed employment stability: secure work, steady saving, eventual pension. Yet the modern economy has upended these assumptions. Automation, outsourcing, and economic shocks render even prestigious roles vulnerable. Layoffs are structural, not personal. Entire sectors can rise or vanish within a decade. To rely on a job as a bulwark is increasingly perilous.

Thus, cultivating an entrepreneurial mindset is essential—not necessarily to start a business, but to internalise adaptability, creativity, and value creation. It is about generating income beyond a single gatekeeper, developing portable skills, credible reputations, and reciprocal networks. These human assets—capability, flexibility, trust—offer far greater hedges against uncertainty than any portfolio alone. Security, reframed, becomes a function of agility rather than accumulation.

This chapter does not proffer a universal checklist for feeling secure; no such list exists. Instead, it invites you to interrogate your own sense of safety. What narratives about money and danger have shaped you? What do you believe will "finally" make you safe, and where are you outsourcing that assurance to ever-elusive numbers? More crucially, which practices and perspectives might cultivate confidence from within?

You will explore why individuals with similar incomes experience dramatically different financial stress, and why psychological safety precedes monetary security. You will learn to navigate uncertainty, understand the limitations of stable employment, and imagine a security anchored not in accumulation or control, but in clarity, competence, and coherence.

The ultimate truth is uncompromising: you will not feel safe merely by amassing enough money to silence anxiety. True security arises when you trust your capacity to respond to life's uncertainties. Herein lies the freedom offered—not guaranteed outcomes, but grounded confidence; not immunity from risk, but a thoughtful, resilient relationship with it; not the illusion of control, but the unshakeable certainty that, come what may, you can manage what arrives next.

Security Is a Feeling, Not a Number

There's an uncomfortable truth buried beneath the surface of modern financial life: most people don't actually want money—they want what they believe money will make them feel. Safety. Control. Certainty. Worth. But money can't deliver those things on its own. Not consistently, and certainly not in the long term. You can have a seven-figure portfolio and still lie awake at night terrified of losing it. You can have nothing but a sturdy backpack and a ticket home and feel grounded, safe, and clear. This isn't a feel-good platitude. It's a fundamental flaw in how we construct the idea of "financial security"—and why so many intelligent, capable people never feel like they have enough.

The prevailing belief is simple: *Once I have more money, then I'll feel safe.* It's intuitive. It's comforting. It's also wrong. Because feelings don't follow logic; they follow meaning. And most people haven't stopped to examine what "security" actually means to them—let alone whether the systems they've built around money are capable of producing it. This is the paradox at the heart of financial anxiety: we chase numbers to solve an emotional equation. We fixate on income goals, emergency funds, and retirement benchmarks, assuming they will protect us from uncertainty. But uncertainty isn't solved by accumulation. It's solved by internal architecture—by building psychological resilience, emotional flexibility, and a personal sense of agency that money alone can't buy.

Consider two individuals with the same net worth. One compulsively checks the stock market, delays every significant purchase, and panics when faced with even modest financial decisions. The other lives with relative ease, makes clear choices without guilt, and doesn't mentally rehearse doomsday scenarios before buying a plane ticket or supporting a family member. The difference isn't how much they have—it's how they relate to what they have. And that difference is massive. Studies in behavioural economics and neuroscience confirm that the human brain is wired to respond far more to perceived control than to objective assets. In other words, *we don't feel secure because we have enough; we feel secure when we believe we can handle whatever happens.*

This belief is shaped not by spreadsheets, but by experience. People who grew up with financial instability—late rent, power shutoffs, stressed parents—often internalise a visceral association between money and fear. Even as adults with well-paying jobs, these individuals may unconsciously relive scarcity patterns. They hoard cash, avoid investments, under-earn, or spend impulsively to soothe the underlying stress. The same is true for those who experienced betrayal—inheritance battles, failed business partnerships, or parents who promised one thing and delivered another. For them, "security" becomes synonymous with control. The irony is that the more they grasp for control, the less secure they feel, because life doesn't operate on guarantees.

Financial advisors and institutional systems rarely account for this emotional complexity. They offer tools—budgets, asset allocation models, insurance products—as though those are sufficient to create peace of mind. But they often ignore the *inner infrastructure* of financial wellbeing: emotional literacy, tolerance for ambiguity, the ability to hold competing truths. For example, it's entirely possible to feel nervous and still invest wisely. To fear volatility and still trust your plan. To grieve past mistakes and still make empowered decisions. These are not contradictions. They are marks of emotional maturity, and emotional maturity is the bedrock of true financial security.

A striking case of this disconnect is the phenomenon of "sudden wealth syndrome." Lottery winners, tech founders post-exit, or even athletes with new contracts often experience profound anxiety after acquiring large sums of money. Why? Because the presence of money amplifies existing psychological patterns. If you didn't feel safe before, money doesn't heal the wound—it magnifies it. Wealth reveals, rather than resolves, our core narratives. And for those who equated financial gain with emotional repair, the result can be disorienting: *I got everything I wanted... so why do I still feel hollow?*

On the flip side, some individuals with modest incomes consistently report high levels of life satisfaction and peace. They structure their financial lives not around conventional benchmarks, but around clarity: What do I need? What matters most to me? How can I honour that with the resources I have? These people may live simply, but not fearfully. They value sufficiency over status, sustainability over optimisation. Their security isn't fragile because it's not externally tethered. They don't outsource their sense of safety to the market or their job title. Instead, they've built a self-trust that doesn't fluctuate with economic news or professional uncertainty.

There is also a cultural component at play. In many Western societies, security has been subtly rebranded as *luxury under control.* Think manicured retirement plans, legacy real estate, passive income flows. These are not inherently problematic—but they are often idolised in ways that suggest anything less is reckless. That if your life doesn't come with stabilisers, you've failed to adult properly. But this worldview makes security conditional, brittle, and exclusionary. It implies that until you reach a certain financial tier, you're not allowed to exhale. It's a dangerous form of delayed life—one where people spend decades waiting for permission to feel safe.

The antidote lies not in dismantling ambition, but in decoupling security from performance. This begins with a reframing: *Security is not the absence of risk—it's the presence of capacity.* Do you trust yourself to navigate uncertainty? Have you cultivated emotional practices—boundaries, discernment, adaptability—that can hold you steady when things change? Have you examined the scripts you inherited about money, failure, and control? These questions matter more than any financial dashboard. Because ultimately, the most enduring form of security is internal—not external.

Developing that internal resilience requires conscious effort. It's not built through lectures or lectures about "being grateful" or "thinking positive." It's developed through lived practice. Choosing to invest even when scared. Saying no to overworking even when the fear of falling behind lingers. Asking for help when your pride says to pretend. Celebrating enoughness when the world screams for more. These moments, repeated and integrated, create a baseline of trust in oneself. And that trust is worth more than any emergency fund.

This is not an argument against financial preparation. Savings matter. Planning matters. Risk management matters. But they are tools—not destinations. They support your life; they do not define your life. And until your emotional foundation is stabilised, no amount of money will ever feel like enough. You'll keep raising the bar. Keep moving the goalpost. Keep living from the myth that safety is one more pay rise away.

True financial security is not a fixed number. It's a flexible mindset. It's knowing you can lose something and not lose yourself. It's choosing presence over panic. It's learning to build your life not on avoidance of risk, but on cultivation of strength. And when that becomes your anchor, your relationship with money changes. You no longer hoard or hustle from fear. You invest, spend, save, and earn from clarity. Not because you're immune to uncertainty, but because you're no longer ruled by it.

That is the shift this chapter invites: from chasing safety in numbers to discovering it within yourself. Not as a platitude, but as a pragmatic, grounded, and ultimately liberating truth. Because when your internal stability leads, your external finances can finally follow.

We Fear Uncertainty More Than Poverty – How Our Minds Exaggerate Risk—and Why Learning to Tolerate Uncertainty Unlocks Wealth

Few forces shape human behaviour more powerfully than the desire to eliminate uncertainty. In financial matters especially, the aversion to not knowing—to instability, fluctuation, volatility—often exerts a stronger influence on decision-making than the reality of the numbers themselves. You can show a person a spreadsheet proving they're solvent, that their retirement is adequately funded, that they could safely invest, quit, or grow—but if their internal narrative is one of fear, hesitation will prevail. The sensation of not being *sure* feels more dangerous than the actual threat of not having enough. This psychological reflex, baked into us through evolution, is one of the most underappreciated forces preventing individuals from building meaningful wealth. Not because they're incapable. Not because they're unqualified. But because they cannot stomach uncertainty.

Poverty, by contrast, is often conceptualised as a fixed and recognisable state. It's definable—no job, low income, few possessions. It feels like a worst-case scenario that the mind can *grasp*. But uncertainty? That's more nebulous. It doesn't just mean danger. It means unpredictability, which is harder to plan around, harder to explain, and far more likely to induce paralysis. Neuroscience supports this: studies have shown that the human brain registers the anticipation of unpredictable negative events as more stressful than the events themselves. In one famous experiment, participants were more agitated when they had a 50% chance of receiving an electric shock than when they were guaranteed a 100% shock. In money terms, this means that a stable but constrained income can feel psychologically safer than the idea of self-employment, even if the latter offers more upside, autonomy, or long-term sustainability.

This aversion isn't limited to lower-income or risk-averse individuals. Even high-net-worth professionals fall victim to it. Consider the lawyer who stays in a toxic firm because her £350,000 salary is "secure," despite the long hours and declining mental health. She has a generous investment portfolio, six months' runway in savings, and offers on the table—but the unpredictability of stepping out, of not knowing what the next year might bring, looms larger in her mind than the certainty of her current misery. Or the entrepreneur who has built a successful business but continues to hoard cash and refuses to invest in growth, paralysed by the what-ifs of recession, regulation, or competition. These individuals aren't struggling from a lack of resources. They're struggling from a low tolerance for ambiguity.

It's important to note that a fear of uncertainty is not the same thing as prudence. Caution can be wise; contingency planning is responsible. But chronically overestimating downside risk and underweighting opportunity is a form of distortion, not wisdom. It's often rooted in past experiences—financial trauma, instability in childhood, or witnessing a parent's job loss—that create an emotional blueprint: unpredictable = unsafe. The adult inherits this wiring and then mistakes it for rationality, never realising that their "caution" is actually a defensive reflex. From this mindset, uncertainty becomes something to eliminate rather than manage.

This manifests in many subtle but costly ways. People will underprice their services just to avoid the discomfort of negotiating. They'll delay investing because they want "just a bit more certainty" in the markets. They'll keep too much in savings accounts, eroded by inflation, because it feels emotionally comforting to "see the number there." They'll avoid starting a side business or charging what they're worth, even if the potential is high, because they can't tolerate the feeling of not knowing exactly how it will play out. In doing so, they trade dynamic potential for static security, often without consciously choosing to do so.

The irony is that wealth creation, by its nature, requires a degree of uncertainty tolerance. All high-yield financial activities—investing, entrepreneurship, negotiation, expansion—operate on probabilistic, not guaranteed, outcomes. If your emotional framework demands 100% clarity before action, you will forever default to low-yield, high-certainty choices. That's not just a behavioural tendency; it becomes a structural limitation on your financial life.

But here's the critical insight: uncertainty is not inherently dangerous. What *is* dangerous is our emotional overreaction to it. Most people assume that fear is a signal of actual external threat. But in many cases, especially in modern financial life, fear is just the residue of an outdated nervous system trying to protect you from tribal exile, famine, or physical danger—none of which apply when deciding whether to raise your prices or allocate capital. The brain's fear circuits evolved long before credit scores and income statements. As such, they are poor judges of modern economic risk.

This means that increasing your capacity to hold uncertainty is not just a psychological preference—it is a financial skill. A skill that, like any other, can be trained. It begins by noticing the stories your mind tells you in the presence of ambiguity. When a new opportunity arises, do you immediately run simulations of worst-case outcomes? When a client pushes back on your fees, do you panic that the work will disappear? When your investments dip, do you catastrophise that you're headed for disaster? These are not facts. They are interpretations. And interpretations can be rewritten.

Training this capacity is not about becoming reckless. It's about becoming resilient. The difference lies in whether you're moving forward with awareness or merely reacting to fear. A resilient person doesn't pretend that risk doesn't exist—they simply learn to distinguish between fear that protects and fear that paralyses. They ask better questions. Instead of, "What if this goes wrong?", they ask, "What is the cost of *not* doing this?" They use buffers—financial, emotional, relational—to take measured risks without placing themselves in harm's way. And most importantly, they remind themselves that not knowing is not the same as being unsafe.

Cognitive behavioural studies have shown that the more often we expose ourselves to tolerable uncertainty and survive it, the more robust our tolerance becomes. A freelance designer who finally raises her rates and survives the first client loss quickly realises she didn't need *all* the clients—just the right ones. A mid-level manager who negotiates a raise for the first time learns that being told "no" is not fatal. The repeated experience of surviving uncertainty rewires the nervous system: not into indifference, but into *courage*.

There is also a deeper philosophical thread to pull here. The pursuit of security is often sold as the goal of financial life—stable job, house paid off, pension fund growing. But if we define security as "the absence of uncertainty," then we've set an impossible standard. Markets shift. Jobs disappear. Economies wobble. The only true security, paradoxically, is internal: the ability to adapt, to endure, to create value in new conditions. Resilience is more durable than savings. And personal agency is more reliable than any employment contract.

The trap of fearing uncertainty more than poverty is that it tricks you into playing small under the illusion of safety. You'll say no to opportunities that could transform your life because they don't come pre-packaged with guarantees. You'll obsess over worst-case scenarios while ignoring best-case possibilities. You'll defer, delay, downplay—until eventually you've crafted a perfectly predictable life that quietly excludes your potential.

True wealth is not just a number—it's a state of internal resourcefulness. It is knowing that you can handle change, risk, ambiguity, and still act with purpose. It is the emotional confidence to walk toward opportunity, even when the outcome isn't assured. That's not recklessness. That's the discipline of mature financial thinking. And it's the muscle that distinguishes those who accumulate real wealth from those who merely preserve the illusion of safety.

So the next time uncertainty whispers its anxious warnings in your ear, don't silence it with false comforts or impulsive retreats. Listen carefully. Ask whether the fear is based in truth—or just habit. And remember: your financial future will not be determined by your ability to avoid uncertainty, but by your ability to tolerate it wisely, and move forward anyway.

Resilience Is Your Greatest Asset – How Emotional Flexibility Beats Any Savings Account

We tend to assess financial preparedness in terms of external assets—cash reserves, investment portfolios, equity holdings, retirement contributions. These are the metrics we learn to monitor, the dashboards we review, the numbers we rely on to feel safe. But quietly, and far more powerfully, there exists an internal asset that shapes not only how we respond to financial setbacks, but how much wealth we ever allow ourselves to generate in the first place: resilience. And unlike your net worth, resilience is not a static figure. It's a capacity—a psychological and emotional flexibility that determines whether you retreat, stagnate, or adapt when circumstances shift. It's the difference between someone who folds under disruption and someone who reinvents, retools, and relaunches stronger than before.

Resilience, as it relates to money, isn't merely the capacity to endure financial stress. It is the willingness to keep engaging with uncertainty, opportunity, and risk without needing complete control. It is emotional elasticity—the ability to bend without breaking when plans unravel, when clients disappear, when economies crash. While most personal finance narratives are built on the assumption that security comes from having "enough," resilience reframes the conversation. *Wealth is not just what you've stored. It's what you're capable of rebuilding.*

Traditional savings accounts, though important, offer only a static form of defence. They sit passively, hedging against a known quantity of financial volatility. Resilience, by contrast, is dynamic. It doesn't just buffer you from loss—it multiplies your ability to recover, pivot, and seize new opportunity under pressure. Consider the entrepreneur whose product becomes obsolete overnight due to regulatory change. One person freezes, clings to the old model, drains savings trying to make it viable again. Another adapts, retrains their team, and finds new application for their expertise within weeks. Both may have started with identical balance sheets. The outcome is determined not by capital, but by emotional fluidity.

The core challenge is that resilience is invisible. Unlike a savings balance or a salary bracket, you can't easily point to it or measure it. But its absence reveals itself acutely when difficulty strikes. You'll hear it in the language: "I can't handle another setback," "I don't know what to do," "It's over." People without resilience often collapse internally long before external circumstances require them to. Conversely, those with deep resilience have an almost unnerving calmness in crisis—not because they're unaffected, but because they trust their ability to respond.

Psychologically, resilience is rooted in two capacities: emotional regulation and cognitive reframing. Emotional regulation is the ability to stay present and calm enough to avoid reactive, fear-driven decisions. It's what allows someone to look at a downsized income or unexpected expense and resist the spiral of panic that might otherwise lead to impulsive loans, self-sabotage, or total withdrawal. Cognitive reframing is the ability to interpret negative events in ways that preserve agency: "This isn't the end," becomes "This is a problem I can learn to solve," or even "This disruption might contain an opportunity I didn't previously see." Together, these abilities turn financial turbulence from a threat into a creative challenge.

Importantly, resilience isn't a fixed trait. It is cultivated. Life doesn't hand it to you in equal proportions. It is often forged through friction—through repeated encounters with difficulty that, when properly processed, expand one's capacity to tolerate ambiguity, loss, or change. The child who watched their parent rebuild after bankruptcy develops a different sense of financial possibility than the one whose household collapsed in silence. The young adult who navigates redundancy and reinvents their income stream will have more confidence facing future economic contractions than someone who has only ever experienced linear growth. What matters most is not the absence of pain but how one metabolises it.

In practical financial behaviour, the presence or absence of resilience predicts wildly different outcomes. A resilient investor doesn't pull out of the market at the first sign of downturn—they adjust strategy, review fundamentals, and stay grounded in long-term thinking. A resilient freelancer doesn't fall apart when a major client disappears—they activate their network, reposition their offer, or double down on skill-building. A resilient employee who's been laid off doesn't internalise the event as personal failure—they view it as a signal to explore new roles, markets, or industries. In all these cases, resilience functions not just as a shock absorber, but as a springboard.

This becomes even more critical in a cultural moment that prizes control. Financial planning tools, predictive algorithms, and AI-based wealth management have seduced many into believing that risk can be eliminated with enough data. But reality remains volatile. Jobs disappear with little notice. Sectors rise and collapse. Illnesses interrupt careers. Policy changes reshape industries overnight. In this context, resilience is not a luxury—it is a *strategic advantage.* If your entire financial identity is built around static control, even a minor shock can destabilise your entire system. But if you've built the inner architecture to absorb impact and reorient, you can remain functional—and even visionary—amid disorder.

There is also an ethical dimension to resilience. When individuals overly rely on savings alone, they often default into hoarding behaviour—delaying generosity, limiting investment, and closing themselves off from collaboration out of fear that "I might need this later." But resilient individuals operate from a different baseline: because they trust in their ability to generate, adapt, and rebuild, they tend to be more open-handed, more experimental, and more collaborative. They are less governed by scarcity because they are not emotionally tethered to static security.

Of course, cultivating resilience doesn't mean ignoring financial fundamentals. Emergency funds still matter. Insurance still matters. Diversified income streams matter. But the presence of those structures without internal resilience can still result in collapse. Think of the high earner who panics during a market dip and sells at a loss—not because they needed the money, but because they lacked the inner composure to weather temporary volatility. Their financial literacy outpaced their emotional fluency. That gap is where damage is done.

Interestingly, the more resilience you build, the less dependent you become on accumulating excessive buffers. If you know you can generate income, navigate loss, and adapt your strategy quickly, you no longer need to stockpile "just in case" resources to the same degree. This reduces financial anxiety, simplifies decision-making, and unlocks more creative, high-upside moves. You stop acting from a defensive posture and start operating from strategic intent.

From a systems view, widespread resilience could dramatically reshape how we think about social mobility, employment, and even education. Instead of training people solely in technical or financial skills, we would focus equal energy on developing adaptability, resourcefulness, and emotional regulation. We'd teach students not just how to budget, but how to navigate uncertainty with composure. We'd prepare workers not just to fill roles, but to respond to disruption with creative initiative. That shift could transform not only individual outcomes but entire economies—by cultivating populations that are not only skilled, but *self-reliant in the face of flux.*

Ultimately, resilience asks us to examine where we place our faith. Is it in static assets, which can erode, vanish, or become inaccessible? Or is it in our own capacity to navigate, to create, to regenerate? The resilient person is not reckless—they are simply less fragile. They are not immune to suffering—they are just not defined by it. And in a world that increasingly rewards those who can adapt under pressure, that flexibility may well be the most valuable currency we ever develop.

The Myth of the Safe Job – Why No Job Is Truly Secure Anymore—and How Entrepreneurial Thinking Can Set You Free

For most of the twentieth century, the job represented more than income—it was a promise. A job meant stability. It meant health insurance, retirement contributions, the possibility of upward mobility and the psychological comfort of knowing what tomorrow might look like. For previous generations, especially in the West, the career path was linear and largely reliable: study hard, get a qualification, join a company, work your way up, and retire with a pension. The steady job was not just practical; it was moralised. Choosing a career was equated with choosing responsibility. Opting for something riskier—entrepreneurship, freelancing, creative labour—was often framed as a deviation from the path of adulthood itself. But that story no longer fits the world we live in.

The idea that a traditional job offers security is not only outdated—it is actively misleading. In today's economy, no job is safe. Not because employers are malicious, but because the conditions that once enabled long-term employment contracts—stable industries, predictable markets, labour protections—have eroded. Globalisation, automation, artificial intelligence, financialisation, and shifting corporate priorities have turned even once-stable professions into precarious arrangements. Whether you're a middle manager, a software engineer, or a university lecturer, there is no such thing as immunity from disruption. *The safe job, as a structural guarantee, no longer exists. Only the illusion does.*

Consider the widespread corporate layoffs during the COVID-19 pandemic. People who had been with the same companies for decades, who had climbed ladders, deferred dreams, and played by the rules, found themselves redundant within weeks. No amount of loyalty or tenure shielded them. Airlines, media companies, law firms, banks, NGOs—all were forced to cut costs, restructure teams, and prioritise efficiency over tradition. These weren't outliers. They were a preview of a broader, accelerating trend. The underlying architecture of "employment security" is fragile because it is built on factors the individual does not control: executive decisions, market fluctuations, technological shifts, and shareholder expectations. You can do excellent work, exceed expectations, and still be rendered expendable by a spreadsheet.

This is not to say that all jobs are inherently bad or that traditional employment is without merit. For many, it remains a valuable platform for skill-building, networking, and short-term stability. But the critical shift is recognising that a job is no longer a fortress—it's a tool. The difference is profound. A fortress implies safety, something you hide inside. A tool implies functionality, something you use strategically. When you treat your job as a tool rather than a guarantee, you begin to think more entrepreneurially—even if you're not self-employed.

Entrepreneurial thinking is not about starting a business per se. It's about cultivating agency. It's the ability to scan your environment for opportunity, to make decisions based on adaptability rather than obedience, and to design a financial life that is resilient not because it's anchored to a single employer, but because it's diversified, dynamic, and underpinned by your own initiative. It's asking: what problems can I solve? What value can I offer? Where can I create leverage, rather than rely on permission?

This mindset is vital because the pace of economic change has outstripped the institutions built to protect workers. Lifelong employment contracts are now the exception, not the rule. Pension schemes are increasingly underfunded. Benefits are conditional and negotiable. Career ladders have been replaced with lattices, gigs, and temporary contracts. According to recent studies, the average person will change jobs between 10 and 15 times in their lifetime. Whole industries can be transformed or erased within a decade. The World Economic Forum reports that 44% of workers' skills will be disrupted by 2027. What this means, practically, is that waiting for a job to make you feel safe is like waiting for a storm to make you feel dry.

Crucially, this shift isn't just about economics—it's also psychological. The people most disoriented by job loss aren't always the ones with the most to lose financially. They're often those who have built their entire identity around their employer, their title, or their role. When those disappear, it's not just a financial hit—it's an existential one. Entrepreneurial thinking addresses this by decoupling identity from employment. It teaches you to derive worth from your capabilities, not your job title. It invites you to see yourself as a value generator in multiple contexts, not just a functionary in one organisation.

Moreover, entrepreneurial thinking fosters a different relationship to risk. Traditional employment teaches avoidance—don't make waves, don't take chances, stay inside the lines. But in a volatile economy, *avoiding risk becomes the riskiest thing you can do*. Entrepreneurial thinkers understand that uncertainty is not a threat to be eliminated, but a terrain to be navigated. They learn to manage downside without shrinking their upside. They diversify income, invest in reputation capital, build networks, and create systems that continue to generate value even when one node—like a job—fails.

This is especially important for younger generations entering the workforce under drastically different conditions than their parents. Millennials and Gen Z are contending with higher education costs, unaffordable housing markets, and global economic precarity—all while being told to "just get a job" and it will work itself out. It won't. What will work is learning to operate with autonomy, flexibility, and creative agency across changing conditions. That's not a rebellion against the old system; it's a rational response to the new one.

It's also worth noting that entrepreneurial thinking does not require you to be self-employed. You can be an intrapreneur—someone who behaves entrepreneurially inside an organisation. You can think like a consultant even within a salaried role. The point is to shift from dependency to dynamism. From passive recipient of income to active architect of value. It's not about rejecting employment. It's about refusing to outsource your sense of safety to structures you do not control.

The irony is that the more entrepreneurial your thinking becomes, the more actual security you tend to create. You build multiple income streams. You develop reputational leverage. You acquire transferable skills. You are better positioned to negotiate, pivot, and recover. You are less likely to suffer total collapse when one platform disappears. In this light, entrepreneurial thinking is not a risky alternative to job security. It is the only form of security left that is meaningfully within your control.

The old contract—loyalty in exchange for security—is broken. What remains is a new contract, written not by institutions but by individuals: *adaptability in exchange for freedom.* This freedom doesn't mean comfort. It doesn't mean immediate wealth. But it means movement. It means strategic agency. It means the power to adjust course without needing to ask permission. And that, in a world where permanence is an illusion, is the most authentic form of safety you can own.

CHAPTER 8
The Self-Made Fantasy

Few phrases in modern finance carry as much allure—and as much deception—as "self-made." It evokes an image of the solitary figure, dogged and unyielding, pulling themselves from obscurity to opulence purely through grit and relentless effort. It is a story that flatters those who succeed and consoles those still striving. Yet peel back the gloss, and the reality is far more intricate: no one achieves real financial success alone. Beyond diligence, there are factors less visible but equally decisive—timing, networks, psychological safety, social capital, and often an inherited safety net. Portraying achievement as purely individual not only misleads—it obscures the structural forces determining who rises and why.

The "self-made" label functions as a protective narrative. It shields the wealthy from scrutiny and absolves systemic inequities from responsibility. If one believes billionaires built their empires entirely independently, it becomes easier to overlook how regulation, public infrastructure, historical hierarchies, and generational wealth confer invisible advantages. This is not cynicism; it is intellectual honesty. To deny context is, in itself, a form of privilege.

Consider the repeated glorification of immigrant success stories in media and political discourse. Certainly, some overcome extraordinary odds, yet the selective spotlight produces survivorship bias so potent it distorts reality. We seldom hear of the countless others who worked just as diligently but remained constrained—not from lack of effort, but from lack of access. Energy is distributed unevenly, but outcomes are never fair. The resulting mythology is corrosive: if you fail, it must be your fault; if you succeed, you deserve it. Complexity collapses into moral judgement.

Central to this myth is the exaltation of hustle. Modern culture romanticises sleep deprivation, overwork, and ceaseless optimisation as the surefire path to wealth. Yet sheer effort has never guaranteed financial freedom. If it did, nurses and teachers would out-earn hedge fund managers. For many, especially those in the working class, hustle yields exhaustion rather than elevation. It ensnares people in a cycle of doing more while achieving little, because the systems around them are designed to extract labour rather than nurture opportunity.

Ironically, hustle can distract from the true levers of power. While individuals scramble to monetise every hour, what is often lacking is leverage. Leverage arises from compounding assets: capital, audiences, data, intellectual property, distribution networks. These are seldom accessed through effort alone. They demand strategy, positioning, and—most crucially—entry into spaces where these tools are shared, inherited, or granted. Hard work alone rarely suffices; one must also be present where it matters most.

Here, the concept of privilege is pivotal—not as a moral indictment, but as a structural reality. Privilege is the absence of barriers, the quiet wind at one's back. It shapes not just wealth, but the mental bandwidth required to pursue it. Someone raised without the chronic stress of poverty approaches opportunities with greater calm, higher risk tolerance, and more strategic focus. This does not diminish their effort; it contextualises it. Financial success depends as much on what one is free to concentrate on as on what one actually does.

Acknowledging this is not a call to abandon ambition, but to recalibrate strategy. If the goal is to build enduring wealth, working longer hours is rarely the solution. Attention should shift to expanding access: to information, mentorship, networks, and scalable platforms. Today's economy rewards asymmetric outcomes, where value produced vastly exceeds input. This is achieved not through linear effort, but through leverage—and leverage begins with perspective.

Look, for instance, at today's tech billionaires. Their ingenuity and persistence are undeniable, yet their stories often omit the insulation they enjoyed: elite education, venture capital access, familial safety nets, and regulatory environments conducive to scale. Their achievements were shaped as much by timing, geography, and ecosystem as by skill. Likewise, digital creators who dominate YouTube, TikTok, or Substack benefit from algorithmic advantage, early adoption, and unequal digital literacy. When examining "success," consider what entrants walked in with that others did not.

This is not about cultivating resentment; it is a strategic realignment. Recognising that systems are not neutral allows one to stop self-blame in constrained circumstances. It shifts the focus from discipline alone to design. Who grants opportunity? Where do decision-makers convene? How do networks transmit trust and credibility? Hard work remains necessary, but without architecture and access, it is often exploited rather than rewarded.

It also forces a reflection on what true aspiration entails. The fantasy of self-made success often comes with the illusion of total self-sufficiency: the notion that one can triumph alone and owe nothing to anyone. This is not only unrealistic, it is isolating. Real wealth is social. It thrives on relationships, trust, collaboration, and reciprocity. Lasting success rarely belongs to the smartest or the hardest working—it accrues to the most connected, the most visible, and the most strategically positioned.

Acknowledging systemic inequities should not justify inaction. Understanding barriers allows for smarter strategy. You stop fighting the wrong battles, cease internalising failure, and direct energy toward moves that compound rather than merely repeat. Sustainable agency emerges not from the myth of solitary conquest, but from informed, strategic participation.

The self-made fantasy seduces because it promises control: work hard enough, and the world bends to your will. Mature financial reasoning recognises that control is never total. What matters is where effort is applied, how access is built, and with whom one aligns. The future rewards not isolation but intelligent collaboration.

This chapter does not seek to diminish aspiration. It aims to refine it, shifting focus from individual heroism to systemic fluency. You will learn why the most successful actors do not simply grind—they engineer conditions in which effort produces disproportionate returns. You will discover how to replace validation-seeking through hustle with leverage achieved via clarity. Ultimately, the question is not "How do I become self-made?" but "How do I become strategically made?"

By chapter's end, the illusion of self-made success will be clear. More importantly, you will be equipped to construct a narrative that honours both ambition and the structural realities of the world you navigate—a narrative that is smarter, truer, and far more effective.

No One Does It Alone – The truth behind every "self-made millionaire" story—luck, timing, privilege, and access matter

For all its mythic appeal, the archetype of the "self-made" individual—the lone genius, the relentless hustler, the bootstrap success story—is among the most enduring and misleading narratives in modern economic culture. It seduces with a sense of pure meritocracy: the belief that talent and hard work alone are the engines of financial success. This idea has been canonised in biographies, business books, and motivational mantras, turning figures like Elon Musk, Oprah Winfrey, and Steve Jobs into secular saints of self-sufficiency. But examine their stories more closely—without the cinematic editing—and a more complicated, more human, and more revealing picture emerges. No one does it alone. Every ascent, no matter how inspiring, is scaffolded by timing, access, social capital, inherited context, and yes—luck.

Start with timing. Being early to a market often confers an advantage no amount of skill can manufacture. Bill Gates, for instance, was born in 1955 and attended one of the few high schools in America with a computer terminal in the late 1960s. He had access to programming tools a full decade before most students touched a keyboard. That head start, invisible in the highlight reels of his rise, wasn't something he created—it was something he received. The same holds for Jeff Bezos, whose parents lent him a quarter of a million dollars to start Amazon. Was he brilliant? Undoubtedly. But so are many others who lacked both the capital and cultural permission to burn through six figures while testing a hypothesis. Behind every "self-made" success is an ecosystem—of capital, connections, early exposure, or cultural conditions—that quietly tilts the playing field.

There is nothing inherently wrong with recognising these background advantages—what's damaging is denying their role. When stories of wealth strip away context, they imply a moral equation: "I worked hard, so I deserve this," which subtly turns into "If you don't have what I have, it's because you didn't try hard enough." This logic is not only false—it's socially corrosive. It obscures the barriers that shape financial outcomes: racial wealth gaps, gender pay disparities, geographic mobility limits, and unequal educational access. The "self-made" fantasy renders these systemic realities invisible, replacing structural analysis with personal judgment.

In practice, this narrative traps both those who aspire to wealth and those who have already acquired it. For strivers, the myth can lead to shame when effort doesn't yield the promised results. If you believe success is purely self-driven, then every failure becomes a personal indictment. It encourages overwork, under-rest, and a dangerous tolerance for exploitation—especially among those trying to outrun generational disadvantage. For the affluent, the same myth can breed delusion: a belief in their own exceptionalism that blinds them to the fragility of their success. This blindness often expresses itself in policymaking, where those in power vote against redistribution or structural reform on the grounds that "If I could do it, anyone can." But that's not just inaccurate—it's historically illiterate.

Consider the role of social networks. Economists have long observed that access to "weak ties"—acquaintances who open doors to new industries, investors, or job opportunities—is a more powerful predictor of upward mobility than raw intelligence or work ethic. A referral to a job at Goldman Sachs, a recommendation to an elite accelerator, a casual introduction to a venture capitalist—these moments are often decisive. But they're not framed as such. Instead, the outcomes are celebrated as genius or hustle, not as the downstream effect of social infrastructure. In this sense, networks are the shadow currency of mobility. They're the accelerators no resume can capture.

Then there's the question of luck. In entrepreneurial circles, invoking luck can feel almost heretical. It disrupts the fiction of control. But study after study confirms what lived experience already knows: randomness plays a larger role than we want to admit. Nassim Nicholas Taleb has argued that survivorship bias—the tendency to focus on winners while ignoring the vast number of similar efforts that failed—distorts how we perceive competence. Many of the most famous tech entrepreneurs could just as easily have failed if one meeting had fallen through, if one investor had declined, or if one algorithmic tweak had gone the other way. They didn't "make it" in a vacuum. They were prepared—but they were also fortunate.

This isn't an argument against ambition or effort. It's an argument for more honest storytelling. When we acknowledge the full architecture of success—when we include the invisible scaffolding of luck, access, and inherited advantage—we don't diminish achievement. We humanise it. And in doing so, we make it more replicable. Aspiring individuals don't need fairy tales. They need roadmaps that include the terrain.

What does this mean practically? It means redefining what it means to "build." Instead of idolising solo achievement, we can start cultivating collaborative advantage. Mentorship, shared networks, mutual visibility—these are not crutches; they are leverage points. Instead of chasing purity in the origin story, we can ask better questions: What doors were opened? Who vouched for you? What safety net allowed you to take a risk others couldn't afford? Instead of lionising individual grit, we can begin building ecosystems that lower the activation energy for others.

It also means rethinking how we use the word "privilege." Too often, it's treated as a condemnation rather than a context. But privilege, properly understood, is not a moral failing—it's a responsibility. If you were lucky enough to be born into a stable family, or to graduate debt-free, or to intern through a family friend, the point isn't guilt—it's awareness. That awareness is what allows for inclusive generosity. It's what helps us design more equitable systems. And it's what inoculates us against the cruelty of judging others for the disadvantages they didn't choose.

There's a final, subtler cost to the self-made myth: it narrows our sense of possibility. If the only valid form of success is solitary, then we miss the power of interdependence. Some of the most transformative ventures—OpenAI, Wikipedia, the NHS—were collective endeavours. They succeeded not because of lone visionaries, but because of ecosystems that allowed vision to scale. If we want to create wealth that endures and uplifts, we need to shift from the solo act to the symphony.

The idea that no one does it alone is not an insult to ambition. It's a safeguard against delusion. It's an invitation to see success in its full complexity—and to participate in creating the conditions for others to thrive. Behind every "self-made" headline is a quieter, truer story. And it's that story, in all its nuance, that deserves to be told.

The Hustle Lie – Why endless grinding won't necessarily make you rich—and often leads to burnout

If hard work alone determined wealth, nurses would be millionaires and hedge fund managers would be bankrupt from idleness. The notion that unrelenting effort guarantees financial success remains one of the most seductive and damaging beliefs in modern culture. It masquerades as empowerment—"you control your destiny"—but functions more like a trap, shifting the burden of systemic inefficiencies and structural inequality onto the shoulders of the individual. The "hustle" mantra, celebrated in social media posts and startup culture, often ignores one of the most essential truths in economics and psychology alike: *labour is not the same as leverage.* And mistaking the two can lead not to wealth, but to exhaustion.

At its core, the hustle ideology confuses activity with impact. It equates being busy with being effective, and equates hours spent with value created. This misalignment has real-world consequences. A delivery driver working 16-hour shifts is exerting far more effort than a venture capitalist who takes three meetings before lunch—but the capitalist may generate significantly more return. Why? Because they are closer to decision-making power, capital, and scalable systems. Hustle, in its purest form, is linear: one hour, one output. But wealth creation, especially in post-industrial economies, is nonlinear. It arises not from grinding longer, but from designing smarter leverage points—equity, ownership, automation, licensing, networks.

The danger of hustle culture lies in its moral framing. It doesn't simply present hard work as a means to an end; it turns it into a virtue signal. You're not just working hard—you're proving your worth. This can lead to a performative version of productivity: staying late not because it produces results, but because it demonstrates commitment. This is particularly prevalent in corporate environments where presenteeism masquerades as dedication. Over time, this performance becomes internalised. People begin to associate their self-worth with their output, their identity with their busyness. When the financial rewards fail to materialise—and they often do—it creates a psychological dissonance: *I did everything I was supposed to, so why am I still stuck?*

Take the case of Lisa, a freelance graphic designer in London. She built a strong portfolio, took on more clients, worked late nights, and doubled her billable hours in the space of a year. Yet, despite the increased effort, her income plateaued. Why? Because she hit the ceiling of personal bandwidth. Her pricing was tied to time, not value. She had no system for scale—no retainers, no subcontractors, no digital products. In short, she hustled harder but not smarter. Only when she began to shift towards productising her services—offering downloadable design kits, creating automated onboarding for clients, and charging for strategy rather than execution—did her income begin to reflect the quality of her work, not just the quantity of her hours.

This is the defining error of hustle culture: it teaches people to optimise for effort rather than ecosystem. Wealth is rarely a direct result of intensity; it's usually a function of positioning. If you're grinding in a structurally low-margin, low-leverage context, no amount of tenacity will convert that into scalable wealth. Conversely, if you're situated in a high-leverage environment—where capital, code, or contracts are doing the heavy lifting—your wealth can grow even when your hours don't. The fundamental asymmetry between hustle and leverage is what makes the former such a poor predictor of financial freedom.

This is not an argument for laziness. Nor is it a dismissal of work ethic. It's an argument for *intentionality*. Strategic effort is not the enemy of success—misdirected effort is. Consider the example of two employees in the same company: one says yes to every task, works late, and prides themselves on being indispensable; the other prioritises fewer, higher-impact projects, and spends time building cross-department relationships. After five years, who is more likely to be promoted, or offered external opportunities? Not the one who hustled the most, but the one who created the most visibility and relational capital. Hustle, when isolated from strategy, becomes self-exploitation.

Burnout, then, is not just a health issue—it's an economic signal. It tells us that the system we are operating within is extracting more than it's returning. It also reveals a deeper cultural failing: the inability to decouple self-worth from financial outcomes. Hustle culture thrives in environments where insecurity is high and identity is fragile. When individuals don't feel secure in their economic future or professional status, they often overcompensate with output. But this leads to diminishing returns—not only financially, but cognitively. Research in organisational psychology shows that overwork impairs decision-making, reduces creativity, and accelerates attrition. A burnt-out brain doesn't build empires; it builds resentments.

Technology, ironically, amplifies this problem. Social media celebrates the "grindset" entrepreneur, the 5am riser, the always-on creative. But it rarely shows the cost: the strained relationships, the neglected health, the eventual plateau. This creates a skewed baseline of what is "normal" or admirable, reinforcing unsustainable patterns. It also distracts from the importance of rest—not as a luxury, but as a lever for better thinking. Sleep, reflection, and whitespace are where strategy is born. Yet hustle culture treats them as indulgences rather than essentials.

To break this pattern, we need a new mental model for success—one rooted in sustainability, not sacrifice. The most successful individuals in the modern economy do not hustle endlessly; they build assets that work when they don't. This might mean intellectual property, digital infrastructure, investment portfolios, or social capital. But the common thread is that they stop trading time for money as early as possible. They shift from operator to owner, from executor to orchestrator. This is not a luxury—it's a necessity in an economy where speed compounds, and burnout diminishes your compounding potential.

The question, then, is not "How hard are you working?" but "What are you working on—and does it have leverage?" Are your efforts building something that will generate returns independent of your effort tomorrow? Or are they simply repeating today's toil at a higher speed? Wealth is not the reward for grinding the longest; it's the outcome of building the smartest systems around your skills.

True financial autonomy doesn't come from exhaustion—it comes from clarity. From designing a life where your energy is applied where it matters most. From decoupling your self-worth from your calendar. And from rejecting the cultural noise that says suffering is proof of seriousness.

The hustle lie dies when we stop worshipping motion and start cultivating mastery. Not mastery of busyness, but mastery of architecture—the kind of thinking that builds systems, scales impact, and protects your time like the scarce asset it truly is.

When Hard Work Isn't Enough – How systemic barriers shape financial outcomes—and why this knowledge empowers smarter strategy

The popular financial narrative rewards grit, glorifies the grind, and promotes the idea that success is within reach if only we work hard enough. It's an appealing story—emotionally resonant, culturally reinforced, and foundational to many modern economies. But it is also incomplete. Because while hard work is necessary, it is not sufficient. If it were, the hardest working people—nurses, teachers, factory staff, small-scale farmers—would be the wealthiest. They are not. That discrepancy demands interrogation. What truly determines financial outcomes is not only effort, but also *access*. Access to networks, information, capital, stable infrastructure, safety nets, and even psychological security. And when access is distributed unequally, outcomes diverge dramatically, regardless of individual effort.

To understand this dynamic, one must first recognise the layers of structural advantage that underlie seemingly meritocratic results. Consider a young entrepreneur with a modest idea but access to family capital, alumni networks, or even a safety net that allows risk-taking without existential fear. Contrast that with an equally talented peer who must work full time to support dependents, has no collateral for loans, and lives in a postcode with underfunded schools and little economic mobility. They may both be hard-working. But one plays the game on an incline, while the other climbs against gravity.

These discrepancies are not always visible. In fact, modern capitalism excels at creating illusions of fairness. The financial press profiles self-made millionaires without referencing inherited privilege. Start-up culture champions underdogs while quietly funnelling resources towards insiders. Career progression is framed as a ladder, not a maze. But when we study outcomes at scale, the data tells a less romantic story. Wealth accumulation is most strongly correlated with *starting wealth*. Social mobility in many developed countries, including the UK and United States, is stagnating or declining. The zip code or family into which you are born continues to influence your earnings more than your individual work ethic.

This is not to suggest that ambition or determination are irrelevant. They matter. But they matter within a context. If that context is shaped by policies, systems, and norms that reward some and marginalise others, then we must reckon with that reality. Financial success cannot be extricated from the scaffolding that supports it. And the myth that hard work alone is the universal ticket to prosperity becomes not just misleading, but dangerous—it creates shame for those who struggle, and entitlement for those who succeed without understanding the scaffolding beneath their ascent.

One of the most powerful tools we can give ourselves is *strategic awareness*. Understanding the landscape in which we operate—its barriers, levers, and patterns—allows us to navigate it more intelligently. Take, for example, a first-generation university graduate entering the workforce with limited social capital. They may lack informal mentorship, exposure to corporate norms, or access to unadvertised opportunities. But once this is recognised—not as a personal failing, but a structural limitation—it becomes possible to counterbalance it. They can seek mentors outside their firm, invest in peer learning communities, or prioritise companies with transparent promotion pathways. Strategy begins with seeing the system clearly.

Another often ignored factor is the psychological cost of financial precarity. Individuals from historically under-resourced backgrounds often carry higher cognitive loads: the mental strain of insecurity, the vigilance required to navigate unfamiliar professional environments, and the pressure of being the "first" or "only" in a space. These invisible taxes reduce bandwidth for long-term planning, risk-taking, or rest—all of which are necessary for wealth creation. Simply put, it is harder to build an investment portfolio when your mental energy is spent on survival. This is not an excuse; it's an empirical truth supported by behavioural economics and neuropsychology.

Understanding systemic barriers is not about fostering victimhood; it is about regaining agency. It allows us to reframe our expectations, reallocate our effort, and design smarter tactics. For instance, someone facing wage stagnation due to industry saturation may shift focus from salary negotiation to asset-building: launching a side business, acquiring real estate, or building a monetisable digital audience. Another person might realise that the highest ROI comes not from additional certifications but from relocating to a region with better cost-to-income ratios or more inclusive policies. Strategy becomes adaptive when it is informed by systemic context—not driven blindly by conventional wisdom.

Critically, this lens also cultivates empathy. In policy debates, in hiring decisions, in how we teach our children about money—it matters whether we understand wealth as a product of both choice *and* circumstance. When institutions ignore systemic forces, they tend to design one-size-fits-all interventions that disproportionately benefit those already advantaged. Financial literacy workshops will not fix pay inequity. Entrepreneurial incubators that require six months of unpaid participation will not help those living paycheck to paycheck. Effective solutions require systemic literacy—not just personal grit.

This understanding is particularly urgent as wealth gaps widen. The pandemic further exposed the fragility of hard work as a security strategy. Essential workers faced the highest risks and often received the lowest pay. Remote-capable knowledge workers, by contrast, saw rising incomes and asset values. The distinction wasn't effort—it was proximity to leverage. Those with assets saw them appreciate; those without worked longer hours with little gain. If our goal is financial agency, we must abandon the idea that hustle is the great equaliser. It is not. Leverage is. And leverage is often a function of access.

So what can individuals do, practically, once they accept that hard work isn't the sole driver of outcomes? First, stop judging your financial position purely through the lens of morality or merit. Guilt and shame are poor tools for growth. Second, audit your access points. What do you currently have access to—networks, platforms, education, capital—and where are the gaps? Then, get strategic about bridging those gaps. That may mean joining affinity groups, learning to pitch to investors, building a public digital profile, or seeking environments that reward results over pedigree. Think like an architect, not just a labourer.

Lastly, acknowledge that systems are dynamic. They evolve—often slowly, sometimes violently. Individuals who understand the architecture of advantage are better positioned to push for change *and* benefit from it. The key is to navigate the now while shaping the next. Knowing that systemic forces influence outcomes doesn't absolve us from acting. It sharpens the way we act. It transforms financial advice from shallow slogans into tailored, context-aware strategies.

The idea that hard work equals wealth is comforting, but it's no longer credible. Our job now is to tell a more honest story—one that integrates effort, yes, but also access, systems, and history. Only then can we design financial strategies that are not just aspirational, but achievable. Not just personal, but powerful. Not just stories of triumph, but maps of transformation.

Building Access, Not Just Effort – Why the Right Networks, Skills, and Positioning Often Matter More Than Raw Hustle

If hard work were the dominant factor in wealth creation, the global economy would look radically different. Farmers, domestic workers, garment factory employees, and sanitation workers would occupy the upper tiers of society. But they do not. In reality, the relationship between effort and financial outcomes is mediated—often eclipsed—by *access*: access to networks, access to opportunity, access to leverage. This is the quiet architecture behind most modern success. And yet, we remain culturally infatuated with the hustle myth—the idea that intensity and hours alone can bridge any economic gap. It's a seductive narrative because it gives us control. But it's incomplete, and for many, deeply misleading.

In the financial stories we celebrate, we often spotlight the visible effort—the early mornings, the sacrifices, the persistence. What we overlook is the hidden scaffolding: the mentor who opened the first door, the university that conferred not just knowledge but credibility, the parent who covered rent so risk could be taken. This scaffolding is not distributed equally. That does not make success illegitimate, but it *does* mean that replicating it requires more than replicating someone's work ethic. It requires *building access*—deliberately, strategically, and with an understanding that wealth compounds through advantage, not just exertion.

Networks are not a bonus; they are infrastructure. In sectors like finance, media, and technology, career opportunities are frequently unadvertised. They travel through informal conversations, backchannels, and introductions. In entrepreneurial spaces, investors fund people they trust, which usually means people they already know. This isn't necessarily malicious; it's human. But it creates a closed loop where visibility and proximity are rewarded more than raw merit. Those outside the loop often work harder just to earn a seat—only to find the decisions were made in rooms they weren't in. Understanding this is not cynical. It's clarifying. And it allows individuals to shift focus from grinding harder to *positioning smarter.*

Positioning is often misunderstood as personal branding, but it runs deeper. It's the alignment of your work, your voice, and your presence with where value is flowing. If you're brilliant but invisible in the wrong room, your value may be capped. But if your competence is visible at the intersection of rising demand and key decision-makers, your growth accelerates. Consider the engineer who builds quietly in a silo versus the one who shares insights on industry forums, collaborates cross-functionally, and is known beyond their title. Same skills. Different outcomes. Why? Visibility. Perception. Access.

Skills are necessary, but they are not neutral. The market does not reward effort—it rewards *perceived value.* And that perception is shaped by context. A designer in Nairobi may be more talented than one in London but earn a fraction due to geographic bias. A coder from a non-elite university may outperform their Ivy League counterpart but be overlooked in interviews because of credential signalling. Recognising this allows us to ask better questions—not just "Am I good at what I do?" but "Is what I do *valued* where I am? And if not, where would it be?" This is not a matter of abandoning core competencies but of adapting them to more fertile ground.

It is also important to distinguish between working *in* the system and working *on* the system. Most people are trained to optimise within existing structures—apply for jobs, impress gatekeepers, follow protocol. But the most significant financial gains often come from stepping outside those boundaries—by building platforms, owning equity, or creating value that bypasses permission. This does not mean everyone should become an entrepreneur. It means understanding *leverage*: time leverage, capital leverage, network leverage. It means asking not just "What can I do with my time?" but "What can I build that multiplies my time?" Hustle may earn you a wage. Access and leverage earn you freedom.

Building access, for those without inherited networks, is entirely possible—but it requires a different mindset. First, it demands intentional social strategy. Many intelligent professionals remain financially stagnant because they treat relationship-building as optional or inauthentic. But every industry has nodes of influence—people who connect others, spot opportunities early, and shape narratives. Mapping and engaging these nodes, sincerely and consistently, is a high-yield investment. This is not manipulation; it's participation. Relationships are not currency. They are *infrastructure.*

Second, building access means investing in *contextual knowledge.* Technical skill is table stakes. What sets individuals apart is knowing *how value is created in their ecosystem.* What drives decisions? What constraints do key stakeholders face? What does timing look like in this space? Too often, effort is misapplied because it is uninformed. A freelancer may cold-pitch dozens of clients without understanding procurement cycles. A jobseeker may submit CVs that never reach human eyes because they don't understand applicant tracking systems. Information gaps drain energy. Access plugs those gaps.

Third, access is reciprocal. Many professionals approach networking transactionally, seeking introductions without offering context or value. But the most resilient networks are built on mutual benefit, intellectual generosity, and emotional intelligence. The best way to gain access is often to *create it* for others. Become a connector. Share resources. Acknowledge good work publicly. These behaviours compound reputational capital, which is a form of wealth no algorithm can quantify but every opportunity algorithmically detects.

Critically, access is not just interpersonal. It is *structural.* Government policy, public infrastructure, and digital inclusion all shape who gets to play the game—and how. Broadband access, for example, is now as critical as transport. Lack of it isolates entire communities from participation in digital economies. Similarly, exclusionary housing policy determines who gets proximity to quality schools or job clusters. If you are building personal strategy in isolation from these systemic factors, you are playing with half the map. Strategic individuals invest not just in self-improvement, but in system awareness—and, where possible, system redesign.

This is particularly true in the emerging creator and digital asset economies, where access has been partially democratised but inequality quickly reasserts itself. Early adopters often benefit most. Those with marketing acumen rise faster than those with core value but poor distribution. And platforms privilege content that performs algorithmically, not necessarily substantively. To navigate these dynamics, creators must treat their content not just as output but as *positioning tools*. Similarly, investors must learn that access to deal flow, not capital alone, determines returns. Money follows access—not the other way around.

It is time to retire the idea that hustle is the most noble path to wealth. Not because effort is useless—but because effort untethered from access is inefficient. And in many cases, exhausting. Financial transformation comes not just from intensity, but from *intelligent exposure*. From knowing where to be, whom to serve, what to say, and when to move. The grind may make you stronger. But access makes you scalable.

The practical question, then, is not "How can I work harder?" but "Where is my leverage—and how do I access it?" That may mean building a personal brand that outlives your current role. It may mean joining an accelerator rather than bootstrapping alone. It may mean mentoring someone who introduces you to an unexpected door. But whatever the method, the insight remains: effort is the engine, but *access is the fuel*. Without it, you're running uphill. With it, momentum becomes exponential.

To build access is to play the game beneath the game. It is not cheating. It is not elitism. It is simply understanding how value circulates in the real world—and learning how to plug yourself into that circuit. Those who do this strategically do not merely chase wealth. They position themselves to *attract* it. That's not hustle. That's architecture. And it's available to anyone willing to stop running—and start building.

CHAPTER 9
The Illusion of Control

Control—of finances, of fate, of life itself—is perhaps the most alluring illusion we chase. It offers the comfort of predictability in an unpredictable world, the promise of safety within systems defined by volatility, the mirage of certainty where none truly exists. Among the disciplined, ambitious, and well-educated, control is framed as virtue: plan carefully, optimise relentlessly, forecast with precision, and stability will follow. Yet beneath that reassuring surface lies a less comfortable truth: control, as commonly conceived, is not only illusory—it can be a liability.

The drive to control often begins with commendable intent: meticulous budgets, granular investment targets, precise market timing, and decade-long plans dissected by the month. These behaviours are socially lauded—they signal responsibility and foresight. But look closer, and fear lurks beneath. Fear of the unknown, of chaos, of losing comfort, status, or identity. When plans become rigid shields against uncertainty, they do not make us safer—they make us brittle. The real danger is rarely randomness itself; it is the fragility bred by attempting to expunge it.

The modern world is not merely fast-moving—it is non-linear. A pandemic can shutter entire industries overnight. A single social media post can launch an unknown artist to international acclaim. Government policies can erase years of planning in a single announcement. Such events are not anomalies; they are the new norm, exposing the limits of prediction. Yet conventional financial advice continues to promote spreadsheet optimism: track meticulously, and protection will follow. The flaw lies not in data but in the assumption that life can be engineered like a machine. People are not machines. Markets are not machines. History is punctuated by random breaks, outliers, and reversals. Real financial wisdom begins with acknowledging this.

Humility—often overlooked in financial discourse—is a virtue of strategic realism. Not meekness, but awareness: "I cannot know what will happen. Yet I can design systems that adapt." Humility enables flexibility, and flexibility breeds resilience. It cushions shocks rather than simply realising ideal scenarios. Nassim Nicholas Taleb's notion of "black swans"—rare, high-impact, unpredictable events—was less a predictive tool than a warning. Most build financial lives that thrive under expectation but collapse under surprise. True wealth is measured by survivability under stress, not comfort.

Here, the distinction between goals and systems becomes vital. Goals indicate direction; systems dictate operation. Traditional advice is goal-centric: save £1 million by 60, retire by 67, purchase a home by 35. But goals without adaptive systems are fragile. Market swings, job loss, illness, geopolitical instability—any can render meticulous plans obsolete. Systems, by contrast, embed adaptability. They ask: which financial practices, habits, and buffers render me responsive rather than reactive? Which automations guard against my worst impulses? Which routines let wealth grow even when plans falter?

Take, for instance, savings. Rather than fixating on an exact target, a resilient system emphasises automatic contributions that scale with income, diversified across asset classes. Success is measured not by beating the market, but by staying engaged with it. Psychological risk is treated as seriously as financial risk, prioritising sustainability over perfection. Budgeting becomes a visibility tool rather than a constraint. Such systems may lack the elegance of a "perfect plan," but they outperform it in reality.

Systems thinking also cultivates optionality: the ability to make high-quality choices at critical junctures. Optionality opposes overcommitment. It maintains career flexibility when industries shift, liquidity when one must pivot or start anew, and freedom when identity is tethered to multiple pursuits. Those who are truly financially secure do not cling to rigid paths; they preserve margin and maintain multiple plays on the table. Wealth, in its most potent form, is as much about options as it is about assets. Choices, not certainties, generate genuine control.

This reframing alters how we perceive failure. In a plan-centric model, deviation signals defeat. In a systems-centric approach, it signals feedback: information for refinement. Failure ceases to mark personal flaw and becomes a mechanism for adaptation. People who overidentify with plans collapse under disruption; those who treat uncertainty as a design constraint remain resilient, recover quickly, and iterate intelligently.

Consider two investors. One commits wholly to a single real estate project, confident in research and conviction. Policy changes devastate the market, and he is wiped out. The other diversifies across property, equities, and digital assets, maintains an emergency fund, and regularly reassesses assumptions. His belief lies not in any single asset, but in solvency itself. Who is truly in control? Not the one with the greatest confidence, but the one with the widest runway.

The logic extends beyond finances to career, relationships, and wellbeing. Individuals anchored to singular identities—"I am a lawyer," "I am a founder," "I am the provider"—risk instability when disruption strikes. Those cultivating multifaceted identities—generalists, collaborators, lifelong learners—possess resilience. Financial health, therefore, is inseparable from psychological diversification: refusing to let a single outcome define your worth.

Here lies the paradox: the more we pursue precision, the more vulnerable we become. Conversely, designing for variability—through systems, optionality, and humility—fortifies our financial lives. This is not surrender; it is the abandonment of the illusion that control equals security. Adaptability equals security.

This insight is liberating. You need not predict every scenario, divine the dominant asset class, or perfect every decision. You need only remain in the game, prepared to respond, equipped with habits that endure stress. You need not command the waves; you need a better boat.

In the chapters ahead, we will explore this thesis: the perils of overplanning, the productive role of randomness, and practical tools to build antifragile financial systems. You will learn not just to manage risk, but to live with it—productively, intelligently, and peacefully. Control is not the goal; capacity is. And it is that capacity which transforms money from a source of anxiety into a source of power.

The Trap of Perfect Planning – Why Obsessing Over Perfect Plans Actually Makes You More Fragile

The modern fixation with perfect planning is a paradoxical pathology: the more we seek to control every variable, the more brittle we become when life refuses to follow our script. In the realm of personal finance, this shows up as meticulously detailed budgets, elaborate retirement calculators, and colour-coded spreadsheets—projects that signal diligence but often conceal a deeper discomfort with uncertainty. We don't just plan because it's rational; we plan because it soothes us. It creates the illusion that if we just input the right numbers, behave consistently, and anticipate every risk, we'll be immune to upheaval. Yet ironically, this very reliance on precision often becomes the source of our greatest vulnerability. Fragility doesn't arise from a lack of effort, but from an overcommitment to an imagined future.

Consider the behaviour of investors who follow a 30-year retirement glidepath, allocating assets based on assumptions made decades in advance. The models they rely on are built atop historical averages, but reality rarely delivers those averages neatly. An economic shock, health event, policy change, or personal transition can render even the most carefully constructed plan obsolete overnight. Planning, in such cases, doesn't protect; it traps. It constrains response flexibility because the person has so over-optimised for a single expected outcome that there is no room to pivot when the unexpected happens. This is a critical flaw in many financial education frameworks: they prioritise precision over resilience, structure over adaptability.

Real life operates under a different logic—one that isn't symmetrical, linear, or fair. Nassim Nicholas Taleb popularised the concept of "antifragility": systems that benefit from disorder rather than collapse under it. Perfect planning, by contrast, is inherently fragile. It assumes stability where there is none and treats volatility as a threat instead of an inevitability. A fragile plan cannot absorb deviation; it demands constant correction. But humans aren't algorithms. We get divorced. We lose jobs. We have children, change careers, make mistakes, fall ill, move cities, grieve, burn out, start over. A financial strategy that can't accommodate real life is not a strategy; it's a story we tell ourselves to feel in control.

Take the example of university graduates who map out their entire career path, complete with expected salary jumps, homeownership timelines, and savings milestones. These plans often unravel within a few years. Not necessarily because of failure, but because of opportunity. They might discover a passion in an entirely different field, get recruited to an unexpected role, or move countries. In such cases, the plan's rigidity becomes a hindrance rather than a guide. Worse, many delay pursuing new opportunities because they are afraid to "abandon the plan." The psychological cost of deviating from what once felt safe can become a form of self-imposed stagnation.

This doesn't mean planning is worthless. But the most effective planning is probabilistic, not deterministic. It's rooted in principles, not predictions. It creates parameters that help guide action without pretending to forecast the future. Rather than plotting one exact course, robust planning defines a range of acceptable outcomes—and builds in the capacity to adapt when conditions change. This is the difference between building a bridge that can withstand earthquakes and building one that collapses if the weather is slightly off-script.

Financial planning, then, must shift from an obsession with certainty to a practice of optionality. Optionality is the capacity to act on opportunity when it arises—not because you forecasted it perfectly, but because you preserved the freedom to choose. In personal finance, this means maintaining liquidity, cultivating diverse income streams, avoiding lifestyle inflation that reduces flexibility, and investing not just in markets but in skills, relationships, and reputational capital. These are the elements that allow someone to pivot with confidence rather than cling to a failing plan out of sunk-cost inertia.

One of the quiet dangers of perfect planning is that it narrows our identity. We become attached not just to the plan, but to the person we imagine ourselves being when the plan succeeds. This is why deviations feel so threatening—not just to our finances but to our sense of self. But if the last decade has shown us anything—from pandemics to economic dislocation to AI disruption—it's that no amount of planning can insulate us from change. The more rigid the plan, the more brittle the person. Flexibility isn't a flaw in financial thinking; it's a prerequisite for surviving the real economy.

Moreover, we need to consider the psychological dimension of planning. Often, what people call "a plan" is a coping mechanism. It's a strategy for managing anxiety, not reality. They feel in control when every step is mapped out, even if those steps are based on faulty assumptions. This is especially prevalent among high achievers, who conflate control with competence. But controlling the future is not a measure of intelligence—it's often a reflection of fear. The real skill is knowing how to proceed without guarantees, how to build systems that thrive amid ambiguity.

This is where systems thinking becomes crucial. A financial system is not a fixed trajectory; it's a set of interlocking behaviours, rules, and routines that self-correct over time. A system might include automatic savings, diversified investments, spending caps, and income buffers. These elements adapt as life unfolds. Unlike a brittle plan, a system doesn't break when circumstances shift. It absorbs shocks and rebalances. It reduces the need for constant vigilance by embedding sound defaults. In this way, systems replace the illusion of control with the habit of responsiveness.

We should also be wary of social narratives that romanticise master plans. Popular media is filled with profiles of visionaries who supposedly followed a perfect blueprint to success. These stories are almost always post hoc constructions. The reality is messier: full of wrong turns, reversals, and recoveries. Successful people don't follow flawless plans—they stay in motion, learn quickly, and preserve options. What appears in hindsight as strategic genius is often just resilience under uncertainty combined with the ability to course-correct without ego.

A final consideration is the emotional fragility that comes with planning obsession. When people derive their sense of safety from the plan, any disruption becomes existential. They're not just losing money or time—they're losing the psychological scaffolding that kept anxiety at bay. This can lead to panic, paralysis, or poor decision-making under pressure. A resilient person, by contrast, doesn't place their trust in the map, but in their capacity to navigate. They feel anchored not by outcomes, but by competence, adaptability, and a calm understanding that change is not a deviation—it's the default.

So what replaces perfect planning? A posture of strategic readiness. An ethos of dynamic alignment. A commitment to direction rather than destination. This means setting priorities instead of rigid goals. Practising reflection over prediction. Valuing clarity over certainty. And most importantly, designing your financial life in a way that stays viable across many possible futures, not just your favourite one.

To be financially antifragile is not to prepare for one outcome, but to stay prepared for many. It's not to seek comfort in control, but to find confidence in capability. Perfection is not resilience. Precision is not power. The future belongs to those who build for variance—not those who pretend to eliminate it.

Chaos, Luck, and Black Swans – The Role of Randomness in Financial Outcomes—and Why Humility Is Financially Powerful

Nothing in modern financial culture is more seductive—and more misleading—than the illusion of total control. We love to tell stories that trace a neat arc: a visionary entrepreneur who saw a gap in the market, took calculated risks, worked relentlessly, and emerged victorious. These narratives have one thing in common: they airbrush out the random, the improbable, and the inexplicable. Yet it is precisely these unpredictable forces—what Nassim Nicholas Taleb termed *black swans*—that so often define who wins, who loses, and who merely survives. If you don't understand the role of luck in money, you're not just misinformed—you're strategically vulnerable.

It's tempting to attribute financial success to skill and failure to bad decisions. We look for causality because it comforts us. If we can trace the outcome to a decision, we believe we can repeat the good and avoid the bad. But financial reality doesn't work like a laboratory. Markets crash for reasons no one foresaw. Start-ups soar not because of visionary leadership, but because a social trend breaks at the right moment. An investor makes a fortune from what, in retrospect, looks like genius—but was in fact a mispriced asset bought during a moment of panic. *The deeper truth is that success in finance is rarely linear, and often far more random than we care to admit.*

Consider Bill Gates—often described as a quintessential "self-made" billionaire. Gates was undoubtedly intelligent and driven, but so were tens of thousands of other students. What distinguished him? For one, he attended one of the only high schools in the United States at the time with access to a computer terminal. That rare exposure, combined with the freedom to experiment with code in his teenage years, set a trajectory others simply couldn't replicate. Gates himself has acknowledged this in interviews, yet his story is still widely cited as a model of individual excellence divorced from circumstance. *What we celebrate as merit often rides on invisible currents of privilege, timing, and chance.*

The financial industry itself reinforces this bias. Fund managers who outperform the market in any given year are praised as brilliant strategists. But when statistical researchers have examined these results over time, many outperformers revert to the mean—or worse. In his classic analysis, economist Burton Malkiel concluded that a monkey throwing darts at the financial pages could outperform most active fund managers over time. This isn't to suggest that all success is luck. It's to suggest that *we systematically overestimate the role of skill in outcomes that are deeply stochastic.*

Our discomfort with randomness isn't trivial—it shapes how we invest, how we work, and how we relate to money emotionally. People who believe the world is largely deterministic are more likely to chase control: they obsess over market timing, over-optimise their portfolios, or panic when forecasts go awry. Ironically, those who understand uncertainty tend to build more robust systems. They don't try to predict the exact path. They build flexibility into their plans. *They aim for antifragility—not precision.*

A striking example of this mindset difference can be seen in how people handle windfalls. Lottery winners, on average, file for bankruptcy at double the national rate within five years. In contrast, individuals who gradually grow wealth over time often build buffers, diversify assets, and prepare for downturns. Why the difference? Windfalls invite the illusion of permanence. They seduce winners into believing they've "solved" money. But if you haven't developed a mindset that anticipates randomness—if you don't expect the unexpected—you'll likely spend as though the future will look like the present. *Financial humility, then, is not modesty—it's strategic intelligence.*

It's also why historical knowledge matters. Throughout the 20th and 21st centuries, some of the most significant economic events came not from the centre of prediction, but from its edges. Think of the 2008 financial crisis. Months before it imploded, celebrated economists dismissed the housing market collapse as "contained." The models didn't see it coming. Neither did the regulators. And yet, millions of families lost their homes, while those few who had bet on systemic collapse—like the infamous Michael Burry—made fortunes. His success wasn't just based on analysis. It was based on *a willingness to think outside the probabilistic consensus.*

This has profound implications for how we define financial wisdom. Traditional advice tells people to set goals, create plans, and stick to them. That's fine in principle—but brittle in practice. A plan that only works under one set of assumptions is fragile. True resilience lies in building systems that can absorb shocks. This is why the concept of "optionality" has gained so much attention in financial thinking. Optionality means designing your financial life to include choices, buffers, and escape valves. It means preferring investments and income sources that leave room for adjustment, rather than locking yourself into narrow corridors of strategy. *It's not about being reactive. It's about being prepared for a wider distribution of futures.*

Humility, in this context, becomes a superpower. Not because it makes you passive, but because it keeps you flexible. Humble investors don't over-leverage. Humble entrepreneurs diversify revenue streams. Humble savers know they might lose a job, face illness, or see a business fail—not because they're pessimistic, but because they understand the real rules of the game. *They don't bet everything on being right—they invest in staying alive long enough to benefit from being occasionally lucky.*

There is also a deeper ethical dimension to this recognition of randomness. If we accept that outcomes are influenced by chance—by where and when we were born, by who we happened to meet, by market timing beyond our control—then our attitude toward others changes. We become less inclined to moralise poverty and less eager to deify the rich. We begin to ask better questions: Who had access? Who had safety nets? Who had to take outsized risks just to survive? This shift doesn't negate personal responsibility—it contextualises it. *It replaces arrogance with empathy, and turns judgement into inquiry.*

Critically, embracing randomness doesn't mean embracing fatalism. It means adjusting strategy. You don't need to predict which start-up will become the next unicorn—you need to invest in enough plausible bets that if one succeeds, it pays for the rest. You don't need to forecast the next crash—you need to keep cash reserves and avoid overextension. You don't need to get every trade right—you need to stay solvent long enough to benefit from long-term compounding. *Control is not about certainty; it's about durability.*

This is why some of the most seasoned investors avoid grand predictions altogether. Howard Marks, co-founder of Oaktree Capital, openly states that "you can't predict, but you can prepare." That's not resignation—it's wisdom. The more we understand the chaotic, often unjust, yet fascinatingly open-ended nature of financial systems, the more we see that mastery lies not in dominating uncertainty but in coexisting with it. Not by eliminating risk, but by building lives that can hold its weight.

So the next time you hear a "how I made it" story, pause. Ask what's missing. Look for the role of timing, of gatekeepers, of capital access, of blind luck. Then ask how you can build a financial life that doesn't depend on any single break, but that benefits from many possibilities. The world is chaotic. Black swans exist. But if you respect randomness, if you design for surprise, and if you resist the impulse to over-credit your own control, you won't just survive chaos—you'll occasionally thrive in it.

Systems Beat Goals – How to Create Flexible Financial Systems That Thrive No Matter What Life Throws Your Way

There's a quiet arrogance embedded in most goal-setting advice: the assumption that life will cooperate. We're told to envision success, reverse-engineer a plan, break it down into daily actions, and stick with it. It's seductively tidy. But life doesn't unfold in tidy increments. It derails, mutates, and occasionally detonates. And in the wreckage of perfect plans, most people discover—too late—that the scaffolding they were relying on was brittle. *This is where systems prove their superiority.*

Goals are seductive because they promise certainty. A six-month savings target. A retirement figure. A debt-free date. Yet the very structure that gives goals their appeal—fixed, measurable, linear—is also what makes them vulnerable. When markets crash, careers stall, health declines, or families unravel, goals fracture under the pressure of reality. Systems, by contrast, are adaptive. They do not care whether conditions are favourable. They are *how* you move, not *where* you're going.

Take two people, each aiming to save £10,000 in a year. One sets a rigid savings goal and auto-debits the same amount monthly. The other builds a living system: a dynamic spending tracker, periodic income reviews, a decision rule for windfalls, and habit loops that favour surplus. If life remains smooth, both may succeed. But when childcare costs rise, or an unexpected move eats into cash flow, the first person's goal risks implosion, while the second can flex without failing. *Systems absorb chaos. Goals collapse under it.*

James Clear, in his work on behavioural change, notes that "you do not rise to the level of your goals; you fall to the level of your systems." It's a profound shift in mindset—from destination to infrastructure. But in finance, this insight is still underapplied. Personal finance discourse remains saturated with fixed targets and finish lines: "£1 million net worth by 40," "retire early," "zero debt by X date." The subtext is that wealth is a linear conquest. It's not. *Wealth, especially sustainable wealth, is emergent. It grows from feedback loops, behaviours, and environments that are calibrated to reality, not fantasy.*

The irony is that systems often *outperform* goals, even by goal-setters' own metrics. They compound small wins. They prevent catastrophic errors. They nudge you back on course without ego. A person with a system of reviewing expenses weekly, investing automatically, and emotionally de-risking large purchases is likely to outperform someone who sets an annual budget and forgets it. Not because they're smarter, but because they've built in *resilience*. Their financial system operates like an ecosystem—not a blueprint.

Systems thinking also reduces decision fatigue. By shifting focus from outcomes to process, it removes the burden of daily willpower. A goal requires you to constantly re-decide: do I skip dinner out? Do I invest this bonus or splurge? A system *pre-decides* for you. It builds in rules that limit friction. If 50% of all freelance income is automatically swept into a tax account, the stress of tax season evaporates. If a pre-committed percentage of your budget is allocated to guilt-free fun, you don't need to agonise over every latte. *Systems honour human limitations. Goals often demand superhuman consistency.*

Critically, systems liberate you from binary thinking. Goals tend to turn progress into pass/fail judgments: you either hit the target or you don't. This fosters perfectionism, discouragement, and abandonment when setbacks occur. Systems focus instead on continuity. If you're running a system of daily micro-investing—say, £5 into an index fund—you're "winning" every day the system runs, even if market conditions are volatile. You may not see immediate results, but the process is compounding beneath the surface. This breeds patience and emotional sustainability, two of the rarest and most valuable financial traits.

Consider a more abstract example: career progression. The goal-oriented person might target a promotion within 18 months, tying self-worth and decisions to that outcome. The system-oriented person builds daily practices: mentoring others, learning new tools, publishing insights, building a reputation across teams. If the promotion comes, fine. If not, the system is still expanding optionality, credibility, and value. One path is a gamble. The other is an engine. *Systems produce results even when they don't produce the intended result.*

Of course, systems are not panaceas. They require design, maintenance, and occasional overhaul. A financial system that once fit your life may become obsolete after a major life change. But this, too, is a feature—not a flaw. Systems encourage *iteration.* You don't need to wait until January 1st to "try again." You just tweak the system and keep moving. This fosters financial maturity: the understanding that wealth is not a sprint or even a marathon, but a form of adaptive navigation.

The broader economic world offers an instructive parallel. Central banks don't issue single goals and hope for the best. They build layered systems: automatic stabilisers, interest rate levers, policy feedback loops. The goal—price stability, for instance—is important, but it's the system that enables response to shocks. Similarly, resilient financial lives are not built by dreaming harder. They are built by embedding mechanisms that make intelligent behaviour easier *especially when conditions deteriorate.*

From a psychological perspective, systems also help insulate us from the destructive effects of uncertainty. Neuroscience shows that unpredictability triggers a stress response. Goals, by pretending to impose order on the future, offer short-term relief. But when that illusion collapses—as it eventually does—the result is panic or paralysis. Systems, by contrast, *acknowledge unpredictability upfront.* They don't attempt to control outcomes, only responses. This reframes risk from threat to variable. It's less glamorous, but far more powerful.

We should also recognise how systems enhance self-trust. When people rely on goals, they often outsource motivation to the finish line. When they miss it, they feel ashamed or demotivated. But when people build systems that reinforce identity—"I am someone who reviews my money weekly," "I am someone who never spends without a 24-hour pause"—they cultivate pride in process. This internal coherence becomes a source of grounded confidence. You are no longer chasing success. You are enacting it.

In truth, most people don't fail financially because they lack ambition. They fail because they rely on plans that require life to behave. They use brute force instead of feedback. They confuse control with effectiveness. Systems, properly built, make these errors irrelevant. They harness randomness. They reduce cognitive load. They turn chaos into fuel. And most importantly, they keep working when you don't.

What would it look like to think of your money life not as a series of targets, but as a system under ongoing refinement? It might mean building in automatic pauses before purchases above £100. It might mean monthly check-ins with a thinking partner, or tiered investing thresholds based on income bands. It might mean using calendar nudges to protect long-term thinking or setting up environmental cues that reinforce saving behaviours. It would certainly mean replacing the question "What do I want to achieve?" with "What conditions make good decisions likely, again and again?"

This shift is not about abandoning ambition. It is about *grounding ambition in infrastructure.* You don't need to predict the future if you're prepared to adapt to it. The only truly reliable financial plan is one built on systems that can flex, evolve, and withstand noise. And if you build systems well, you may discover—almost accidentally—that you surpassed the goals you thought you needed in the first place.

Optionality: The Secret Lever – How Building Choices Into Your Life Creates True Control, Even in an Unpredictable World

Control, for many, is the holy grail of financial planning. We chase it through spreadsheets, five-year strategies, emergency funds, and career ladders. But the future does not respect our certainties. Markets shift without notice. Industries become obsolete. Illness strikes. Families fracture. A single phone call can rearrange your next decade. In this volatile landscape, the kind of control worth pursuing is not prediction—it's optionality.

Optionality is not about having a rigid plan; it's about preserving the power to choose when the unexpected arrives. It's the ability to pivot, adapt, or walk away—not because life went to script, but because you built space for alternatives. At its core, *optionality is a form of freedom born from intentional design.*

The concept is rooted in financial theory. Options are contracts that give their holder the right, but not the obligation, to buy or sell an asset at a set price. In real life, optionality works the same way. The more high-quality options you hold—career opportunities, skill sets, relationships, savings buffers, geographic mobility—the less fragile your life becomes. You can tolerate surprises not because you control outcomes, but because you've engineered resilience into your structure.

Consider two people with similar incomes. One lives paycheck to paycheck, locked into a single employer, with debt obligations and fixed costs that allow no deviation. The other lives well below their means, has diversified skills, a side income stream, and minimal fixed expenses. If both are laid off, the second person doesn't just survive—they choose. They may take time off, pursue a passion, start a business, or retool their career. Same shock. Radically different outcomes. *Optionality doesn't make you invincible—it makes you manoeuvrable.*

The myth that optionality is a luxury of the wealthy is dangerously misleading. It is often *the foundation* of wealth creation, not a byproduct of it. The working-class immigrant who acquires a trade and moves cities gains optionality. The student who learns to code and freelance alongside university work gains optionality. The single mother who builds a local network of support for shared childcare is building options into her daily survival. Optionality is not about privilege—it's about leverage. And leverage is scalable.

In a world where institutions are increasingly unreliable—where job security is fragile, pensions are eroding, and governments are politically gridlocked—individuals must learn to create their own shock absorbers. This isn't about cynicism; it's about strategy. Your capacity to generate, recognise, and act on options will determine not only your financial wellbeing, but your psychological stability.

Nassim Nicholas Taleb, who popularised the term "black swan" to describe rare, high-impact events, argues that optionality is the antidote to fragility. His insight is elegantly simple: you cannot predict black swans, but you can position yourself to benefit from them. A person with options doesn't need to guess the future—they're simply more likely to benefit from positive randomness and survive negative shocks. Optionality, in Taleb's framing, is a strategy for dealing with uncertainty by embracing *asymmetry*—capping your downside while leaving the upside open-ended.

This has profound implications for how we build our financial lives. Too often, people pursue narrow optimisation—maximising returns, minimising taxes, eliminating all "waste." But the most optimised system is often the least robust. The real question should be: *How many pathways do I have if this fails?* A life engineered for maximum efficiency but zero flexibility is a life teetering on the edge of collapse. Optionality may look inefficient from the outside—but it is profoundly anti-fragile.

Entrepreneurs understand this intuitively. A failed product can be catastrophic for a rigid business, but irrelevant for one with multiple income streams, a loyal customer base, and low overhead. Similarly, in personal finance, the person who creates optionality through diverse income, mobile skills, and lifestyle flexibility can absorb more risk—*and* seize more opportunity—than someone who locks their life into a single narrative.

Importantly, optionality is also psychological. Some people have the means to pivot but not the mindset. They cling to sunk costs, fear reputational damage, or equate status with permanence. They've built golden cages. True optionality requires *permission to change direction*—to detach identity from any one outcome and reframe quitting not as failure, but as reallocation. This demands ego discipline. It also demands a broader definition of success: not dominance, but durability.

Let's consider a practical application: career design. Many are taught to climb a single ladder. The unspoken rule is that credibility accrues through linear progression. But this model is collapsing. Skills are becoming obsolete faster than ever. Roles are unbundling. Freelance, fractional, and project-based work are surging. In this environment, a portfolio career—where one builds multiple roles, revenue streams, and reputations—is no longer a hedge. It's a necessity. It maximises *optionality* in an unstable landscape.

Similarly, in investing, optionality is often misunderstood as speculative gambling—buying call options or chasing asymmetric bets. But true investment optionality means maintaining *liquidity*, resisting over-concentration, and preserving the ability to act when the world shifts. The investor who is 100% locked into real estate during a credit crunch, or whose net worth is tied up in illiquid private ventures, has little manoeuvrability. By contrast, one who holds some dry powder—cash equivalents, low-correlation assets, or short-term vehicles—has choices when others freeze.

Optionality also invites us to revisit how we think about lifestyle. A life maxed out with car payments, high fixed expenses, and social commitments that require constant performance leaves little room for spontaneity or risk-taking. Conversely, designing a life around mobility, simplicity, and strategic slack means you can say yes to things others can't: an unpaid sabbatical, an overseas opportunity, or a high-risk, high-reward venture. *Control, in this sense, isn't about stability—it's about range.*

Crucially, optionality is not the same as indecision. It's not about keeping all doors open forever or fearing commitment. It's about *strategic reversibility*—the ability to test, iterate, and retreat without collapse. Amazon, famously, distinguishes between "Type 1" and "Type 2" decisions—those that are irreversible versus reversible. Optionality encourages you to keep Type 2 decisions light, fast, and frequent—while guarding your exposure to Type 1 risks. It's the same in life: build light bets, not heavy certainties.

Education is another arena where optionality is misunderstood. Students are often pressured to specialise early, incurring massive debt for credentials that may not guarantee employability. But those who cultivate *meta-skills*—learning how to learn, communicating with clarity, managing ambiguity—retain optionality across contexts. In a world where entire industries can vanish, transferable skills become the currency of mobility. They don't just buy you jobs—they buy you time, reinvention, and resilience.

There is also a moral dimension to optionality. If we want to build more equitable societies, then expanding access to optionality—through education, financial literacy, fair credit, mobility infrastructure, and legal protections—is a crucial task. When optionality is reserved for the already advantaged, volatility becomes a weapon rather than a test. But when more people hold meaningful options, a society becomes more robust, less polarised, and more adaptive to change.

In the end, optionality is a mindset as much as a mechanism. It asks: *How can I make decisions today that expand my future choices?* It invites you to measure wealth not by what you own, but by how many quality moves you can make. It shifts the axis of success from control through prediction to control through preparedness. The world will always be unpredictable. But your response to it doesn't have to be reactive. With optionality as your lever, you gain something far more powerful than control—you gain *leverage without fragility*.

CHAPTER 10
The Lie of Straight-Line Success

If one were to sketch the typical mental image of success, it would resemble a neat, upward-sloping line: steady, predictable, reward perfectly mirroring effort, hour for hour, year for year. There's a seductive comfort in that idea—especially for those navigating salaried work, formal education, and the familiar cadence of incremental promotions. The problem? It's largely a fiction. Real wealth—whether financial, creative, or reputational—rarely progresses in straight lines. It surges, it stalls, it leaps unexpectedly and sometimes retreats without warning. Its trajectory is jagged, erratic, and often invisible until, suddenly, it manifests.

The myth of straight-line progress is not just inaccurate—it can be actively damaging. It fosters unrealistic expectations, leads even intelligent individuals to misinterpret plateaus as failure, and volatility as incompetence. Worse, it prompts many to abandon their efforts precisely when compounding is poised to begin. The truth is that meaningful success often feels like nothing is happening—until everything happens at once. This chapter explores why.

It starts with a vital distinction: income versus wealth. Income tends to be linear. For salaried professionals, it is a predictable exchange of time and expertise for monthly deposits. Raises arrive at intervals, reinforcing the illusion that effort and reward scale neatly together. Wealth, by contrast—assets that appreciate, compound, or generate returns independent of labour—obeys a far less polite logic.

Consider an investor: years may pass with little apparent movement, only for a market surge to multiply capital overnight. An entrepreneur may labour for half a decade on infrastructure before achieving product-market fit. A writer or creator might toil in obscurity until one essay, video, or talk goes viral, opening opportunities and income streams far beyond prior efforts. These are not anomalies; they are the structural realities of nonlinear systems. Early grind may appear unrewarded, not because effort is wasted, but because value is accumulating beneath the surface.

The principle of compound interest illustrates this well. In year one, £1,000 growing at 10% becomes £1,100; in year two, £1,210. Hardly transformative. Yet by year 20, it's £6,727. By year 30, over £17,000. Most give up long before the inflection point—not due to system failure, but expectation failure. Delay is mistaken for deficiency.

This principle extends beyond money. Skills, relationships, trust, and credibility compound in similar fashion. Writers cultivate audiences post by post; freelancers build reputations job by job; leaders earn loyalty decision by decision. Compounding occurs not merely in creation, but in the doors those creations open. Networks deepen; opportunities self-perpetuate. Each action generates future leverage without additional effort. This is the flywheel effect—and it requires patience during the stretches that appear stagnant.

Patience, of course, is difficult in an age addicted to immediacy. Digital media has shrunk our timelines while inflating expectations. Social feeds highlight overnight IPOs, viral creators, and meteoric careers. Rarely do we witness the relentless, often dull persistence that precedes breakthroughs, or the willingness to honour the unglamorous middle, where foundations are quietly laid.

The middle is crucial because it is the realm of systems rather than sprints. Goals—"I want to earn £100,000," "launch this product," "retire by 45"—give direction but lack durability. Systems, however, are repeatable structures that generate momentum even when motivation wanes. A gym-goer with a routine will outperform one chasing target weights. An investor who automates savings triumphs over time, regardless of short-term fluctuations. A writer committing to two pieces a month, inspired or not, surpasses sporadic brilliance. Structure sustains; spark alone rarely does.

Nonlinear success also relies on asymmetric opportunities. Traditional thinking suggests effort scales linearly with reward: work twice as hard, earn twice as much. Reality is more capricious. A single investment, relationship, or platform choice can yield returns far exceeding input. A developer's open-source project may secure a role at a unicorn startup. A teacher's short video might reach millions, generating unforeseen income. These are modern realities, dependent on exposure to optionality and the willingness to place intelligent small bets.

The emphasis here is on small. Asymmetric returns do not demand outsized risk; they reward environments engineered for upside without catastrophic downside. This is the mindset of the tinkerer, the builder, the curious explorer. They iterate, test, and experiment—rarely waiting for perfect conditions. Massive change often begins with modest trials.

Tolerance for failure is equally essential. Linear models treat setbacks as derailment; nonlinear thinkers interpret them as feedback. A failed startup educates more than a cushy job. A rejected pitch refines strategy. Closed doors may force one to innovate. Failure becomes input, not verdict.

Identity itself must shift. The most successful seldom see themselves as finished products—they are evolving platforms. Pivots are expected; reinvention welcomed. Titles, roles, and plans are temporary scaffolds. Motion, not trajectory, defines worth. This mindset cultivates resilience: discouragement loses its grip when immediate results do not dictate value.

Flourishing in a nonlinear world is not the abandonment of planning, but the replacement of rigid plans with flexible frameworks. Progress is measured not in tidy milestones, but in capacity: am I more capable, better connected, more resilient than six months ago? If so, the slope ascends, even if graphs have yet to reflect it.

Rejecting the straight-line myth brings liberation. By releasing the demand for constant visible progress, one can build enduring structures. Daily metrics lose tyranny; long-term leverage gains prominence. One stops comparing early chapters to others' climaxes and begins to prepare for leaps when they arrive.

This chapter delves into how wealth and progress truly unfold: the traps of linear thinking, the mechanics of compounding, the reality of delayed returns, and the power of small, consistent action. It offers practical tools for designing life around systems rather than outcomes, cultivating the strategic patience needed to weather plateaus and capitalise on spikes.

Above all, it teaches a critical lesson: real success, like real wealth, is never linear. It is jagged, dynamic, and richly uneven—and all the more potent for it.

Wealth Doesn't Grow Like a Salary – Why Real Wealth Builds in Non-Linear Ways: Plateaus, Leaps, Setbacks, and Sudden Jumps

Most people are conditioned to think about money in predictable, linear increments. Earn a degree, get a job, work hard, receive annual raises, and gradually climb the income ladder. This model—so deeply embedded in the wage-based economy—is the mental template most apply when they think about building wealth. Yet this assumption is misleading. *Real wealth, unlike a salary, does not grow in a straight line.* It accelerates, stalls, reverses, and then explodes without warning. Understanding this erratic and often uncomfortable rhythm is essential not only to growing wealth—but to staying committed when nothing seems to be working.

At the heart of the linear mindset is a simple narrative: you get out what you put in. It's a story that fits well in classrooms, HR policies, and performance reviews. It offers a sense of fairness, control, and reassurance. But wealth creation—true, generational, or financial independence-level wealth—is governed by a different logic. *It is governed by volatility, optionality, asymmetry, and compounding—forces that do not respect neat timelines or tidy effort-to-reward ratios.* The uncomfortable truth is that wealth behaves far more like a biological system than a spreadsheet. It is complex, lumpy, and non-linear.

This is not just a philosophical abstraction. The evidence is everywhere. Consider entrepreneurs. Many spend years building infrastructure, credibility, and product, with little to show for it financially. Then one contract, one distribution channel, or one market shift changes everything overnight. The same holds for creators, investors, or startup employees. They grind through long periods of marginal growth, only to experience outsized gains in brief windows. These inflection points are not flukes—they are features of the system. *The slow years are not wasted; they are foundational.*

The problem is that most people are never taught to expect this pattern. Instead, they internalise the salary logic: you do the work, and you get the raise. They monitor progress monthly, quarterly, annually—expecting incremental improvement. When those improvements don't appear, they assume something is broken. Often, they quit. They exit a compounding system prematurely because it hasn't yet shown its hand. What looks like stagnation is frequently a prelude to breakthrough.

This confusion is compounded by how we measure success. Salaries reward time, reliability, and adherence to structure. Wealth, by contrast, rewards leverage, ownership, risk tolerance, and timing. You can clock in for 40 years and never become wealthy. Conversely, you can make one asymmetric bet—a business idea, a property, an equity stake—and see your financial trajectory change dramatically. *The real difference is not work ethic; it is the type of engine you're building.*

To understand non-linear wealth, one must first appreciate compounding—not just mathematically, but emotionally. Compound growth is deceptive at first. It begins so slowly as to appear irrelevant. If you double one penny every day, you only reach £1.28 by day eight. But by day 30, you have over £5 million. The early days are silent, unrewarding, and discouraging. If you quit at day 20, with only £5,243, you miss the explosion. This is precisely how many abandon entrepreneurial, creative, or investment pursuits. They misinterpret the quiet phase as failure, when it's simply pre-compounding.

Compounding also occurs in skills, reputation, relationships, and trust. A freelancer who builds deep credibility with clients over time finds that projects begin to arrive unsolicited. A content creator who publishes consistently for years suddenly breaks through not because of a single viral moment, but because the back catalogue earns newfound attention. *Wealth is often the delayed dividend of consistency in invisible arenas.*

This brings us to another vital truth: the growth of wealth is *non-linear not only in pace, but in emotion.* It includes setbacks, reversals, and plateaus. Many of the most successful investors or entrepreneurs have lived through gut-wrenching downturns—failed launches, economic recessions, personal crises. They did not escape volatility. They developed the emotional stamina to endure it. If anything, non-linear wealth creation *demands* a higher tolerance for uncertainty, ambiguity, and psychological discomfort than wage work. But the upside is that it eventually liberates you from time-based earning altogether.

It's also worth acknowledging the role of luck and randomness. The linear narrative suggests that if you follow the rules, good things will follow. But wealth creation is entangled with variables outside your control: the timing of a market trend, a chance introduction, an algorithm shift, or a global crisis. These forces can collapse or supercharge your trajectory. This does not mean that hard work is irrelevant—but that *hard work is not always the determining variable.* This can be demoralising for those who've built their identity around effort. But it is also liberating. It invites you to focus on *exposure to upside* rather than pure effort.

One of the most practical ways to embrace non-linearity is to create systems that keep you in the game long enough to see the spikes. This means building financial resilience, yes—but also psychological resilience. It means detaching self-worth from short-term results. It means redefining progress as *capacity-building,* not just earnings. Are you better positioned than you were last year? Do you have more skills, more leverage, more access? These are the indicators that matter in a non-linear world.

Let's take a concrete example: equity. Earning equity in a business—whether as a founder, early employee, or investor—creates a path to non-linear upside. It is unpredictable, illiquid, and often valueless for years. But one exit, one acquisition, or one market boom can render it life-changing. By contrast, salary provides steady cash flow but no ownership, no compounding, and no explosion. Many people reject equity early in their careers because they crave predictability. But the long game favours those who can handle uncertainty.

Similarly, small bets and side projects often produce disproportionate results. A coder launches an app that fails, then reuses the code to build something better. A writer starts a newsletter that stagnates for 18 months, then gains traction when a single post goes viral. A property investor buys a low-yield property, learns the mechanics, and leverages that learning into a more profitable portfolio. These stories share a common pattern: a willingness to start, a tolerance for delay, and a readiness to seize opportunity when it appears.

Critically, the shift from salary-think to wealth-think is not just tactical—it is psychological. It requires patience, risk literacy, emotional regulation, and the humility to admit you don't fully control outcomes. You stop obsessing over fixed timelines. You start optimising for resilience and staying power. This shift is what separates those who build durable wealth from those who simply earn well but remain financially fragile.

Indeed, one of the defining differences between income and wealth is that *income ends when you stop working; wealth endures*. But it doesn't arrive on a neat monthly schedule. It trickles, then floods. It disappears, then resurfaces. It is slow, then sudden. To thrive in this environment, one must build a different mental map—one that sees volatility as signal, not noise.

This is not to diminish the value of steady work or salaried income. For many, these provide the base stability from which risk can later be taken. But to mistake linear income growth for wealth-building is to confuse motion with leverage. Wealth, in its truest sense, is not about how much you make this month—but about what you've built that will *continue to produce*, even when you stop.

In the end, embracing the non-linear nature of wealth is not about chasing drama or abandoning discipline. It is about recognising the rhythms that govern real success—and adapting your expectations, strategies, and psychology accordingly. It means preparing for plateaus, planning for volatility, and positioning yourself for leaps. Most importantly, it means staying in the game long enough to see that what looks like a flat line today might, with time and patience, reveal itself to be the base of a dramatic curve.

The Magic of Small Consistent Moves – How Tiny Changes Compound into Massive Results Over Time

If there is one principle in finance that is both underappreciated and overestimated, it is compounding. Underappreciated because few people are patient enough to let its effects accumulate; overestimated because many misunderstand what truly compounds—thinking only in terms of interest rates or investment portfolios. In reality, *everything compounds*: habits, knowledge, decisions, and relationships. And in the world of wealth, those who master *small, consistent moves* often outperform those chasing dramatic breakthroughs. This is not poetic optimism. It is a practical, strategic truth rooted in systems theory, behavioural science, and financial history.

The modern mind is trained to chase immediacy. We expect performance reviews to yield promotions. We associate long hours with rapid returns. We seek diets that show visible change within weeks and investment strategies that beat the market in days. Against this backdrop, the idea of making tiny improvements daily—so small they seem insignificant—feels quaint, even delusional. Yet *compound impact is a silent force*: it does not beg for recognition, but it reshapes everything over time.

Consider this: improving by just 1% per day—whether financially, physically, or intellectually—doesn't yield a 365% improvement over a year. It yields a 3,778% gain. The mathematics are exponential, not additive. But more importantly, the psychology is transformative. *Consistency beats intensity over time.* One well-managed budget, one extra read before sleep, one mindful spending choice—these do not change your life overnight. But over years, they sculpt a trajectory that diverges massively from peers relying on intermittent intensity.

Take personal finance as an example. Most people wait for a windfall to begin saving seriously. But financial independence rarely stems from sudden jackpots. It stems from consistent behaviour: automatic transfers into investment accounts, choosing a modest car instead of financing a luxury one, reinvesting dividends rather than extracting them. The boring stuff. But the boring stuff *works*, because it stacks. What begins as a £100 per month investment becomes, over decades, a six-figure portfolio. And more importantly, it builds identity—a self-image of someone who behaves with future returns in mind.

This principle extends far beyond money. Careers, too, are shaped by compounding. The professional who takes one extra hour a week to deepen a technical skill or refine their writing style doesn't outperform others in three months. But in three years, their fluency, speed, and credibility eclipse their peers. They are invited to bigger tables not because they are louder, but because they have quietly become irreplaceable. *Reputation compounds*. So does trust. So does intellectual capital. These are slow assets, but when built, they create escape velocity.

The trouble is that compounding is invisible at first. It often feels like nothing is happening. You start a content project and no one reads it. You launch a side hustle and earn pennies. You try budgeting, but your bank balance still feels thin. This is where most give up—at the flat part of the curve. But this flatness is deceptive. It hides momentum gathering beneath the surface. The early phase of compounding is not a test of skill—it's a test of *patience*. This is why belief matters. Not the kind of belief you chant in front of a mirror, but belief in systems. Belief in arithmetic. Belief in time.

A common mistake is to confuse smallness with insignificance. Saving £5 on lunch by packing your own meal seems pointless in a world of six-figure incomes. But it's not about the £5. It's about the habit, the intention, the act of choosing awareness over autopilot. These choices become grooves in your behavioural wiring. They define your relationship with money, with time, with consumption. *Small doesn't mean weak; it means manageable*. And manageability is the first prerequisite of consistency.

This is also why unspectacular beginnings are often superior to grand launches. People who go to the gym twice a week for five years outperform those who go daily for two months and burn out. Writers who commit to publishing one thoughtful piece per week for three years build bigger followings than those who publish erratically when inspiration strikes. Investors who dollar-cost

average through bull and bear markets end up wealthier than those trying to time perfect entries. *Rhythm matters more than fireworks.*

Yet we are bombarded with outliers. We see viral stories of creators who "blew up overnight", startups that scaled to unicorns in 18 months, or traders who doubled their money in a week. These stories distort our expectations. They imply that massive action, taken quickly, is the true path. But most of these stories omit the years of groundwork, failed experiments, and invisible effort. There are no overnight successes—only long-term players whose work finally became visible.

To embrace the power of small consistent moves, you must shift your definition of success. Instead of measuring success by immediate output, measure it by *sustained input.* Did you make the tradeoff that aligns with your long-term values? Did you maintain the practice even when no one noticed? Did you stay in the game when others quit? These are better metrics of wealth—because wealth, properly understood, is not just a number. It is *autonomy over time*, and that autonomy is earned through habits that compound quietly until they no longer can be ignored.

One powerful real-world example comes from Warren Buffett—not because of his investment picks, but because of his timeline. More than 90% of his net worth was generated after the age of 60. Why? Because he began investing as a child and never stopped. His genius isn't just stock selection; it's *duration.* The compounding curve did most of the work. This is what most people miss. The real advantage is not brilliance—it's *not leaving the game.* And to not leave the game, you need a strategy that is not exhausting. *Sustainability is underrated.*

It's worth stating clearly: small consistent moves are not about being unambitious. They are about *strategic ambition.* It's the discipline to play a longer game, to anchor to process over peaks, to understand that outperformance comes not from exceptional moments, but from a foundation that has been laid brick by brick. Over time, those bricks become castles.

Another nuance worth exploring is emotional compounding. Every time you follow through on a small commitment—whether it's saving, investing, publishing, exercising—you build *trust in yourself*. That trust then makes future decisions easier. You no longer have to fight internal resistance at every turn. Decision fatigue decreases. Momentum increases. *You become the kind of person who follows through*, and that identity is worth more than any single achievement.

The opposite is also true. Inconsistency compounds—but in reverse. Skipped actions, broken commitments, and scattered focus don't just reduce output; they erode confidence. And once that confidence is gone, even the right tactics stop working. You second-guess yourself. You abandon plans. You chase novelty. That's why it's not enough to know what works. You must build the *psychological infrastructure* to keep doing it.

Ultimately, wealth building is less about breakthroughs than it is about behaviour. And behaviour, at scale, is a product of routines, not revolutions. The small decisions you make when no one is watching—the £20 saved, the extra paragraph written, the call not made out of FOMO—these are the architects of your future financial reality. They are boring, repetitive, and often thankless. But they are *real*. And they work.

If you want to build a fortune, change your daily cadence. If you want to shift your trajectory, shrink your focus. Ask not what will double your income this year—but what habit, if maintained, would multiply your wealth over a decade. That's where the power lies. Not in epiphanies. In *deliberate, consistent moves*, made with clarity and patience, compounding until the results are too massive to ignore.

Surviving the Boring Middle – How to Stay Focused During Plateaus When Nothing Seems to Be Happening

The most dangerous phase in any meaningful pursuit is not the beginning, when enthusiasm is high and novelty energises progress. Nor is it the end, when results provide motivation and success begins to feel inevitable. The real test is the middle—the long, unremarkable stretch when progress is incremental, feedback is scarce, and motivation starts to wane. In finance, careers, entrepreneurship, and personal growth, this *boring middle* is not a detour. It is the path. And those who learn to navigate it intelligently often separate themselves not by raw talent or strategy, but by endurance of what feels like stagnation.

The middle phase is deceptive. On the surface, nothing appears to be happening. You've been budgeting diligently for a year, but your savings still feel meagre. You've invested in index funds monthly, yet your net worth barely moves. You've published fifty articles, but none have gone viral. You've built habits, read the books, avoided frivolous spending—but still, your financial life seems unimproved compared to the hustle culture success stories on your feed. This is where most people falter—not because they lack intelligence or discipline, but because they *underestimate how long the quiet phase lasts.*

Progress in most high-leverage domains is nonlinear. The beginning offers visible returns because you're correcting obvious inefficiencies. The end offers excitement because compounding has become visible. But the middle offers neither. It offers repetition, delayed gratification, and the psychological discomfort of *uncertainty without feedback*. This discomfort tempts people to abandon long-term strategies for short-term novelty. They start over, try new systems, or chase higher-risk tactics that offer the illusion of momentum. But true compounding rewards the boring middle. It punishes restlessness.

Consider how this dynamic plays out in personal finance. The early stages of saving and investing feel thrilling: your first emergency fund, your first stock purchase, your first budget that works. But after the first twelve months, progress slows. Gains accrue, but imperceptibly. You're no longer correcting dysfunction—you're simply maintaining discipline. The returns don't yet feel transformational. But abandoning the process here is like pulling up seeds before they sprout. *Financial transformation is invisible before it becomes inevitable.* And the only way to make it inevitable is to *not stop* when it feels unrewarding.

There is a psychological toll to plateaus. Humans are wired to respond to feedback. We crave signs that our efforts matter. But the most valuable efforts—saving consistently, developing expertise, mastering risk, cultivating trust—are often invisible in the short term. Worse, the world offers no shortage of visible distractions: people who appear to succeed faster, systems that promise shortcuts, trends that claim to bypass effort. This contrast erodes our confidence. It makes us doubt strategies that are *slow but true* in favour of those that are *fast but fragile.*

Staying focused during the boring middle requires an unusual kind of discipline: *process-oriented thinking.* That means shifting your identity from someone chasing outcomes to someone refining systems. Instead of asking, "Is this working?", ask, "Am I doing the right things consistently?" Because in plateaus, feedback will lie to you. You'll feel like your investments are underperforming, your efforts are wasted, your opportunities are passing you by. But if you are executing a sound plan, the absence of progress is not failure. It is *friction.* And friction is part of the ascent.

An illustrative example comes from software development. Many engineers report that 80% of the work happens in the middle of the project—where there is little to demo, no clear deliverables, and no user excitement. Yet this is where the architecture is stabilised, the systems are debugged, and the product becomes reliable. The user only sees the final release, but the team knows that the *middle made it possible.* Similarly, financial freedom is often built not in the breakthroughs, but in the silent middle phase—when you keep budgeting, keep investing, and keep avoiding self-sabotage.

This is also where emotional resilience matters. Without a strategy to manage boredom, the mind seeks drama. You may find yourself checking your portfolio daily for a dopamine hit. You may become obsessed with market news, tempted by speculation, or convinced that you need to do something—anything—to move faster. But the mature response is restraint. *Boredom is not a signal to change your plan. It is a signal to master your impulses.* In this sense, boredom becomes a training ground. If you can stay disciplined when there's no applause, you've built real strength.

Plateaus are also fertile ground for introspection. When external rewards are minimal, you are forced to examine internal alignment. Do you actually believe in your strategy, or were you just hoping for quick returns? Are your habits sustainable, or are they performative? The middle asks hard questions. It tests whether your systems were built for visibility or for durability. This period offers an opportunity to refine your financial philosophy—not because you're failing, but because plateaus reveal what matters *when momentum disappears.*

For those building businesses, the boring middle is especially treacherous. The launch is thrilling. The first customer is validating. But then comes the grind—months of refining your offer, building an audience, improving operations, and enduring dry months. Many founders abandon ship here, pivot endlessly, or chase external validation. Yet the most enduring companies are those that outlast boredom. They keep solving problems no one sees. They build processes that seem unremarkable but compound silently. They survive long enough for leverage to kick in.

One counterintuitive insight is that progress during plateaus *often accumulates below the surface.* Just because you can't see it doesn't mean it isn't happening. For example, the person who builds a habit of reading for 30 minutes a day may feel like it's yielding nothing. But a year later, their worldview has shifted. Their articulation improves. Their strategic decisions become sharper. These second-order effects are hard to track, but they are real. The same holds true in finance. Diligent savers and investors often underestimate the *emotional fluency* they are developing—patience, discernment, and resistance to hype. These traits become invaluable when complexity arises.

To survive the boring middle, it helps to introduce periodic reviews. Not to measure short-term success, but to reaffirm process fidelity. Ask yourself: Have I followed my plan with integrity? Are my assumptions still valid? Are my behaviours aligned with my values? These reviews prevent you from being seduced by noise. They re-anchor your strategy in intentionality, not reactivity. Over time, this reflection becomes a source of quiet confidence. You begin to trust your trajectory not because it looks dramatic, but because it's *unshakable.*

Perhaps the most important truth is this: *the boring middle is not a punishment; it is a filter.* It weeds out the impatient, the inconsistent, and the overleveraged. It rewards those who can operate without applause. If you can persist during this phase—maintaining your systems, resisting distraction, and staying emotionally grounded—you reach a threshold few do. Eventually, the curve bends. Results accelerate. Outcomes compound. And from the outside, it looks like success arrived suddenly. But you'll know better. You'll know it was earned—in silence, in boredom, in persistence.

The financial world rarely celebrates those who endured the plateaus. But those who do emerge with more than wealth. They emerge with mastery—over their money, their habits, and themselves. That is the real prize. Not the number in the account, but the *character you build* on the way there. So if you find yourself in the boring middle, don't run. Don't reinvent. Don't despair. Sit with it. Trust it. Work it. That is where real transformation hides.

Asymmetric Opportunities – How Small Bets on the Right Things Can Change Your Life More Than Years of Hard Work

Most people are conditioned to believe that results are proportional to effort. Put in more hours, receive more pay. Stay disciplined longer, accumulate more wealth. The linear model of cause and effect dominates both the workplace and the classroom—and it's reinforced by traditional financial advice that rewards predictability over upside. But wealth, influence, and transformative outcomes rarely unfold linearly. They're often the result of *asymmetric opportunities*: low-cost, low-risk bets with disproportionately high potential upside. Understanding and leveraging this asymmetry is one of the most underappreciated skills in wealth building.

An asymmetric opportunity does not simply mean "getting lucky" or finding a shortcut. It refers to a situation where the potential gains vastly outweigh the potential losses, regardless of whether the success rate is high. In traditional economic terms, it's about achieving a high expected value—*not through certainty, but through leverage of outcomes*. A small bet on the right startup, the right asset, the right relationship, the right skill—executed with discernment—can alter the trajectory of your life in ways a lifetime of safe, hard work cannot replicate.

The most instructive examples of asymmetry come from venture capital. VCs know that most startups fail. Yet they invest in dozens, sometimes hundreds, of early-stage companies because they only need one to succeed massively. That one success can return 10x, 100x, or more—offsetting every loss and creating generational wealth. This model isn't reserved for Silicon Valley insiders. The core insight is portable: *you don't need everything to go right—you just need one thing to go exceptionally right.* This principle scales down to individuals who learn to make asymmetric life bets.

In personal finance, asymmetry shows up in behaviours like investing early. Consider someone who, instead of waiting until 40 to begin investing substantial amounts, begins putting away £200 per month starting at age 20. Thanks to compounding, this small, consistent action can result in a portfolio equal to—or greater than—someone who invests five times as much starting later. The bet is small in real-time cost, but it compounds over decades. *Time is the lever. The cost is low. The upside is enormous.*

Another domain rich in asymmetric opportunity is skill acquisition. Learning to code, understanding financial modelling, developing public speaking, or mastering a second language—these are not inherently expensive or risky endeavours. But the payoff can be extraordinary, not just financially but also in terms of autonomy, leverage, and optionality. For example, the ability to automate a repetitive job task might free up hundreds of hours annually. A single technical skill might unlock freelance income streams or lead to a six-figure role. *Skills are bets. Many offer limited downside and unlimited upside.*

Too often, people focus on improving their effort rather than increasing their exposure to asymmetry. They double their working hours, accept lateral promotions, or budget aggressively—not realising that *perfect execution of a linear plan will rarely outcompete an imperfect bet on exponential returns.* A side project that succeeds can eclipse years of dutiful employment. A cold email to the right person can open a door no credential ever could. An afternoon spent deeply understanding a new technology can be more valuable than a semester's tuition. The asymmetric thinker asks: where is the upside greatest relative to the cost?

This doesn't imply abandoning prudence or recklessness. The goal is *not* to chase moonshots or lottery tickets. It's to structure your time, money, and attention in a way that makes room for non-linear gains. Traditional systems—like formal employment and academic pathways—rarely reward this thinking because they're designed for averages. Asymmetric thinking resists averages. It embraces *power law dynamics*, where a small percentage of inputs drive a massive share of outcomes.

Asymmetry also rewards those who manage psychological risk. Most people avoid placing unconventional bets not because the financial cost is high, but because the emotional cost is uncomfortable. Launching a niche newsletter, asking for equity instead of a raise, building a product, approaching a mentor—all involve the possibility of looking foolish. But the upside in each case is orders of magnitude larger than the downside. *Fear of embarrassment, not rational cost-benefit analysis, is often the limiting factor.*

Contrary to popular belief, asymmetric opportunities are not scarce. They are miscategorised. They are dismissed as distractions, hobbies, or long shots because they do not follow institutionalised paths. But they are everywhere—for those trained to look. The internet has dramatically lowered the barrier to entry for experimentation. You can test an idea, publish insights, launch a product, or reach global audiences with minimal cost. Yet most people never act, paralysed by the illusion that outcomes must match inputs. This is not just a missed opportunity—it's a missed mindset.

A powerful question to ask regularly is: *what is something small I can try that, if it works, changes everything?* That question alone reframes your orientation from labourer to strategist. It invites you to stop maximising for certainty and start maximising for *exposure to positive convexity*. Convexity refers to the shape of the return curve—where the upside curves upwards while the downside flattens. In such situations, failure is tolerable, but success is transformative.

Consider the story of someone who built a simple app for personal use and shared it online. The app gained traction, attracted users, and was acquired within a year. The initial bet? A weekend of effort. The return? Financial independence. Not because they worked harder than anyone else, but because they were willing to make a small, asymmetric bet when the opportunity surfaced. Stories like this are often dismissed as flukes, but what they truly are is *evidence of leveraged insight meeting execution.* The lesson is not to replicate the app. The lesson is to become someone who recognises and acts on such leverage when it appears.

The same dynamics apply to relationships. A single introduction to a person with insight, resources, or networks can accelerate your learning, connect you to rare opportunities, or help you avoid costly mistakes. The effort might be a short conversation. The return could be exponential. Those who cultivate asymmetric relationships—not in a transactional way, but through genuine curiosity and contribution—often find themselves riding tailwinds others never even saw.

To embrace asymmetric opportunities fully, you must also build *optionality* into your life. Optionality is the ability to change course when favourable opportunities emerge. This means not locking yourself into inflexible financial obligations. It means keeping your schedule, your capital, and your identity slightly looser than social norms encourage. Those who optimise for optionality—who have the time to pivot, the capital to experiment, the network to amplify—are better positioned to act when high-leverage situations appear.

Ultimately, the asymmetric mindset is not about gambling—it is about *engineering your environment* so that upside has room to emerge. This requires a shift from the predictable comfort of effort-based thinking to the strategic discomfort of probabilistic thinking. Not everything needs to succeed. Most things won't. But *if you place enough well-chosen small bets, one of them eventually will.* And that one success can buy you a freedom that no salary, no degree, and no incremental promotion ever could.

The real work, then, is not grinding harder. It's learning to see asymmetric opportunities, and cultivating the courage, patience, and flexibility to act on them. It is training yourself to tolerate uncertainty in exchange for upside, and structuring your life not around maximising effort—but around increasing your exposure to luck, leverage, and convexity. Do this well, and one well-timed bet might do more for your future than a decade of doing everything "right."

CHAPTER 11
The Myth of the Finish Line

Modern financial thinking is haunted by a persistent illusion: that there exists a day, a precise moment, when we will finally "arrive." Retirement. The big exit. The fabled finish line. We are trained—by advertisements, advisers, and cultural storytelling—to imagine a future where effort, striving, and even worry are no longer required. A future in which a single figure—your "retirement target"—unlocks a life of leisure and security. Yet for those who reach it, the reality often diverges sharply from expectation. Liberation is frequently replaced by disorientation; fulfilment, by restlessness. The notion of permanent, static victory is an economic mirage, collapsing under the weight of lived experience.

Retirement, as popularly conceived, is largely a modern construct—and a commercially convenient one. It exists to sell pensions, mutual funds, annuities, even holiday packages. Rooted in an industrial-era mindset, it frames work as something to be escaped rather than engaged with as an evolving pursuit. For the curious, ambitious, and purpose-driven, "stopping" is seldom satisfying. What they seek is sovereignty: the ability to choose what work to pursue, when, and why. Financial freedom, in this sense, does not mark an end; it signals the opening of a new chapter.

This chapter challenges the misconception that wealth-building is a linear march toward a static endpoint. In truth, it is far more complex—and far more empowering. Wealth, when cultivated with intentionality, evolves alongside our values, relationships, and sense of purpose. The objective is not merely to earn, save, and retire. It is to become someone who uses resources wisely, creatively, and generatively. The real destination is not rest—it is relevance.

To grasp this, consider what people typically envision when they hear "retirement." For some, it is the ability to stop working at 65 and subsist on investments. For others, the early-retirement ideal—quitting a conventional job by 35 and living frugally on passive returns. In both cases, the implicit promise is the same: once a threshold is crossed, striving ceases. But human psychology undermines this assumption. Stagnation is rarely peace; it is boredom. And boredom, left unchecked, erodes vitality.

Retiring from something only makes sense if one is retiring to something equally compelling. Without this, financial independence quickly becomes a void of structure, motivation, and purpose. Many who reach conventional retirement find themselves adrift, even depressed. Their spreadsheets may balance, but their sense of contribution remains incomplete. What seemed like a finish line proves to be a mirage.

So what replaces the myth of the finish line? Not the abandonment of goals, but their evolution. True financial maturity is not about halting work but refining it. Accumulation becomes a tool, channelled toward projects, causes, and communities that reflect identity and values. Wealth ceases to be a destination; it becomes a medium of impact, enabling influence, amplification of voice, support of others, and challenge to existing systems. The most effective people are rarely those with the most; they are those who most skillfully align capital with purpose.

Consider those who continue to build, create, and lead long after they "need" to. The founder mentoring new talent; the investor funding climate-tech ventures instead of retreating to a villa; the mid-career professional leaving corporate security to pursue educational reform. These are not anomalies—they are indicators of a fundamental truth: the real question is not when to stop, but how to choose. Financial optionality shifts focus from relaxation to deliberate engagement on one's own terms.

Financial freedom is often framed as a point—a dollar figure, a spreadsheet target—but it is more accurately conceived as a spectrum of agency. At its simplest, it liberates from bills; at its most profound, it transforms the individual into a steward of capital, capable of shaping systems, funding innovation, and leaving institutions improved. This reframes the individual from passive consumer to active contributor.

This perspective also demands clarity on why wealth is sought. If success is measured merely by the cessation of work, ambition stalls at comfort. But if capital is viewed as a lever for amplifying values and effecting systemic change, the relationship to money becomes dynamic, integrated, alive. Money becomes less an end than a tool—and tools, after all, are meant to move things.

Emotional patterns complicate this phase. Satisfaction may be tinged with guilt for "having enough" while others struggle, or anxiety over potential loss. Disorientation can arise from uncertainty about the next step. These feelings are normal but not failures; they are invitations to evolve. The next stage is defined not by bigger portfolios, but by clearer intent. What problem will you tackle now that you possess genuine choice?

Some may retreat, de-risking their lives into comfort. Others will recommit to projects that matter: long-horizon, uncertain, socially impactful initiatives. Here, the concept of financial sovereignty becomes essential. Sovereignty is not about isolation or control; it is the capacity to deploy resources according to conviction, even along unconventional paths.

Achieving this also requires letting go of the illusion of completeness. One will never feel "finished." Hunger does not vanish—it matures, shifting from validation to contribution, from proving to building something enduring. This is not a failure of the original plan; it is evidence of growth.

Rejecting the finish-line myth invites a new form of questioning. "How much is enough?" transforms into "Enough for what? Enough to serve whom? Enough to leave what behind?" This recalibration fosters a richer life, driven by meaning rather than metrics.

While economic systems will continue to market retirement as the ultimate prize, those who feel most alive—and most financially powerful—are not the ones who purchased that dream. They are the ones who replaced it with something resilient: a life of aligned action, perpetual growth, and intentional contribution. For them, the question is never when it ends, but what is possible now that the game is theirs to shape.

This chapter examines how to transcend the finish line. It explores why humans chase endpoints, how to structure financial life for continuous evolution, and what it means to become a sovereign economic actor—not merely secure, but catalytic. Real freedom is not a destination. It is an open field. And the significance lies in the moves you make within it.

Retirement Is a Marketing Fantasy — Why Aiming for a Mythical Retirement Number Often Leads to Disillusionment

There is perhaps no financial narrative more culturally entrenched, yet intellectually hollow, than the modern myth of retirement. It presents itself as a rational, attainable goal: work hard for 40 years, contribute dutifully to a pension or retirement fund, and one day, at a socially sanctioned age, you will unlock the gates to permanent leisure. This idea has been so heavily marketed, so deeply internalised, that most people accept it without scrutiny. It is, after all, the reward we're promised for being economically obedient. But peel back its polished surface, and the illusion begins to show. Retirement, as commonly sold to us, is not merely outdated—it is strategically misleading.

The origins of retirement as a concept are neither ancient nor organic. In fact, they are startlingly recent. The formal idea of retirement was popularised in the late 19th century when German Chancellor Otto von Bismarck introduced a pension scheme for citizens over the age of 70. At the time, average life expectancy was significantly lower, meaning most people would never live to claim this benefit. It was a political manoeuvre more than a social good. In the mid-20th century, Western industrial economies adopted similar models, encouraging the idea of stepping away from work at a fixed age. Yet what began as a social policy evolved into a commercial product. Retirement became a marketing category, an aspiration embedded in everything from financial services to holiday brochures.

Today, we're bombarded with the notion that retirement is not only desirable but essential. We are instructed to calculate our "retirement number"—a mythical figure at which work ceases to be necessary and life begins to resemble a permanent holiday. But this fixation distorts more than it illuminates. It treats life as a linear sequence: education, employment, retirement. It presumes we all aspire to escape our work. And most dangerously, it trains us to delay meaningful living until some deferred future—without acknowledging that neither the future nor the satisfaction it promises is guaranteed.

Financial institutions benefit enormously from perpetuating this fantasy. The more afraid people are of an insecure retirement, the more they save, invest, and purchase financial products. Retirement is, to a large extent, a fear-based sales funnel. We are told to accumulate aggressively, warned that we might "run out" of money if we don't hit the right number, and lured into obsessing over performance metrics that rarely reflect our actual needs or desires. The industry sells comfort—but trades in anxiety.

This dynamic becomes especially problematic when we consider how ill-suited the traditional retirement model is to modern life. People live longer, change careers more frequently, and seek purpose well beyond the age of 65. Moreover, in knowledge-based or creative work, experience often amplifies value. Yet the dominant script still suggests that our most valuable years end precisely when we reach peak insight and competence. This is not just wasteful—it's dehumanising.

There is also a philosophical cost to structuring life around retirement. It subtly devalues the present by casting it as a means to an end. It trains us to see time as a sacrifice we must make today in order to enjoy it later. This mindset is particularly corrosive when extended over decades. People delay hobbies, travel, family time, even health, because they've been told the payoff will come later. But the deferred life plan rarely delivers. Retirement, once reached, often feels hollow, even aimless. Many retirees report a loss of identity, a decline in mental health, or a sense of purposelessness that no amount of leisure can resolve. Because work, for many, is not merely about income—it is about contribution, structure, and meaning.

Of course, none of this is to argue against financial independence. It is wise, even necessary, to accumulate assets that give you choice. But that's precisely the distinction: *retirement is not the same as freedom.* Freedom is the ability to decide what to do with your time, energy, and talent—whether that's continuing to work, starting something new, or dedicating yourself to a cause. Retirement, by contrast, is a culturally sanctioned halt, a prescribed life-stage that often fails to account for the complexity and dynamism of real human lives.

This misunderstanding leads to misaligned strategies. People optimise for a finish line instead of building sustainable systems that support ongoing agency. They accumulate financial capital without investing in social capital, health capital, or intellectual capital—all of which are required for a fulfilling post-career life. They treat retirement as a cliff, not a continuum, and are therefore unprepared for the psychological transitions it entails.

Critically, the fantasy of retirement also reinforces class-based inequities. For those in high-income roles with generous pensions, "retiring early" may be viable. But for the majority of the global workforce, retirement is less a reward than a threat: a future in which the body slows, income disappears, and support systems crumble. The image of golden years spent on yachts or golf courses reflects a narrow slice of society—and yet it shapes policy and aspiration far beyond its relevance.

There is a better way to think about our financial futures—one that doesn't rest on a binary notion of working vs. retired. We can think in terms of phases, not finish lines. There may be periods of intense professional engagement, followed by sabbaticals, retraining, or reinvention. There may be moments when income generation is central, and others when meaning or impact takes precedence. This fluid model recognises that humans evolve, that purpose changes, and that financial decisions should be designed to support a life of unfolding possibility—not a single moment of withdrawal.

To live this way requires different questions. Instead of asking, "When can I stop working?" we might ask, "What kind of work would I never want to stop doing?" Instead of asking, "How much do I need to retire?" we might ask, "How much flexibility do I need to shape my life meaningfully over time?" These questions shift the emphasis from accumulation to autonomy, from anxiety to alignment.

They also demand a more holistic view of wealth. Real wealth is not just stored money—it's stored *capability*. It's the ability to adapt, to contribute, to recover, and to reimagine. These attributes are not the exclusive domain of the elderly or the young. They are cultivated continuously. And they are more likely to flourish when we build our financial lives around systems of choice and purpose—not arbitrary age milestones or external benchmarks.

There is, ultimately, something deeply liberating about abandoning the retirement fantasy. It opens space for more authentic planning, more honest conversations, and more sustainable ambitions. It allows us to design lives in which money serves the individual, not the reverse. And it empowers us to stay relevant—not because we have to, but because we want to.

This subchapter aims to dismantle the myth of retirement, not by discarding its underlying desire—freedom—but by exposing its flawed assumptions and replacing them with a more flexible, human-centric model. You will encounter alternative frameworks, challenge prevailing narratives, and explore how to structure your finances around ongoing autonomy rather than terminal withdrawal.

The goal is not to shame those who aspire to stop working. It is to ask deeper questions about what kind of life we are building—and for whom. Because the real endgame is not to retire. It is to remain *sovereign*—over your time, your decisions, and your purpose—for as long as you are alive.

Why Growth Never Ends — How Wealth-Building Evolves as Your Values, Purpose, and Identity Change

The common depiction of wealth-building suggests a finish line: an ideal figure reached, a lifestyle secured, and a sense of closure attained. But in truth, wealth is not a destination—it's a dynamic reflection of who we are, what we value, and how we move through the world. The reason growth never ends is not because we are endlessly greedy or insatiable, but because our definitions of "enough," "freedom," and "success" evolve with us. Financial evolution mirrors personal evolution. It's not a linear accumulation of money; it's an ongoing calibration of meaning, purpose, and identity.

Most traditional financial planning assumes a fixed self. You, the investor, are imagined as a stable unit: your preferences are knowable, your goals are measurable, your risk tolerance is static. You set targets in your thirties, aim for them in your forties, and expect to arrive fulfilled by your fifties or sixties. But life resists such choreography. Who you are at 35 is rarely who you are at 50. And if your financial life doesn't adapt to those internal shifts, it starts to work against you—even if the numbers look right on paper.

Consider someone who builds wealth with the singular goal of early retirement. In their twenties and thirties, the motivation is clear: escape corporate constraints, buy back time, travel. But once that target is hit, something unexpected often happens. Restlessness sets in. The same person, once obsessed with spreadsheets and withdrawal rates, begins to crave purpose, connection, or impact. The original plan—perfectly executed—now feels like a cage. This is not failure; it is a natural response to identity expansion. *Wealth without relevance quickly turns into a burden.*

This is why true financial wisdom requires not just planning, but re-planning. The capacity to revisit, reframe, and reorient your financial trajectory in light of changing values is not a weakness—it's a strength. Static goals, no matter how well crafted, become obsolete when they no longer align with your internal compass. Real growth occurs when your money is shaped by who you are becoming, not who you were.

One of the most underdiscussed features of wealth-building is *identity drift.* As people gain financial agency, they often encounter a surprising dilemma: the habits that got them here no longer serve them. Scarcity mindsets that once fuelled savings now provoke anxiety. Hustle patterns that built capital now erode energy. Friends, careers, even geographies may feel outgrown. Yet letting go is hard, especially when those earlier strategies brought visible results. Financial maturity, then, is not about refining techniques—it's about recognising when you've outgrown them.

This inner realignment plays out in every life stage. A young entrepreneur may initially pursue wealth for independence but later discover they want to fund creative or social ventures. A mid-career executive might start valuing time over title and reorient towards part-time consulting or advisory roles. A retiree may feel called to mentor, teach, or launch a passion project that never fit into the earlier income-maximising framework. Each evolution demands not just money, but meaning.

It is no accident that some of the world's most successful investors and entrepreneurs frequently change their metrics of success. They move from income to autonomy, from autonomy to impact, from impact to legacy. Each stage carries its own set of financial strategies. But more importantly, each stage requires a different kind of internal clarity. If your wealth-building doesn't adjust to your shifting centre of gravity, it begins to ossify—even if your net worth keeps growing.

This also explains why chasing the highest return isn't always the smartest move. Optimising purely for financial gain can trap you in pursuits that pay well but cost too much in time, energy, or integrity. *Sustainable wealth is built not just on high-return assets, but on high-alignment choices.* These are the choices that reflect your evolving sense of what matters—where you're willing to trade yield for autonomy, or risk for resonance.

There's a practical corollary here: portfolios should be designed for fluidity, not rigidity. A system that allows for sabbaticals, career pivots, or family caregiving is often more valuable than one that merely optimises for a number on a screen. The capacity to move—to downshift, to experiment, to change your mind—is a powerful form of financial resilience. It's the difference between wealth that owns you and wealth that serves you.

Moreover, growth is not always vertical. There are seasons where financial progress plateaus, not because of poor decisions, but because priorities have shifted elsewhere—health, caregiving, learning, healing. These are not detours from wealth-building; they are investments in forms of capital that cannot be measured in spreadsheets. Emotional clarity, spiritual alignment, relational strength—these are assets too, and they often determine how wisely your financial capital gets used.

Culturally, we underestimate how much wealth-building is shaped by context. A person's strategies in their twenties are shaped by student debt and career instability; in their thirties, perhaps by family obligations; in their forties, by burnout or reinvention. Each phase requires different forms of intelligence—sometimes strategic, sometimes emotional, sometimes social. The illusion that a single financial blueprint will carry us smoothly across decades is not only naïve; it's dangerous.

This is also where the idea of "enough" gets complicated. What feels sufficient at one stage can feel restrictive at another. A modest life may be ideal for a writer seeking solitude, but insufficient for someone hoping to fund large-scale community projects. Equally, a large fortune may feel hollow to someone whose deeper desire is simplicity. The point is not to moralise one form of wealth over another, but to emphasise *alignment over absolutism*. You are allowed to change your mind. Your financial plan should too.

At its most powerful, wealth becomes a mirror. It reflects back the person you've become and offers tools to express that identity more fully. It gives you the ability to fund what you believe in, protect what you love, and shape a life that feels internally coherent—not just externally validated. But to get there, you must remain agile. *Growth isn't about more—it's about deeper integration between your money and your evolving self.*

This demands a new literacy—one that fuses financial competence with philosophical depth. It's not enough to know how to invest. You must also know what you are investing *for*. It's not enough to save aggressively. You must also understand what you're saving *from*, or *towards*. This literacy is rare because it requires introspection, not just information. But it is precisely this form of inquiry that protects you from the traps of comparison, drift, and regret.

The irony is that most people assume the financial journey ends with success. They believe the point of wealth is to stop worrying about wealth. But the truth is more nuanced. Once basic needs are met, money becomes a vehicle for expressing deeper values: freedom, contribution, creativity, love. It becomes a canvas for identity, not a scoreboard for achievement. And as long as your values evolve, so too will your relationship to wealth.

Ultimately, the reason growth never ends is because the self never stops becoming. Every financial milestone reached gives rise to new questions, new ambitions, new configurations of meaning. Real financial mastery is not the ability to predict every future outcome—it is the capacity to adapt as your inner world shifts. It is recognising that money, like you, is not fixed. It is fluid, responsive, and most powerful when it moves in sync with who you are becoming.

This subchapter is not about tactics. It is about orientation. It invites you to view wealth not as a static accumulation, but as a living conversation between your finances and your unfolding identity. It asks you to replace rigidity with reflection, strategy with self-awareness, and arbitrary goals with aligned growth. Because true wealth-building doesn't stop when you hit a number. *It deepens as you do.*

Money as a Tool for Impact — How Wealth Can Be Used to Create, Serve, and Contribute Far Beyond Yourself

The pursuit of wealth, when disconnected from purpose, quickly becomes hollow. Despite the pervasive cultural script that frames money as an end in itself—a sign of status, power, or personal achievement—the deeper truth is that money derives its greatest meaning when it becomes a tool for agency, contribution, and long-term impact. The financially literate know how to grow capital; the financially wise ask what capital is *for*.

Modern personal finance often stops at optimisation. It teaches how to save more, earn more, invest smarter, and retire earlier. Yet few frameworks address the more profound question: once financial security is achieved, *then what?* Beyond consumption and comfort lies a broader opportunity—to direct capital in ways that influence systems, uplift others, and align with values that transcend the self.

The idea that wealth can and should be generative—used to empower, support, and serve—is not new. But it is often drowned out by more dominant narratives: wealth as competition, wealth as escape, wealth as insulation. In reality, those who sustain satisfaction through wealth tend to orient it as *a conduit, not a container.* Their money moves with intention. It enables rather than encloses.

One of the most significant reframes in financial thinking is to view money as stored potential energy. On its own, it is inert—numbers in an account, digits on a ledger. But when activated with purpose, it becomes kinetic. It can fund education, launch businesses, back movements, amplify voices, or restore ecosystems. *The utility of wealth multiplies when it is paired with vision.*

This is where traditional models of "retirement" or passive accumulation often fall short. They promote stasis: a cessation of effort, a withdrawal from productive life. But impact demands engagement. It is not built from the sidelines. The wealth you accumulate over decades is not merely a reward for past effort—it can be the most potent asset you bring into your second act: as a mentor, investor, creator, or catalyst.

Consider the real-world examples. A software engineer exits their startup with a significant windfall. Instead of disappearing into leisure, they establish a coding school for marginalised communities. A doctor who achieves financial independence in midlife decides to offer care to refugee populations at no cost. An investor retools their portfolio to back climate-tech start-ups instead of extractive industries. These are not acts of charity in the traditional sense. They are expressions of alignment—money deployed in service of conviction.

This shift requires a new kind of financial literacy: not just how to build wealth, but how to *deploy* it with sophistication. Strategic philanthropy, impact investing, social entrepreneurship, donor-advised funds, foundation creation—these are tools of advanced financial expression. But their effectiveness depends not just on technical knowledge, but on clarity of values.

Indeed, some of the most transformative uses of capital are small and hyperlocal. A community microloan scheme. A friend's tuition. A grant to a young artist. A donation that prevents eviction. *Impact is not always scale; sometimes it is precision.* And sometimes, the most powerful form of economic agency is *proximity*: using your financial position to bridge gaps, remove frictions, and build ladders for others.

That said, using money for impact is not about self-congratulation or saviourism. It demands humility—recognising that you are not fixing the world, but contributing to it in your own deliberate way. It also demands nuance. Not all giving is helpful. Not all investing is virtuous. Effective impact requires discernment—understanding systems, listening to communities, and sometimes being willing to support unglamorous work over headline-grabbing causes.

Moreover, directing wealth for impact is not the exclusive domain of the ultra-rich. Even modest surplus can be leveraged for significant effect. The key is not size, but intentionality. A recurring £50 donation to a scholarship fund. Lending rent-free workspace to an emerging nonprofit. Using your financial cushion to take career risks that enable meaningful work. *The magnitude of impact is rarely proportional to the size of the cheque—it is tied to the clarity of purpose and the courage to act.*

This reorientation also alters how we view risk. In conventional investing, risk is something to be minimised. But when money is a tool for impact, risk can be reframed as a necessary cost of innovation. Many high-impact initiatives—whether in art, activism, or entrepreneurship—would not survive under traditional risk metrics. They require capital willing to absorb volatility in service of longer-term change. *Deploying wealth for good often means stepping outside of institutional thinking and into personal conviction.*

There is also a personal evolution that occurs when money is viewed as a mechanism for service. It reduces the existential anxiety that often clings to wealth. When capital is hoarded out of fear—fear of scarcity, fear of decline—it begins to corrode the spirit. But when it is moved with intention, it creates momentum. You start seeing your resources not as things to defend, but as energy to direct. *Security, paradoxically, is strengthened by contribution, not clinging.*

This dynamic is especially vital for those who have achieved some level of financial independence. Without a broader horizon of meaning, wealth can produce boredom, guilt, or a creeping sense of purposelessness. The hedge against these is *agency with consequence*—using your financial freedom to build, uplift, repair, inspire.

It also means reframing legacy. Not as the assets you leave behind, but the influence you exert while still alive. How you use your wealth shapes how people see themselves, what they believe is possible, and what they are empowered to do. Your impact can echo long before your estate is ever distributed. *Money in motion often creates more lasting change than money in trust.*

To build a life where money is a tool for impact, start with clarity, not capital. What causes stir you? What futures do you believe in? What gaps do you see that others ignore? What injustices anger you? What beauty moves you? Let your financial decisions reflect those internal answers. Over time, even small actions compound—don't just think of compounding in terms of interest, but in terms of influence.

There's a cultural shift underway: from wealth as display to wealth as utility. From "how much can I accumulate?" to "how well can I use what I have?" This shift is not just more ethical—it is more *satisfying*. It connects the quantitative with the qualitative. It makes finance human again.

And perhaps most importantly, it breaks the myth that money is a zero-sum game. That for someone to win, someone else must lose. In reality, money directed toward genuine impact often creates exponential value—new businesses, stronger communities, safer environments, healthier lives. When wealth serves, it doesn't shrink; it amplifies.

The question is no longer just how to become wealthy. It is how to become *usefully* wealthy. Not because the world demands it of you, but because you will not feel whole if you don't. Impact is not an obligation; it is a privilege. It is how money becomes meaning. It is how the abstract turns into something real. And it is how the financial chapters of your life turn into something far more lasting than numbers. They become the architecture of a legacy worth building.

The Art of Financial Sovereignty — Financial Freedom Isn't an End, It's the Start of Your Most Powerful Work

The most dangerous assumption in modern finance is that freedom is the finish line. People chase it as if it were a destination—an endpoint where work ceases, stress dissolves, and life finally begins. The rhetoric of "early retirement," "passive income," or "financial independence" is everywhere, often fuelled by fantasies of beaches, silence, and disengagement. But what happens after the goal is achieved? For many, disillusionment. The problem isn't with financial freedom itself. The problem is the belief that *freedom is the reward.* In truth, it is the raw material. *Sovereignty begins where security ends.*

Real financial sovereignty is not about the absence of work—it's about the presence of power. The power to choose your problems. The power to walk away. The power to redirect your time toward things that carry intrinsic meaning. The end of mandatory work is not the start of idleness. It's the start of responsibility—the chance to shift from survival economics to legacy economics. From reaction to creation. From extracting value to building it.

For the time-conscious, ambitious reader, this idea should reframe every decision: wealth is not just a shield; it is a lever. What you do with that leverage defines whether you have achieved sovereignty or simply secured safety. Most financial plans aim to eliminate discomfort. Sovereignty invites you to embrace discomfort on your own terms—through meaningful risk, original thinking, or system-level contribution.

The challenge, however, is psychological. A person who has spent decades optimising for accumulation often struggles to pivot toward activation. Money, once hoarded, can become a prison. Risk aversion calcifies. Identity becomes anchored to frugality or asset preservation. Ironically, the fear that once kept you hustling now keeps you stagnant. *Freedom requires courage not once, but continually—especially after you've won the right to stand still.*

Consider the artist who stops creating after their work becomes profitable, the entrepreneur who sells their business and then flounders in purposeless consumption, the investor who reaches their number and yet obsesses daily over market fluctuations. In each case, the mistake is the same: believing that the point of financial independence is to *retreat*. But retreat is not sovereignty. Sovereignty is the conscious, strategic use of your resources to shape the world as you believe it ought to be.

This is where traditional financial advice often fails. It's mechanistic, goal-oriented, and devoid of existential context. It assumes that once you reach your number, your life will sort itself out. But money doesn't answer questions of meaning. It amplifies what's already there—or what's missing. *The absence of necessity does not automatically produce clarity.* You still have to decide: what is worth doing when you no longer *have* to do anything?

To build financial sovereignty that matters, start by redefining the endgame. Ask what kind of problems you want to be working on for the next ten years. Ask what trade-offs you're finally ready to reject. Ask what pursuits you would double down on if income were irrelevant. Wealth doesn't erase the need to choose. It simply gives you the bandwidth to choose better.

It also reconfigures your relationship with time. For most people, time is an economic constraint—they sell it to meet obligations. Sovereignty shifts this entirely. You begin treating time as your *primary asset*, not something you liquidate for short-term gain. That shift enables deeper work, longer horizons, and more intentional living. You stop being reactive. You start designing.

But this design process isn't abstract. It requires infrastructure. Financial sovereignty is sustained not just by having assets, but by having systems that convert those assets into sustainable autonomy. That includes:

Low-burn living expenses that protect you from market volatility.

Flexibility in income sources—consulting, equity, royalties, or intermittent entrepreneurship.

Psychological readiness to operate without external validation or a rigid schedule.

Strategic allocation of time toward projects that compound in value—whether intellectual, creative, or social.

These aren't fringe ideas. They are the architecture of post-capitalist agency. They reflect a growing awareness that the traditional career ladder doesn't deliver the autonomy or impact many high performers seek. So they build parallel lives—structured not around retirement, but *regenerative output.* They move from labourer to architect. From schedule-taker to schedule-maker.

And yet, sovereignty should not be romanticised. It is harder than it looks. You must decide what matters without external pressure. You must build your own accountability frameworks. You must find energy in purpose, not just incentives. This is where many falter. The absence of structure feels like liberation for a month—until it becomes chaos. That's why sovereignty isn't just about permission; it's about *practice.* You must learn to direct your attention deliberately. You must master internal discipline. You must tolerate uncertainty without drifting into paralysis.

It is in this light that sovereignty becomes not just a financial concept, but a *spiritual* one. It requires deep honesty—about your strengths, your compulsions, your ambitions. It reveals what parts of your identity were tied to obligation versus desire. It calls on you to *create* rather than consume, to *engage* rather than escape.

Some of the most sovereign individuals you'll encounter are not the wealthiest, but the most aligned. They have used modest means to exit systems they found extractive. They have redefined success as control over their inputs. They build, not out of desperation, but out of design. Their lives are tailored, not templated.

This orientation toward sovereignty also reshapes how you evaluate opportunities. You stop asking, "What does this pay?" and start asking, "Does this expand my influence? Does it align with my compass? Will I care about this ten years from now?" You become more selective—not because you are arrogant, but because you understand the cost of distraction.

Moreover, you begin to differentiate between income and leverage. Sovereignty doesn't just flow from earning more. It flows from *controlling more of what you earn*, and ultimately from *earning in ways that reflect your values*. For some, this means solo consulting. For others, it's angel investing in underrepresented founders. For others still, it's writing books, building tools, or funding long-overdue institutions. *The point is not the format—it's the autonomy and integrity behind it.*

Perhaps most radically, financial sovereignty allows you to operate outside of urgency. Urgency is the default setting of modern capitalism—everything must be fast, scalable, monetised. But when you don't need immediate returns, you can think generationally. You can invest in long arcs. You can write things that don't sell today but matter deeply tomorrow. You can build institutions that serve, not extract. *You no longer need to chase trends because your capital structure supports patience.*

This is why sovereignty matters at a systemic level. It allows talented, thoughtful people to remain independent of institutions that would otherwise dilute or distort their work. It's not just personal freedom—it's the preservation of intellectual and creative integrity. Sovereignty isn't selfish; it's strategic. *It enables people to remain uncompromising where it counts most.*

Of course, all this requires you to unlearn deeply ingrained scripts. The script that says busy is good. That success is visible. That time off is wasted. That value equals effort. But the sovereign person doesn't perform for applause. They perform for purpose. Their output is quieter, but more enduring. Their wealth is not just financial—it is cognitive, relational, and reputational.

So don't chase sovereignty as a trophy. Build it as a platform. Not so you can do nothing, but so you can finally do *everything that matters.* When your money serves your mind, when your time reflects your truth, when your work is your choice—that is sovereignty. It is not the end of ambition. It is where the most meaningful ambition begins.

CONCLUSION
Write Your New Money Story

The most profound transformation in your financial life begins not with mastering budgets, maximising savings, or refining investment strategies. It begins with the stories you tell yourself—the unconscious narratives that have quietly guided your choices. Money is rarely just arithmetic; it is identity, fear, approval, worthiness, legacy. For decades, many of these stories have been inherited rather than authored, and their influence is far-reaching.

In the preceding chapters, we have dismantled the invisible scaffolding behind your financial decisions: inherited beliefs, cultural biases, myths of linear progress, illusions of control, and the fantasy of a final arrival. Each insight has chipped away at the assumption that financial struggle is merely a product of ignorance. More often, it arises from these ingrained stories, absorbed so thoroughly and early that they masquerade as truth.

Now, you have encountered a different paradigm—one that does not promise instant wealth or certainty, but clarity, agency, and strategic humility. You have seen why the pursuit of perfect plans makes us fragile, why randomness carries more weight than we acknowledge, why systems outpace goals, and why small, consistent actions often triumph over heroic sprints. You have explored what true sovereignty entails: that wealth, once secured, demands purpose rather than escapism.

This chapter is not a summary. It is a bridge from understanding to authorship. Knowledge alone does not transform financial life; transformation begins when knowledge becomes narrative. Your task is to craft a money story that reflects your values, context, and evolving ambitions. This is not cosmetic branding; it is a philosophical act of self-definition.

To write a new story, you must first interrogate the old one. What patterns did you inherit? Scarcity, shame, the compulsion to prove yourself, the urge to avoid discomfort? Who shaped your earliest lessons about money, and how—by instruction or example? Who benefits if you remain tethered to that narrative? Whose approval are you still chasing in your pursuit of milestones?

Most people never pause to ask these questions. They optimise according to unconscious scripts that are outdated, unexamined, often harmful. Some hustle because they equate money with safety. Others self-sabotage because they deem wealth selfish. Some fear isolation; others quietly assume they are undeserving. These beliefs are rarely spoken, but they animate every hesitation, every impulsive choice, every rationalisation.

Rewriting your story means naming these ghosts. It means moving from reactive management of finances to intentional design. You are reclaiming authorship over how you approach risk, time, status, generosity, and ambition. The shift is existential: from character in another's script to architect of your own.

A meaningful money story does not promise ease; it aligns incentives with identity. Decisions are evaluated not solely by returns, but by coherence with values. If the old story was externally dictated—by family, market norms, or cultural myth—your new story must be internally grounded. Who are you when no one else's rules apply?

This question carries tangible consequences. The entrepreneur who builds ventures aligned with principles rather than profit. The investor willing to accept modest short-term gains for greater long-term impact. The parent teaching children that success is agency, not possessions. These are not romantic gestures—they are strategic choices enabled by a story that serves you, not inherited expectations.

Rewriting your story does not reject ambition, growth, or wealth. It reframes them. Wealth becomes a tool, not a scoreboard. Enoughness trumps appearance, discernment trumps urgency, contribution trumps competition. Financial success is liberated from mimicry and embedded in conviction.

The process demands emotional discipline. Shedding old scripts creates a void. Here, true authorship begins: deciding what "enough" looks like, what freedom feels like, what impact matters. This work is deliberate, slow, sometimes solitary. It is unrewarded publicly, yet it forms the foundation of lasting sovereignty.

Pragmatically, a clear story sharpens decision-making and reduces friction. When priorities are defined, you waste less time. When what is unimportant is acknowledged, strategy becomes more effective and sustainable. You stop imitating and begin curating.

Life changes, and your story must adapt. What mattered at thirty may not matter at fifty. Roles, responsibilities, and relationships evolve. A strong money story is flexible yet anchored in clarity, agency, and alignment.

This is the distinction between those who sustain success and those who burn out. Growth is iterative, not linear. Build, pause, recalibrate. Move from accumulation to activation, from strategy to stewardship, from proving to serving. In this framework, financial life is not about status—it is sovereignty in motion.

As you reach the close of this book, the work is yours to define. You have the frameworks, clarity, and permission to question, reject, and reconstruct. No longer must you follow another's blueprint.

Start now. Define what matters. Commit it to writing. Iterate without shame. Remember: a money story is not static. It is rewritten each time you choose alignment over obligation, integrity over imitation, autonomy over approval.

Let this be your power—not simply to grow wealth, but to live it.

Write Your Own Money Story

The most dangerous financial beliefs are not the ones we consciously choose. They're the ones we inherit silently, absorb unquestioningly, and carry for decades without scrutiny. These beliefs—about what success looks like, what wealth requires, who deserves it, and what it should be used for—are rarely stated aloud. They are passed through glances, habits, social norms, and quiet assumptions. And because they arrive so early and feel so normal, we rarely see them as beliefs at all. We mistake them for truth. This book has been a sustained effort to dislodge that illusion.

By now, you've unlearned more than you may realise. You've seen why hard work isn't always enough, how systems often override individual willpower, why control is a myth, and how wealth actually accumulates in jagged, often unpredictable ways. You've dismantled the fantasy of linear success and retirement as a finish line. You've examined the role of randomness, luck, bias, and access—not as excuses, but as *real forces* shaping outcomes. And perhaps most importantly, you've been given frameworks to replace inherited myths with evidence-based clarity.

What remains is not simply new information—it's the open field of authorship. This is where the real work begins: crafting a money story that is yours, and yours alone. A story not designed for optics, approval, or conformity, but calibrated to your values, your circumstances, and your evolving sense of meaning. *That* is financial freedom—not a number, not a milestone, but the ongoing act of choosing what your money is for.

Most financial advice stops at tactics—how to budget, invest, reduce debt, or optimise taxes. And while those are essential tools, they are not sufficient for transformation. You could master all the mechanics and still feel out of control. You could hit your "number" and still feel insecure. Because beneath the spreadsheets lies the software: the worldview that governs how you interpret success, risk, sacrifice, and value. If that software is inherited and unexamined, no amount of optimisation will create freedom.

Now that the myths have been named, the illusion lifted, and the old defaults disrupted, the question is no longer *what should I do with my money?* The deeper, more empowering question is: *What kind of life do I want my money to support—and who am I willing to become to create it?* That's the question a personalised money story answers.

To be clear, writing this story isn't a one-time exercise. It's a living document. It adapts as you do. Your priorities at twenty-five may differ dramatically from those at fifty. A story that once revolved around financial security may evolve into one centred on creative freedom, service, or legacy. The power lies not in perfecting the story—but in claiming authorship over it. You no longer need to outsource that narrative to employers, banks, industries, or cultural scripts designed to keep you consuming.

Writing a new money story also means confronting trade-offs with clarity. When you stop chasing vague ideals like "more" or "enough," you begin asking more useful questions: What is this money actually for? What am I no longer willing to sacrifice? What kind of problems am I willing to have? These questions don't have easy answers—but they reveal your true metrics of success. Without them, you're vulnerable to chasing someone else's finish line indefinitely.

Consider the traditional retirement narrative: grind for decades, delay gratification, and finally cash out into a life of leisure. For many, this isn't just outdated—it's a trap. It assumes that meaning and purpose can be deferred without cost. It assumes that identity, creativity, and ambition will still be waiting for you at the other end. But humans don't work that way. Growth doesn't pause at sixty-five. Fulfilment isn't a reward for enduring decades of misalignment. And the tragedy of waiting is that by the time you arrive, you may no longer remember what you were waiting for.

By contrast, a self-authored money story integrates wealth-building with life-building. It prioritises energy, alignment, and design over deferral. It treats freedom as a daily practice—not a deferred reward. It's not anti-discipline or anti-structure—it's about *intelligent structure* that supports the life you want now and evolves with you as you grow. In practical terms, that might mean building income streams around your health and energy, not just market demand. It might mean declining high-paying opportunities that cost too much time or integrity. It might mean choosing a simpler life not out of scarcity, but from clarity.

One of the core lessons of this book is that *money multiplies agency*. It doesn't invent purpose—but it enables it. Once you stop seeing wealth as a scoreboard or a safety blanket, you start seeing it as a lever. A tool to deepen relationships, amplify your work, and fund causes you care about. A tool to protect your attention, say no to misaligned demands, and yes to ideas still forming. A tool not to escape life—but to enter it more fully.

But to use that tool well, you must be honest about what matters to you—not what should matter, not what impresses others, not what aligns with someone else's version of success. That kind of honesty is hard. It requires stripping away the armour of comparison and the seduction of consensus. It demands that you confront your own contradictions, rewrite your own metrics, and tolerate the discomfort of forging a unique path.

That discomfort is worth it. Because once you've named your money story—and built a system to support it—you become unshakable. Not because nothing can go wrong, but because you are no longer living reactively. You are no longer measuring your progress by borrowed standards. You have stepped into authorship—and with that comes the rarest kind of power: the ability to define what enough means, and to live accordingly.

You will still face uncertainty. There will be plateaus, setbacks, and doubts. That's not failure—that's the terrain. The goal isn't to avoid these moments, but to navigate them with alignment. To ask, in each decision: *Does this serve the story I'm writing?* If the answer is yes, you keep going. If it's no, you adjust—not from panic, but from authorship.

Some people will resist your story. They may not understand why you've opted out of certain norms, declined certain opportunities, or prioritised what they can't measure. That's fine. Your story is not a performance. It's not for them. It's for you—and for those you're here to serve. Financial sovereignty is not just about freedom from work or constraint—it's about freedom to contribute, to build, to shape.

At the end of this book, you are not simply more informed. You are more *equipped*. Equipped to think critically. To see clearly. To design consciously. You are not free from responsibility—but you are free from fiction. You are no longer bound to play a part you didn't audition for. You are not chasing someone else's dream—you are articulating your own.

Write your story. Let it be honest. Let it be flexible. Let it be alive. The work isn't over—but for the first time, it's *yours* to shape. That's not a burden. That's the deepest kind of freedom.

About the Author

Eleanor Whitmore is a financial behaviorist, researcher, and cultural critic who has spent over a decade studying the hidden forces that shape our relationship with money. Combining insights from neuroscience, behavioral economics, cultural anthropology, and personal narrative, her work exposes the invisible money myths we inherit—and shows how they quietly dictate our earning, spending, and investing decisions. Eleanor's approach is rooted not in dry financial formulas but in the emotional and psychological realities that drive financial choices. With a background that bridges both finance and the social sciences, she has helped thousands of individuals and organizations rewrite their money stories, reclaim agency, and build wealth that aligns with their deepest values. The Inherited Lie is her defining work—a powerful roadmap for anyone ready to break free from limiting beliefs and step into true financial sovereignty.

www.ingramcontent.com/pod-product-compliance
Lightning Source LLC
Chambersburg PA
CBHW031343230926
51848CB00002B/358
* 9 7 8 9 3 7 1 7 7 8 4 4 2 *